A QUAKER C
NAZI GEI
Leonhard Friedrich sur ⌐uchenwald

THE AUTHOR, BRENDA BAILEY, the daughter of Leonhard and Mary Friedrich, was born and educated in Britain. During the war she served with the Friends Ambulance Unit. She married Sydney Bailey, a writer on UN and international affairs. She worked with him at the Quaker UN Office in New York.

On returning to London in 1960, Brenda helped in the formation of two Community Relations Councils and initiated several multi-racial community projects in Islington, including a new building and local management structure for Caxton House Settlement at Archway.

She then served as Development Officer for Quaker Peace and Service, working with American and European Quaker groups to raise money for community work projects in the developing countries of Africa, the Indian sub-continent, and the Middle East.

Mary Friedrich, née Tupholme
b. 6th Aug 1882 at Sheffield
d. 9th Nov 1970 at Bridport

Leonhard Friedrich
b. 22nd Nov 1889 at Segnitz-am-Main
d. 15th March 1979 at Bridport

Both were interred at Bad Pyrmont Quaker burial ground.

A Quaker Couple in Nazi Germany

Leonhard Friedrich survives Buchenwald

by

J. E. Brenda Bailey

William Sessions Limited
York, England

© J. E. Brenda Bailey 1994

ISBN 1 85072 131 9

Printed in 10 on 11 point Plantin Typeface
by William Sessions Limited
The Ebor Press
York, England

Dedicated to:

Elena Rose Johnson

our grand-daughter

And heartfelt thanks to the co-operative effort of all my family. My husband Sydney Bailey, who never tires of teaching me to write. My daughter Marion Bailey and her husband Syd Johnson, and my cousin Margaret Burgoyne, who all encouraged me in the early stages. To my son Martin Bailey and his wife Alison Booth, both journalists, who have spent much time improving the text.

Contents

Chapter		Page
	Acknowledgements	viii
	Introduction	1
I	Life in Nuremberg 1931	7
II	Nuremberg: Last days of Weimar Republic 1932	24
III	Hitler becomes Chancellor 1933	34
IV	The Move to Bad Pyrmont 1934	51
V	Consolidation of Nazi Regime 1935	60
VI	Bad Pyrmont 1936	68
VII	Mary's Commitment to the Jews 1937	72
VIII	Annexation of Austria and the Munich Crisis 1938	78
IX	Kristallnacht 1938	89
X	War becomes Inevitable 1939	97
XI	Hitler's Domination of Europe 1940	111
XII	The Suffering Intensifies 1941	128
XIII	Expulsion of the Jews 1942	135
XIV	Leonhard's Arrest 29th May 1942	141
XV	Initiation to Buchenwald 1942-3	160
XVI	Mary on her own 1943	171
XVII	The Allied Invasion of Europe 1944	184
XVIII	Final Year in Buchenwald 1944-5	195
XIX	Ending of the War 1945	209
XX	Leonhard Comes Home 1945	218
XXI	Post-war Chaos 1945-6	229
XXII	Picking up the Broken Threads 1946-9	240
XXIII	The Later Years 1950-79	248
XXIV	Perspectives from the 1990's	262
	References	270
	Bibliography	277
	Index	281
	Jews and non Aryans assisted by Mary Friedrich	296

List of Illustrations

	Page
Quakerhouse, Bad Pyrmont	Front cover
Buchenwald Gate House	Back cover
Brenda Bailey	i
Leonhard and Mary Friedrich	ii
Mary, Brenda and Leonhard beside the summerhouse, 1932	11
My playmates, 1932	11
Nuremberg Friends Meeting Rooms	20
The original Pyrmont Meeting House	32
The Catchpool family, 1932	39
Bertha Bracey, 1927	42
Dr Willi and Edith Straus, London 1933	45
Elizabeth Fox Howard	45
Four Friends at Yearly Meeting, 1934	56
Seebohm family house, Kirchenweg, Pyrmont	58
1936 Yearly Meeting catering group	71
Heinrich Otto with daughter Dietgart and Brenda	71
Friends World Committee Conference, Swarthmore 1937	76
Leonhard's brother Bernhard and son Martin in America	76
Pyrmont street sign – Dr Gustav Sturmthal and family	92
Edith Straus and son, Edgar	117
Marie Pleissner and Joan Mary Fry, 1939	121
Cilli and Hans Seutemann	123
Dr Otto Buchinger and son Dr Ott Buchinger, 1942	147
Buchenwald site plan	161
Site of Block 45	163
American guns outside Buchenwald Gatehouse	205
Leonhard's friend, Salomyxin	205
FAU friends visiting Leonhard and Mary	227
Brenda at Einbeck station handing clothing to Polish families	235
Tony Trew and sick children outside FAU team house	238
Wolfgang Mueller, standing behind Mary and Leonhard	241
Leonhard Friedrich, Emil Fuchs and Friends, 1951	249
Friends World Committee in Pyrmont	254
Dr Paul Oestreicher Snr.	256
Leonhard reading the newspaper by unknown artist	260

Acknowledgements

I GIVE HEARTFELT THANKS to the many people who have made it possible to write this book. The recollections of people who knew Leonhard and Mary Friedrich and the problems of the Nazi times have added vivid detail.

Among those in Britain who have helped are Hannah Blum, Tessa Cadbury, Roger and Julia Carter, Enid Huws-Jones, Grigor McClelland, Ted Milligan, Deryck Moore, Rev Paul Oestreicher, Hilde Sturmthal and her daughter Elga Isom, Edgar Straus and Tony Yelloly.

German Quakers whom I wish to thank are Annemarie Blanke, Dr Ott and Marlies Buchinger, Lutz and Ute Caspers, Giesela Faust, Annetta Fricke, Anna Sabine Halle, Eva Hermann, Lore Horn, Hannah Jordan, Etta Klingmueller, Brunhild Mueller, Inge Specht.

Friends House Library is not far from my home, enabling me to make frequent use of their material, with the particular help of Josef Keith, who has also done the index. I have also been helped by Jack Sutters, the AFSC archivist, and the Wiener Library in London. The Public Library in East Finchley has willingly obtained many books for me to read. The Bad Pyrmont Library helped with material about the Jewish cemetery.

Claude Julian-Waring of QPS and Patrick Auld and others of Universal Office Equipment patiently helped me to get the best out of my computer. Thanks are also due to eleven Quaker Trusts who helped with grants and loans to meet publication costs.

BRENDA BAILEY

Introduction

I AM WRITING SO THAT others may understand the experiences of my parents, Leonhard and Mary Friedrich, who lived as Quakers in Nazi Germany, through the grimmest of times. They held onto their faith in God and humanity during a period when millions of Jews, Gypsies and other people regarded as 'sub-human' were deliberately annihilated. Democratic and cultural values, which had developed over centuries of civilisation in Europe, were destroyed.

We need to know about the past in order to understand the present and prepare more sensibly for the future. Dictatorial regimes continue to exist because ordinary people can be intimidated into keeping quiet. Just minding our own business and looking after our own affairs can be disastrous for society.

I have written about the experiences of my German father and English mother during the Nazi years and have also tried to cover the historical context of the period. Their life story comes alive through the accounts of people I knew, using their own words wherever possible. I remember how hard it was for my parents and other German Quakers to stand up for those who were being victimised by the Nazis. I myself might sometimes have made different choices, but their attitudes always seemed fearless and without hatred.

In 1931 I was a child of eight, living with my parents in Nuremberg. Two years later I came to a Friends boarding school in England, but regularly returned home to Germany during the holidays. In 1939, we decided I should complete my schooling in England, though this meant being separated from my parents for the war years. I was settled and married in Britain when we met again at the end of the war in 1945.

Leonhard and Mary Friedrich were employed as the first wardens of the newly-built Quakerhouse in Bad Pyrmont in 1933. Leonhard also managed the Quaker publishing business, which aimed to spread the ideas of Quakerism throughout Germany. Leonhard and Mary were both deeply committed to the Society of Friends and to supporting people who were in trouble, who had family problems, were unemployed, were engaged in a spiritual search or were in difficulties with the authorities for political or racial reasons. They were particularly concerned about the suffering inflicted on the Jews, and on people who although no longer of the Jewish faith, were defined as such because they had a Jewish parent or grandparent.

Mary's professional experience in social and industrial personnel work enabled her to present the personal details needed to obtain overseas guarantors for would-be emigrants and she succeeded in arranging for 59 individuals to leave before the war began. She had many overseas contacts, and wrote hundreds of letters to find families abroad sufficiently caring and financially able to support a refugee family. Similar work on a greater scale was undertaken from the Quaker offices in Berlin, Frankfurt and Vienna, with sponsorship links being arranged by the Germany Emergency Committee at Friends House in London.

When the outbreak of war put an end to this work, Mary helped organise social occasions for the Pyrmont Jews at the Quakerhouse. This was done at considerable personal risk because associating with Jews carried severe penalties. Once the war had started and emigration options were closed, she continued to visit them in their homes and hear of their experiences. Friends eventually helped them prepare themselves with dignity for the journey to Poland and the concentration camps in the East.

In the summer of 1942 Leonhard was arrested whilst in Stuttgart on Quaker business. In a lecture he gave in 1947 entitled 'Guest of Adolf Hitler', which was subsequently published in *Der Quaker*[1] he describes how he survived 92 days of solitary confinement and interrogation, followed by two-and-a-half years in Buchenwald. His concern was not to burden the audience with the details of his suffering, but to endorse the truth of the disclosures appearing in the press. In the years immediately after the war the general public in Germany, and to some extent outside Germany, could not really believe what had happened. Those in Germany who remembered the flamboyant anti-German propaganda abroad which followed the First World War suspected that the victorious Allies were promoting similar lies. Television did not exist for ordinary people, but gradually newspaper pictures appeared and newsreel film was shown. Visual journalism has a greater emotional impact than the written word. Leonhard wanted people to recognise the truth of these horrific revelations, in the hope that such cruelty could be prevented from ever happening again.

Most of the survivors of the concentration camps felt a deep obligation to tell of their experiences for the sake of their fellow prisoners who had died. Many experienced a sense of guilt about being alive, while their relatives and comrades had not survived. The psychologist Bruno Bettelheim who had been in Dachau and Buchenwald, wrote that his concern was not so much for the past, but to help us recognise the dangers of our own destructive tendencies for the future.[2]

When we learned about the death camps at the end of the war, we were told how many Jews had walked solemnly without resistance into the gas chambers. The torture, desperation and hardship they had been through had separated them from all that had given meaning to their lives, so that some felt that their own impending release by death, was almost preferable to life.

At a time when we in Europe are making it increasingly difficult for asylum seekers to come to our countries, we also need to remember the obstacles the outside world created for Jewish emigrants trying to escape from Nazi Germany. The lack of support from abroad had the psychological effect of reducing the strength of the oppressed to resist and struggle to stay alive. Leonhard frequently said he retained his determination to survive because he knew that his family and friends were praying for his return. This is a lifeline we need to offer to victims of oppression today. The Beirut kidnap victims, Terry Waite and John McCarthy, have spoken of the renewed strength they felt when they heard of the support of distant friends.

Whilst Leonhard was in Buchenwald, Mary often felt extremely isolated and threatened. She had to cope with countless Gestapo and police interrogations. Her home and the Quakerhouse were frequently searched. It was very hard being a lone Englishwoman while Britain and Germany were at war. The Society of Friends in Germany provided her with basic financial and much personal support. But in the local group, where she most needed friendship, she sometimes experienced painful misunderstandings and differences of opinion about what action should be taken. After Leonhard had been arrested, Mary had little privacy at home because evacuees were billeted in her small flat by the town housing department. There were also the innumerable Quaker visitors whom she encouraged to come for rest and recuperation from the bombed cities. Some were in great distress because their relatives were lost, in trouble with the Gestapo or bombed out. Mary, who still felt herself to be the caretaker, kept a close watch on Quakerhouse, which was first commandeered for the use of the Hitler Youth and later used as emergency accommodation for the elderly. She reported damage or misuse of the premises to the Burgermeister and her vigilance contributed to the respect for the cemetery and the eventual return of the building to the Quakers.

There was immense joy when the war ended and Leonhard returned home to pick up the pieces of their former life. Hitler was dead and gone for ever and the British Military Occupation encouraged Friends to re-open their activities. The longed-for contacts with family and Friends from abroad were facilitated by many visits from young Friends Ambulance Unit members and the Friends Relief Service. Pyrmont Friends organised a sewing room and relief centre for refugees and needy people, and also a youth club in the prestigious Kur Hotel. Quaker work began again, Leonhard resumed publication of Quaker literature and Mary's last effort in her eighties was to start an annual seminar on Quakerism, which still continues as a regular feature of the Yearly Meeting.

Source Material

Mary recorded the events of her life in a series of pocket diaries from 1901 onwards, surprisingly keeping this up at considerable risk during most of the war years. She wrote in both languages, used code words, and made occasional entries in an early style of Pitman's shorthand. She recorded the names of the people she had written to each week and kept a visitors' book. After Leonhard and Mary died I found several boxes of letters, photos and neatly-kept records.[3]

For the early chapters I have used the Minute Book of the Nuremberg Friends Meeting from its founding by Leonhard and Mary in 1924 until the book was filled in 1935.[4] A similar Minute Book for the Bad Pyrmont Meeting, which began in 1934, has disappeared and was presumably taken away by the Gestapo when they cleared out all the Quaker books and files. I have copies of several of Mary's reports written to supporters of the work, and to the Germany Emergency Committee in London. But most interesting are the letters and reports of meetings with the Gestapo which Mary wrote immediately after her attempts to get Leonhard released from Buchenwald.

In order to describe Leonhard Friedrich's experiences in Buchenwald, I have made full use of his article published in *Der Quaker* 1975: 'Leonhard Friedrich as Guest of Adolf Hitler 1942-5'. The text of the article originated in a talk he gave at the Quakerhouse in October 1947. Leonhard re-wrote the material for various occasions. Soon after their 1968 retirement to England, we made a translation and duplicated an English version. I have selected the fullest materials for quotation in this book.[1]

These family sources are supplemented by contemporary articles in *Der Quaker* and articles written for *The Friend* by the Quaker Representatives appointed to Berlin, from Britain and the USA. Some paragraphs describe the awful struggles on the Eastern Front, which British newspaper readers were barely aware of at the time. Now, 50 years later, I can understand how profoundly this battlefield affected the development of Europe and the Soviet Union. The fall of the Berlin Wall in the winter of

1989 and the subsequent unification of Germany finally mark the end of the war and its legacies for my generation.

I have begun the story in the year 1931, when the Quaker relief work which had followed the First World War was largely completed and the Nuremberg Friends Meeting was well established. At this time there was a discernible anxiety in the Quaker group about the growing menace of the Nazi party.

Friends had discovered an old Quaker Meeting House built in 1800, with a burial ground, first used in the 17th century, at Bad Pyrmont, some 50 miles south-west of Hanover. A number of old leather-bound volumes relating to the life of a Quaker community in Minden were also found at this time. The evidence of an earlier generation of Friends rooted in Germany meant Quakerism could not be dismissed as a recent foreign import.

Efforts began in 1932 to purchase the derelict building with the idea of starting a Meeting for Worship there and rebuilding the Quakerhouse as a conference centre. In 1933 Leonhard and Mary moved to Bad Pyrmont, to be the wardens and to create a Quaker base in this small town, away from the political tensions of the big cities.

Herta Israel, a German Friend of Jewish origin who had worked in the Berlin Quaker centre and was living as a refugee in Britain, wrote:[5]

> There is a difficulty for those of us who are not British in accepting Quakerism, because Friends value characteristics that are in some measure Anglo-Saxon. As far as I can see these are reservedness and caution, a clear sense of proportion and serenity, confidence that enables the spiritual holding up of one's head, through a heavy tempest and storm. This is exactly what we German Friends need most desperately.

Then I cover the war period, including Leonhard's time at Buchenwald. This became more vivid for me after a visit to the concentration camp in the spring of 1989, in what was then the German Democratic Republic. I have written about the period when Mary was on her own and of Leonhard's homecoming, and post-war experiences.

I have mentioned little about Leonhard and Mary's childhood and young adult experiences. Mary had been the seventh of fourteen children. Her father Beeston Tupholme (1851-1914) had worked as a draughtsman and engineer until 1896. Mary was brought up as a Baptist and had childhood dreams about undertaking mission work in China. However, she began work as a secretary in the City of London, soon after typewriters came into general use. She then moved to Liverpool and became secretary to a childrens' charity. The job involved travelling to Canada for six months of the year, to settle Liverpool orphans on farms there.

Leonhard, whose parents Martin and Christina Friedrich had died when he was young, had been working in London since 1911 representing a German firm and first met Mary in a boarding house there in 1912. At the outbreak of the First World War in 1914, Leonhard was interned as an enemy alien for four years on the Isle of Man. This was where he first met Quakers, who were concerned for the welfare of interned prisoners. Mary had by now become an industrial welfare worker and assisted in the founding of the Institute of Personnel Management. She had worked at Needlers and Reckitts in Hull and with C. & J. Clark in Street, all Quaker firms in those days. To the end of her life, Mary had wonderful support from Street Meeting, where she joined the Society of Friends in 1920. Soon after this, she went to Germany, to work for the Friends War Victims Relief Committee in Frankfurt and Nuremberg. On 3rd August 1922 Mary and Leonhard were married at the Sheffield Friends Meeting House and returned to Nuremberg.

CHAPTER I

Life in Nuremberg 1931

LEONHARD AND MARY FRIEDRICH had lived in Nuremberg since their marriage in 1922. Leonhard was by this time 42 years old. He had grown up in this medieval city, though he had been born in the village of Segnitz-am-Main. He worked as export sales manager for a firm named Huber Jordan Koerne, making transfer designs for decorating porcelain. He spoke English fluently, after working in Hatton Gardens for a German stationery firm called Kara, from 1911 until his internment on the Isle of Man during the First World War.

His wife Mary was 49 years old in 1931 and I was their only child, aged eight. In 1924 they had started a Friends Meeting for Worship at 13 Theresien Strasse, where they also opened a Quaker relief centre, known as the Depot. This was supported by the Friends Service Council in London. The Depot provided subsidised food and clothing to help some 700 families recommended by the town welfare department as being hungry and poor, but ineligible for official benefits.

The reparations imposed on Germany by the Versailles Peace Treaty 1919, had included sanctions against the import of essential raw materials and food, leading to a great deal of malnutrition, rickets and TB among children. Hunger diseases unknown in England were frequently diagnosed, and were of particular concern to the German immigrant community in America. President Hoover, a Quaker, responded to their lobbying with the provision of a very large-scale school feeding programme, and 11,000 school feeding centres were opened. The President asked the American Friends Service Committee (AFSC) to administer the programme, which required the presence in Germany of many American Friends and non-Quaker staff. At one time the *'Quakerspeisung'*, was providing a meal-a-day for a million undernourished children. The legendary Quaker school meals programme is remembered to this day.[1]

British Friends hoped their work in Germany would achieve some reconciliation and bridge-building with the people, to overcome the enmity engendered by war. From 1922-7 they operated similar Depots in Frankfurt and Leipzig, where poor people could obtain food and clothing at a quarter of the shop prices.[1] The Depots served children suffering from deficiency diseases and hungry students, as well as some unemployed professional people, who could get no help elsewhere. Problems of poverty had been made worse by a hyper-inflation, with money losing virtually all its value. For instance in December 1923 Mary had to take a shopping-bag full of paper money to the market in order to return home with half a bag of food. At that time US $1 was worth 4,200,000,000 marks.

Reparation payments to the Allies after the 1914-18 war exacerbated the problems of the world-wide economic depression, which hit Germany harder than other industrial countries. Unemployed youth were creating mayhem in the streets and fears of political upheaval were growing. Emil Fuchs, a theologian who later became a Friend, warned that this would strengthen the forces of Communism. Hans Albrecht, the Clerk of the German Yearly Meeting, warned that on the German side of the border areas between France and Germany there was smouldering discontent. Richard Cary, a journalist and Representative of the American Friends Service Committee in Berlin, wrote in *The Friend*: 'Of the twenty million unemployed in the industrial world, five million are in Germany'.[2]

The German government provided a meagre dole for the first six months of unemployment, but thereafter those without work had to depend on charity. Hitler's growing political influence stirred up discontent, but President Hindenburg and the army were reluctant to stop him.

Hungry people were ready to listen to Hitler's promises of a brighter future. The Nazi leaders travelled tirelessly all over the country to make speeches, which were reported in the newspapers and heard over the new radios which had recently become widely available in public places and many homes. The Nazis were gaining in strength and were visible on the streets wearing the brown shirt and breeches of the Sturm Abteilung (SA). Unemployed youth signing up with the SA were given a uniform, canteen meals and pocket-money allowances. They took part in Nazi indoctrination and filled the streets during political demonstrations. There was also the Security Service (SS) elite corps wearing black uniforms bearing a Death Head symbol, created as Hitler's bodyguard.

Elizabeth Fox Howard who visited Germany in April 1931 reported that conditions were worsening and despair was driving people to the Nazis. She said people were operating on a short fuse, there were pent-up feelings of injustice among people of all walks of life. In retrospect we know that it was a deliberate part of the SA training to fan the flames of any small disturbance into a public brawl.

The year 1931 had been difficult for Leonhard and Mary and the Quaker group in Nuremberg. Several members of the Friends Meeting had lost their jobs and were very poor. Mary wrote to Helen Dixon, at the Friends Service Council in London, asking if she could send them 18lb packages of cheese, butter and tea. In response, English Friends organised a 'Group Parcels Scheme' for German Friends. Germans became anxious about the future, though they believed that law and order would be maintained so long as Hindenburg was President. They were, however, aware that he was 84 years old and his days were numbered.

Leonhard and Mary wrote to Clarence Pickett (1884-1965) of the American Friends Service Committee on 31st May, asking if they could consider sending a Friend to come and live with the Nuremberg Group:

> To demonstrate that the love of Christ is the foundation of all our activities to counter evil. You may think we German Friends should be able to do this for ourselves, but we are few, and do not have the tradition. We do not feel strong and are all suffering materially. It would be of great help if a concerned Friend could live amongst us and stay for a longer period, giving us the Quaker message quite simply as the early Friends did.[6]

Our Home Life

My parents lived in a top-floor walk-up flat, at 25 Wetzendorfer Strasse, on the northern edge of Nuremberg. The building was one of a block of 60 flats, built around 1910. From our fourth floor bedroom window to the north, one could see for miles over flat farmland, with the occasional old farmhouse and trees growing beside small streams, where we picked cowslips in the spring.

Just across the road and below our window, we looked onto the steep roof of an old farm and could watch the farmers wife draw water from her well. To the right was the Bieling School where I had started in the first class at the age of seven the previous September. The massive building had been erected in about 1910 to provide primary and secondary education for 1,200 pupils, in classes of 50 or more children. From the kitchen and balcony on the south side of our flat we looked down onto our garden, which was one of a fenced group of allotments. This separated us from the town and thousands of other four-storey flats which were typical of the early 20th century working-class housing. Our flat was five minutes' walk to the shops, and to a frequent rattling tram service to the town centre, Leonhard's office and the Friends Meeting Rooms.

This was a lovely home for me as an eight-year-old girl. There were lots of families in neighbouring flats where I was always welcome and Mary encouraged the neighbourhood children to use our garden as a play area. The mothers could see us from their balconies and call us back for meals. I have photos to remind me of a happy childhood playing in the sandpit, the summerhouse, the swing, ball-games on the lawn, and hide-and-seek in the bushes (illustrations 5 and 6). We took great delight that winter in tobogganing and skating on a frozen lake. There were seven of us children from five families who were the closest of friends, until the divisions of the Nazi world affected us too.

Mary met two of these families again after the Second World War, in December 1951 when she was visiting New York and wrote in her diary:

> I stayed a few days with our Friend Anna Curtis, who had been a Quaker relief worker in Germany in the 20's. She now lives in a tiny down-town apartment, where I slept on the sofa. Anna arranged a meeting with two Jewish women who had lived in our block of flats in Nuremberg. Frau Wuga and Frau Fleishman came together and were delighted to remember happier times. Being Jewish they were thankful to have got away from Germany, but it was difficult to earn enough to live on in New York. They both said how much our friendliness had transformed life in the block of flats.
>
> Frau Wuga remembered how some of the parents wanted me to stop Heinz, then aged five, from playing in our garden. When I heard it was the mother of Ella, Brenda's best friend, who was complaining, I had apparently said: 'That is just too bad, it will have to be Ella who stays out of the garden, because I am not stopping Heinz from coming'. Mary went on to ask about the rest of the family. The father had apparently died in the 30s. Heinz, the son, had gone to England with a Jewish group in 1938.
>
> Frau Wuga stayed in Nuremberg to look after an elderly mother, who had died on the journey to Theresienstadt concentration camp. Frau Wuga then changed her name, identity and appearance, and worked in a restaurant. She had no food coupons and was often hungry. The place she had lived in was bombed and for two years she shared a room with several others, without cooking facilities, heating, or even a door. In 1947 her son Heinz, who was working as a cook in Scotland, was able to bring her out of Germany. He remained in Scotland, but Frau Wuga later joined her sister in New York, where she is employed for 14 hours a day as a cook in a boarding house.
>
> Frau Fleishman had come to the States with her husband just before the war, but had not received much help from the Jewish organisation which brought them there. They were still living in the same two-roomed flat they had found the week they arrived and her husband was no longer well enough to work.

5. Mary, Brenda and Leonhard beside the summerhouse, 1932.

6. My playmates, 1932.
Heinz Wuga (Jewish child),
Irmgard Zantner, Brenda
Friedrich and Ella Roetzer.

Our flat in Wetzendorfer Strasse may not have seemed quite such an idyllic home for Mary who had to carry all the shopping, coal and refuse up and down four flights of wooden stairs. She also had to manage with fewer household conveniences than her sisters' families living in suburban England. The first improvement to our flat was to install a bath in the long narrow toilet, but as there was no hot water system every drop had to be heated in pans on the cooker, which was fuelled by soft powdery brown coal. This must be why I remember spending most Saturday afternoons having a luxurious bath in the home of my mother's closest friend, Edith Straus. When domestic gas became available later that year Mary was very glad to be able to install a gas cooker and a rather terrifying geyser to heat the bath water. It was a remarkable year for improvements in our flat, because we also acquired a telephone. Leonhard bought our first radio so that he and Mary could listen to the BBC news, and I enjoyed hearing Uncle Mac on Children's Hour.

Our flat had three rooms plus a small kitchen, balcony and bathroom. I slept in a corner of my parents' bedroom and the best room was kept tidy for frequent callers. Perhaps there was less need for a child to have her own room because we had fewer toys and there was just enough space for my newly acquired Victorian doll's house. Mary had bought it in 1908 for her nieces, Constance and Margaret Tupholme, who lived in Sheffield. They kindly had it crated and sent by rail to me for Christmas 1930. It is now in the care of my grand-daughter, Elena, who lives in the Isle of Skye.

Each of our rooms was heated separately by huge ceramic tiled stoves, burning wood and coal. The climate of southern Germany is more extreme than England's, the winter is cold and snowy, the summer is warmer with much less rain. Each flat had a fenced and padlocked area in the attic for drying clothes and storing cases. There were similar areas in the cellar for storing coal and wood, as well as potatoes and apples, which were carefully laid out on shelves. Most families preserved eggs, fruits and vegetables. Beans were cut up and salted in tall earthenware containers and other items were bottled. There was also a meat-safe kept near a window, which served as a refrigerator for milk and butter and other perishables.

In the 1930s, before domestic washing-machines were generally available, my aunts in England boiled their coppers for the weekly wash. In Nuremberg Mary found housewives had a different approach to dirty linen. Each family had sufficient linen for washdays to be held at intervals of six or eight weeks. There was a laundry room and yard in the basement, which could be booked by tenants for two days at a time. On the first day Mary carried down the dirty linen which had accumulated in the attic, and soaked it in cold water and soda in five huge galvanised baths. She then prepared the fuel for the boiler which Leonhard lit early in the morning before going to work. The washerwoman Mary hired to help arrived at 7 am, and they worked together in hot steam, all day long. The wash-house floor sloped down to a central drain which enabled the women, wearing wooden clogs, to slop the water around in a way which seemed a pure delight to me. The soaking sheets were transferred to the copper for boiling, after which they were lifted out with strong sticks and hung over trestles to drain. After a cold rinse some 20 sheets and shirts and underwear were put through a huge wooden mangle and hung on the line in the yard to dry. There was never quite enough space on the line for everything, so those items dry enough for ironing were taken down and rolled up. If wash-day turned out to be rainy the wet clothes had to be carried up five flights to the attic, where there was an indoor washing line. When almost dry, the sheets and pillow cases were taken up the road on a little cart to the steam mangles for ironing. Finally, shirts and the starched collars and dresses were ironed in the kitchen, and the linen cupboard was filled up once more. The whole process took most of a week, and was frequently referred to in Mary's diary. Washdays were much like this to the end of Mary's housekeeping days in 1968.

Milk and fresh breakfast rolls and farmhouse rye bread were delivered daily. A delicious aroma came from the bakery near the tram-stop, where customers brought their own cakes to be baked. At Christmas Mary took a huge *stollen* on a metre-length board. Her weekly shopping expedition was to Tietz, a large department store in town with a grocery section, rather like Selfridges. It was owned by a Jewish family with English connections and the managing director was Wilfrid Israel, who was born and partly educated in England. He had had contacts with English Quakers such as Ruth Fry and Marion Fox because he had assisted them in relief work in Germany following the First World War. In the 1930s he became a discreet but remarkable leader of the Jewish community.[3] I doubt that Leonhard and Mary knew him personally, but they went out of their way to patronise Jewish stores.

In May Leonhard's cousins Lily Rupp and Kaetchen Schelleman came visiting from Marktbreit. They brought 400 fresh eggs with them and these were preserved and kept in the cellar for use in the winter. Leonhard kept in close touch with his cousins from the village on the Main where he was born. He sometimes took us visiting there for short holidays. I learned to swim in a sheltered bay of the River Main.

Mary missed good Ceylon tea until she discovered a shop in England willing to send one or two large containers at a time. She sold quarter-pound packets to her friends who greatly appreciated it, making a little money on the transaction.

The winter of 1930-1 had been particularly severe. Mary suffered repeated bouts of ill-health, although she was naturally a very energetic person. In February the doctor X-rayed her, fearing gall stones, but found none. He prescribed castor oil, a treatment guaranteed to make anyone feel worse. Mary was also very short of money and was most grateful to a visiting Philadelphian Quaker who paid for some dental treatment.

As a small child I was often off school for weeks with bronchitis. The prescribed treatment was to put steaming hot compresses right around the front and back of my chest, and around my neck, secured with flannel bandages to keep in the heat. The whole process was repeated every four hours. I was also anaemic and had rickets like so many children living in Germany at this time. I was given plenty of cod liver oil and attended remedial exercise classes to correct curvature of the spine and knock knees.

We spent much of our leisure time in the home of a gynaecologist, Dr Willi Straus, and his English wife Edith. Like Mary, Edith never spoke German very well and spent a few weeks in England every summer. She was very friendly and hospitable in arranging social evenings at her home for young people. She often rolled back the carpet for dancing because she loved the newly-introduced foxtrot. Leonhard enjoyed playing bridge with Willi and on one occasion went with him to see a performance by Charlie Chaplin at the Phoclus Theatre. Edith and Mary remained lifelong friends and Edith was the safe anchor for me when the war years separated our family. Edith shared the responsibilities of running the Depot and the British Wives Club with Mary. On 6th May 1931 Mary and I went to the Nuremberg airport to see Edith off to Berlin. This was the first time we had seen an airplane on the ground, or heard of anyone we knew travelling this way; it was very exciting and we admired her courage.

Leonhard loved to take us for country excursions. Sometimes it was with a large group from the Quaker Meeting or with visitors from abroad. We would travel on a local train which had an open viewing platform at each end of the carriage. We walked through lovely pine forests and sometimes stopped for lunch at a country inn.

Mary's Quaker Work

Mary was always deeply interested in people and got to know the members of the Meeting well. She had a gift for listening to others, and for helping people discover their own inner resources. She made useful suggestions towards finding solutions to practical problems and made those who came to Meeting feel welcome and valued.

During the earlier post-war years when the Friends Service Council (FSC) and the American Friends Service Committee (AFSC) supported relief work, it had been necessary to monitor and report on the changing welfare needs. In 1931 Mary was still keeping in touch with city officials, and she regularly visited Herr Hoffman of the Welfare Department, Dr Fischer at the Employment Department and Dr Meyer in the Statistics office. She then wrote quarterly progress reports to the London and Philadelphia Quaker offices, also describing the Meeting's activities. Copies were sent to Effie McAfie at the AFSC office in Paris and to Emma Cadbury, the AFSC worker at the Vienna Quaker Centre. Emma was the sister of the Quaker historian Henry Cadbury.

Leonhard and Mary were in close touch with the FSC and AFSC Representatives at the Berlin Quaker Centre, who were Corder and Gwen Catchpool from London, and Richard and Mary Cary from Philadelphia. These Friends visited Nuremberg several times a year to encourage the group and gather information for their assessment of the political situation in Germany. The Representatives frequently wrote articles for Quaker journals about the economic and social consequences of the Versailles Treaty, reporting the feelings of foreboding which Friends held about the rise of Nazism.

The British Wives Club had developed out of Quaker welfare work with the internees and POWs in Britain during the First World War. When Leonhard had returned to Nuremberg after his own four years of internment in the Isle of Man, he found that many returning POWs felt strange in their own home town, having had very different war-time experiences from their relatives. A number of the men had also returned with British brides. These young women spoke little German, were shocked by the austere living conditions, and welcomed the opportunity to meet together. The formation of the club was a very natural project for Mary and Edith Straus, although other members of the Meeting also participated.

Mary and Edith helped many club members through periods of trouble. One of these was Mrs Gehringer, who had made a disastrous marriage. Her husband was one of the unemployed who signed on with the SA and wore their brown uniform to intimidate those around him. He was just the kind of bully the SA encouraged. Mary wrote in her diary:

> Edith and I visited Mrs Gehringer in Mai Strasse, where she lives in a street of temporary wooden huts provided for the unemployed. She and the children were hungry and shivering with cold. We listened to the story of her husband's cruelty and beating, and felt very distressed for her.

A few weeks later Mary records that all the Gehringers' furniture was taken by the bailiffs, in payment for debts her husband had incurred. Mary appeared in court to support her.

The Friedrichs visitors' book lists the names of 37 Friends in 1931. Most of the guests were from America or Britain, but Chester and Minnie Pickett Bowles came from Japan and Heinz and Karen Tucher were from a noble family, some of whom were famous Nuremberg brewers, on home leave from their assignment as Quaker missionaries in India. Friends came to see the Quaker work, but also wanted to see the sights of the picturesque medieval Nuremberg. Among them was Effie McAfie, formally Professor of Archaeology at Hunter College in New York, though at this time she was AFSC Representative in Paris, where a great deal of Quaker relief work was taking place.

In April, an English Friend arrived saying he had no money. Mary invited him to stay. She also reported a few weeks later looking after two tramps who were friends of Alfons Paquet. In June Dr Alfred Garrett and Elizabeth Goodhue, Mary Cary's mother came again, but these Friends were not short of money, and Mary enjoyed being taken out to meals and using taxis with them when she arranged visits to the city officials and the youth services.

Summer visits to England

Mary and I usually visited England for about six weeks in the summer, returning to Germany in time for the Yearly Meeting at the end of July. Leonhard sometimes organised a walking holiday in the mountains, acting as a courier to earn his expenses.

In 1931 Mary and I left on 25th May to stay in Paris with Effie McAfie and to learn about Quaker work there and meet French Friends at their centre in Guy de la Brosse. I had been having private French lessons since the spring in preparation, but neither of us could cope with the language when we were on our own. Toot van Oordt, a Dutch worker at the Quaker Centre, took us sightseeing to Les Invalides, the Champs Elysees and the Louvre. Mary went to Versailles to see the table on which the famous treaty of 1919 was signed. I was left with a French family while Mary attended meetings and I discovered the difficulties of making myself understood.

On 3rd June we crossed the English Channel and stayed with Mary's eldest sister at Southgate. We visited Aunt Ellie and old friends from the Hornsey Lane area where Mary's Tupholme family had lived.[4] Mary visited Joan Fry at Friends House where she was working at the Germany desk, and was invited to join the FSC Germany Emergency committee meeting.

On 11th June we travelled to Peterborough to stay in the house where I was born at 76 Lincoln Road East. This was where my grandmother Sarah Tupholme was looked after by Mary's youngest sister Margaret and her husband Wilfred Harbour. Granny was 78 years old and very stout. She always wore a richly embroidered black satin dress with a white frill around the neck and a gold brooch of four interlocking rings under her chin. She was confined to the ground floor in a wheelchair. Since other people did the housework, Granny always had plenty of time to listen to the chatter of children, to play cards or to produce an interesting button box. Occasionally we took her out in an enormous bathchair. It had a small steering wheel in front which Granny manipulated, while we pushed from behind.

Visits to Peterborough were the most enjoyable part of our holiday. Mary adored looking after her mother, and I loved the easy atmosphere there. This year Aunt Margaret said the new puppy she had acquired was to be my very own dog, though it sadly had to live in Peterborough. We went swimming in the River Nene and I enjoyed donkey rides up and down Lincoln Road East. Occasionally Aunt Margaret took me to a fairground at Skegness, though Mary rather disapproved of such a frivolous time and money-wasting activity. Mary's sister Jessie Holland and my cousins Philip and Denys were also staying with Granny, so there was even more fun. We also visited Great Aunt Kathleen Watson who wore a black velvet choker round her neck and lived two doors down the road. One day Mary took us children to the cemetery to weed and put new plants on the graves of her father Beeston Tupholme and her mother's parents, Henry Watson and Anne Bird, who had been confectioners in Long Causeway, Peterborough.

After Mary was rested we went to stay with her brother, Bert Tupholme and his wife Amy, in Sheffield. Their adult children, Norman and Margaret, were also at home. Mary's father, Beeston Tupholme, had grown up in Sheffield and he returned to live there after he married Sarah Watson in Peterborough in 1872. Amy was a wonderful dressmaker and always made something new for me. These annual visits were very important to Mary as a reminder of a more normal and less stressful life than she was experiencing in Germany. Her brother Bert was recognised as the businessman in the family, so she sought his advice about the investment of small savings she had from before her marriage. He had a lovely dry Yorkshire sense of humour and was skilled at all kinds of wood and metalwork, especially at repairing old clocks.

This year Mary took me to visit Osbourne's, the steel mill in Sheffield where she had worked as a welfare officer during the First World War. It was a hot and frightening place where buckets of molten steel were carried on overhead rails with chains and pulleys, and finally poured into moulds and beaten into shape with huge hammers.

In August Mary went to Birmingham to attend a Woodbrooke Summer School, leaving me in Peterborough. She was thrilled about the opportunity to attend this Quaker college. In her diary she described a visit to Cadbury's chocolate factory. She also mentioned a peace demonstration addressed by Norman Angell, who called for the League of Nations to re-negotiate German reparation payments, despite opposition from America.

Mary gave a talk at Woodbrooke entitled 'Germany in Distress'. She reported that the audience were critical because she appeared not to understand how bad conditions were for the unemployed in Britain. She was also challenged by a German student at Woodbrooke who appeared to have Nazi sympathies.

Mary's friend Edith Straus from Nuremberg was also in England at this time, visiting her mother in Milverton Road in Kilburn. She had the use of the family car and when Mary returned from Birmingham we had a pleasant few days together, visiting Jordans Friends Meeting House in Buckinghamshire and Windsor Castle, where we saw Queen Mary's amazing dolls house. Another day Edith drove us to Broadstairs where we stayed with Mary's childhood friend Muriel Neal. The sandy beach was cold and windy. On 3rd September we returned to Nuremberg, a 30 hour journey by boat and train. Leonhard was there to meet us and had also had a very cold time in the Tyrol.

Leonhard's Employment and Quaker Work

Since June 1921, a year before they were married, Leonhard had worked as export manager for the firm Huber Jordan Koerne. He used to bring home samples of floral designs on Thomas/Rosenthal porcelain for Mary's comments. But the 1931 world-wide recession caused a severe reduction in orders for the firm from England and America. In October his wages were cut by 10%, as part of a national policy to reduce the pay for salaried workers.

Leonhard had become very interested in Quakerism while he was interned during the war in the Isle of Man. James Bailey and other Friends visited the prisoners and provided books and craft materials. When the German Yearly Meeting was started in 1925, Leonhard was one of the first 40 members of the *Gesellschaft Der Freunde* (Society of Friends) and served as Treasurer and a member of the Executive Committee for 35 years. Quarterly Executive meetings were held in various parts of Germany where Quaker Meetings had been established. In the Nuremberg group he held many responsibilities, leading the youth group or Bible study, acting as Clerk, caretaker and Elder of the group.

German Friends became increasingly uneasy about the situation in Europe. There was poverty, fear of rearmament, racial injustice in the world, and in Germany against the Jews. Quakers believed in the power of love giving strength to the powerless, and wrote letters to Chancellor Bruening and President Hoover. A few weeks after the Yearly Meeting, on 21st September, the world economic problems were exacerbated by Britain's renunciation of the Gold Standard.

Many of the Friends attending Yearly Meeting were teachers with a real commitment to liberal Quaker educational methods who wanted their children to have the chance to grow up in a Quaker environment. There was much discussion about the possibility of opening a German-speaking Quaker school, which to be free of Nazi influence was later established at Ommen in the Netherlands.

Some weeks after Yearly Meeting, on 12th September, a Nazi *pogrom* was directed against a Berlin Synagogue. This prompted the Berlin Meeting to write a letter of sympathy to the Jewish community. The matter was taken further by the Executive Committee which sent 300 letters to other Churches and to the Catholic and Evangelical Bishops. Unfortunately only seven replies were received. The letter asked the Christian community to stand firm against this outrage directed towards fellow citizens, saying there was great urgency to take measures to end the growth and virulence of anti-Semitism.[5]

The Nuremberg Friends Meeting

The Minute Book entries for 1931 show an astonishing amount of activity, and a wide interest in world events. The Meeting rented two large ground floor rooms at 13 Theresien Strasse, a 15th century four-storey building within the walls of the old city, bombed during the Second World War. It was situated on a busy city road where noisy trams and horse-carts travelled among the motor cars. On Sunday mornings it was quieter, unless the church bells from Frauen Kirche or Sebaldus Kirche were pealing. Regular Sunday Meetings for Worship were held and there were two children's classes, following lesson plans. On Thursday evenings Leonhard enjoyed leading the youth group, combining discussion and singing with social activities. German Friends of all ages were sensitive to any authoritarian attitudes and appreciated the democratic Quaker style.

The monthly Bible study evening was occasionally led by a visiting Friend, but more often by Adolf Bauman, who lived in nearby Fuerth. He had joined Friends in England many years earlier, when he was working at Dewsbury, and had a scholarly understanding of the Bible. At each of the monthly business meeting, the Advices and Queries were read. These are a series of questions about the application of Quaker beliefs to everyday life, to which written answers were regularly minuted.

7 and 8. *Nuremberg Friends Meeting Rooms, exterior ground floor, and interior.*

In April, members of the Meeting were out on the streets like many Quaker groups in other countries, collecting signatures for a petition in support of the World Disarmament Conference, to be held in June at Lausanne. With President Hoover's concurrence this conference finally agreed to suspending war reparation payments in return for a substantial terminal sum, which was never paid. This agreement greatly enhanced the reputation of Chancellor Bruening.

Open Meetings were organised by Friends on a wide variety of subjects, attracting up to a hundred people. Among the topics for 1931 were:

Chester Bowles	Friends in Japan
Effie McAfee	Perspectives from France
Magda Durrbeck	Christ in the Present Day
Tony Napits	Race Problems
Dr Alfred Garrett	The Psalms
	Unity in Christendom
	Quakerism: A Religion of Experience
Elizabeth Goodhue	The True Religion
	Setting Goals for Life
	The Meaning of Marriage
Dr Zayd	International Reconciliation
Ruth Pumphrey	Mission Work in Labrador
Louisa Jacob	Ireland
Gertrud Jacob	Palestine and Syria
Carolina Wood	China, Japan and India

In the autumn Louisa Jacob, a retired American teacher Friend from Moorestown, New Jersey, came to Nuremberg in response to Leonhard's request to Clarence Pickett earlier in the year. She stayed for several weeks getting to know Friends and returned later for visits lasting many months. She was dearly loved. Louisa was very interested in supporting the international peace movement, focussing on the League of Nations in Geneva. In November 1931, she wrote the following letter to Clarence Pickett at the AFSC:

> Whilst still uncertain about how to spend my retirement, I received a letter from Mary Friedrich saying how much they would appreciate help in the many activities of the Meeting. I arrived on 4th November and found one is not asked what one can do, but during the notices at the end of Meeting one hears: 'Our Friend from America will do so and so . . .' and one has to accept to do the best one can. I led a class for some young people giving ideas for running children's classes.

Anna Brandstetter has been teaching for eight years, but now a promising young Friend, Sophie Schubert, who has a real gift for understanding children, has come forward. There is a fortnightly social evening on Sundays. The event of the month was when the Executive Committee met in Nuremberg, and we entertained visitors from all over Germany.

Other activities include a monthly social for some of the former members of the Depot, and also the British Wives Club. Mary Friedrich keeps in touch with many individuals in need who visit her at any time in her home. Her mother-heart is big enough to receive and comfort them. She feeds them from whatever she has available, and often sends them home with little surprises such as half a pound of butter 'for the children'. One learns what true sharing means living in a place where poverty lies behind almost every door. Leonhard and Mary have set themselves the difficult task of keeping this little group of Friends together in the spirit of peace and brotherhood.[6]

Christmas

At Christmas Louisa wrote and produced a nativity play for the youth group to perform to an audience of 60 people. I was proud to be the angel Gabriel. Afterwards we paid our eighth annual visit to a home for crippled children bearing toys and presents. The usual Christmas parties for the British Wives Club and a group of needy elderly people who used to depend on the Depot had been pleasant occasions. Each departing guest went home with a parcel containing cheese, tea, butter, *Lebkuchen* etc, in Christmas wrapping with a sprig of fir and a candle.

This Christmas was one of the highlights in the life of the Friedrich family. Mary was looking forward to the arrival of Ru Schuleman from Holland and Florence Livingstone from England, colleagues from her former factory welfare employment. They arrived for our family Christmas Eve celebrations. Real candles were lit on a sweet-smelling fir tree which filled a corner of the room from floor to ceiling. There were plenty of presents for me and modest gifts for the adults.

On Christmas Day we all went to Willi and Edith Straus's home. At least a dozen of us sat down to an elegant Christmas dinner, which ended up with dishes piled high with fruit, among which soap and marzipan replicas were hidden. After dinner there were games of bridge for the older generation and party games and dancing for the younger ones. Amongst this gaiety Mary caught Edith in a pensive mood, wondering if this would be their last such Christmas together. They felt Germany was heading for a civil war between the Communists and Fascists, which would break up the kind of life they knew. Edith and Willi were both from Jewish families and felt it would be impossible to stay much longer. Their son Edgar had already left for England a year earlier, in 1930, when the secondary school he attended created two streams, one for Protestants and another for Jews and Catholics.

Directly after Christmas we went on a winter holiday in the nearby Frankische Schweitz with Livy and Ru, who had joined us for Christmas. We travelled by train to Grafenberg and piled our rucksacks on two sleighs for the three-hour walk through the snow to the Hotel zur Post at Eggloffstein. The next day we had planned to walk to the village of Grossweinstein, pulling our luggage on the sleigh. We never got there. There had been a heavy snowfall overnight, though the morning had been sunny and bright. After walking for hours, we could find no village with a Gasthaus willing to serve lunches or provide accommodation. We only just survived by eating huge quantities of chocolate bars. By five on a dark evening we managed to return to our previous nights lodging at Hotel Zur Post. We were frozen and our chilblains burned when we reached the warm rooms. Our host advised us to rub our chilblains in buckets of snow which he brought to our room.

On New Year's Eve we climbed the hill to the village church for the candle-lit midnight mass. The church was warm and filled with people and there was only standing-room at the back for us. The singing was beautiful. But we were anxious about Mary who had fallen on the icy metal shoe-scraper in the porch. She later had a great deal of pain from a bone splinter on her patella. It should have been removed surgically, but no one thought to do so and it troubled her for years.

CHAPTER II

Nuremberg: Last Days of Weimar Republic 1932

Leonhard to Lose his Job

WE RETURNED TO NUREMBERG from our brief winter holiday in a crowded yellow post bus on 2nd January. Mary's friends who had been holidaying with us returned to their work in England and Holland. At home Leonhard found a letter from his employers waiting for him, saying:

> In view of the further economic and political developments we cannot avoid cutting down our staff to the absolute minimum. We therefore have to give you six-months notice to take effect from 30th June 1932.

This was devastating news. Although the recession was cited as the reason for his dismissal, Leonhard felt it was because he would not join the Nazi Party. The next day, while he was at work, Mary registered him at the Employment Exchange and also went to the Welfare Office to find out what benefits they could expect. After having shared their problems with the Meeting on 10th January, Mary wrote in her diary:

> There was a warm feeling of friendship and support. We will help each other in these hard times, and make our Meeting for Worship the bright spot in our lives.

Later that month Headley and Bep Horsnaill, British Quaker representatives at the Vienna Centre, came to stay. They were in a state of near panic, fearing a civil war in Germany. They had not intended to return to England until May, but were now planning to do so immediately and this added to Mary's anxiety.

Many people with foreign connections were thinking of leaving the country. Out of loyalty to German Quakers, Mary did not see this as an option for us. However, to give some measure of family security, she wrote to Street Meeting in Somerset, where she had become a Quaker, to ask for birthright membership in the Society of Friends for me. Leonhard and Mary had become members of Germany Yearly Meeting when it was established with a membership of 40 at Wartburg in 1925. There was no

24

provision for child membership among German Friends, and Mary felt she wanted me to be linked to Quakers in case anything should happen to them.

The Rise of Hitler, through Five Elections

1932 was a critical year in which Hitler exploited the political and economic problems of the Weimar democracy. Early in the year there was speculation as to whether the 84-year-old Hindenburg would stand for a further term as President. He had served honourably as a General in the First World War and had hoped to retire, but in view of the growing political extremism of both the right and the left, he felt duty-bound to continue. Hindenburg's support came from the traditionalists, industrialists and the Junkers, the titled Prussian landowners. Chancellor Bruening of the Catholic Centre Party fought a strong campaign for Hindenburg's re-election. Hitler's strategy was to stay out of Berlin and build support throughout the country. He led a campaign in every small town with amazing energy and had the intimidating support of the brown-shirted SA. The Nuremberg newspaper *Der Stuermer* was strongly pro-Nazi. The national election results on 13th March gave Hindenburg 49% of the votes, against Hitler's 30%, but the vote for Hitler had increased by five million since the previous election in 1930. A second national election was held on 10th April because Hindenburg had just fallen short of an outright majority. The electorate again re-affirmed Hindenburg's Presidency, whilst also increasing support for Hitler.

The government uncovered evidence that the SA, under the leadership of Captain Roehm, were planning a putsch. Chancellor Bruening therefore signed a decree to suppress Hitler's uniformed para-military organisations on 14th April. The Nazis reactions against this banning measure in the Reichstag, led to Chancellor Bruening's resignation on 29th May and his replacement by Franz von Papen, who governed by Presidential decree rather than through Parliament.

Street violence perpetrated by the SA then broke out, in which 86 people were killed. This led to a third election for the Reichstag held on 31st July. During the election campaign, Hitler spoke to large mass rallies in sports stadia throughout the country. The National Socialists won 230 of the 608 seats in the Reichstag and became the largest party, although the majority of voters were still against them. Hitler had now increased his votes to seven million. He visited Hindenburg to demand the Chancellorship, but was received very icily by the President who wanted a coalition government.

Although Hitler's supporters were impatient, they arranged a coalition with von Papen to ensure the election of Goering as President of the Parliament. Neither of the parties concerned had confidence in democratic institutions. Goering managed to double-cross von Papen and set the date of 6th November for the Reichstag's fourth national elections. There was a poor electoral turn-out, resulting in a loss of 34 seats for the Nazis in the Reichstag.

The German people were fed up with so many elections in one year. All the parties were running short of funds for campaigns. Von Papen had lost all credibility. After weeks of confusion, on 2nd December President Hindenburg chose General von Schleicher to be Chancellor, though there seemed little public support for this appointment. Hitler was in real difficulties because he could not find sufficient money to keep his paramilitary forces in their uniforms. He cut the salaries of party workers and sent them onto the streets with collecting boxes. But surprisingly, on 16th January 1933, Hitler announced that generous financial support had been obtained from German businessmen in the Ruhr.

Chancellor Schleicher realised he would be unable to create employment or improve stability while the Junkers and industrialists supported Hitler. Their support for Hitler was given when they realised the Communists were gaining strength from the misery of unemployment and recession. The Junkers anticipated that Hitler would counter-balance this trend. Nazi intrigues eventually forced Chancellor Schleicher to resign on 28th January 1933.

Over the next two days there was a struggle for power between the politicians, the army and the police. In the final crucial hours, the army sided with Hitler and on 30th January 1933, Hindenburg named Adolf Hitler as Chancellor to form a coalition government with von Papen. They both privately resolved 'to end this democratic nonsense', thereby ending 14 years of the Weimar Republic and marking the beginning of the Third Reich.[1]

Mary's Life with the Meeting in Nuremberg

Germany's economic situation remained very bleak. There were many bankruptcies among small businessmen and the first of the big bank crashes occurred. In her report of February 1932 to Friends in London and Philadelphia Mary wrote:

> In Nuremberg there are 88,000 people registered as unemployed, and a quarter of the population are dependent on the city for welfare. Many more men are working on short-time with reduced wages and are not much better off than the unemployed. The weather is bitterly cold and there is much suffering. During this year there are increasing requests to Friends to give relief, especially for people who had taken a firm anti-Nazi stand or for people who were suspected to be Communists.

Edith Straus and Mary were active in supporting the British Wives Club. They were visiting each other frequently to share their worries, to help with the ironing, or to plan another activity for the Club. At this time one member of the Meeting locked his wife in the toilet, and would not let her out, until she had written a hundred lines saying: 'I will be obedient to my husband'. Mary must have dealt with this example of male dominance quite well, because the man became a good friend and loyal Quaker for the rest of his life.

At the end of April Edith had an acute gall bladder attack and her husband Willi took her to England to recuperate. On his return he told Mary that England felt like a completely different world from Germany. Street violence was escalating and Mary confessed in her diary: 'I felt unwell and nervy, I was so anxious about the future'.

In May, Manfred and Lily Pollatz and their four children visited from Dresden. They were both fine teachers and had for some years considered starting a Quaker school, possibly in the Netherlands. Two years later they left Germany, taking six adopted Jewish children, in addition to their own four, to start a home school in Haarlem. With some financial support from the Friends Service Council in Britain and from individual Friends, they eventually provided a refuge and school for some 20 Jewish children, and were recognised by the Dutch education authorities.

Disarmament – Nuremberg Friends

The Meeting had been very interested in a further session at the Disarmament Conference held in Switzerland in February, where Chancellor Bruening fought hard for recognition of Germany's right to re-arm as France had done. The French resisted, but eventually there was a compromise in Germany's favour. Louisa Jacob had been in Geneva as one of the Quaker observers, and reported on her experiences to the Nuremberg Meeting. Mary had heard the inaugural speech by Arthur Henderson, the Chairman of the conference, on the radio. The Nuremberg Friends then held a public peace meeting with the Womens International League for Peace and Freedom on 15th June. Mary wrote in her diary:

> Leonhard was away in Berlin. The authorities feared a disturbance might occur and posted police guards to patrol outside, while two armed policemen sat with us in the Meeting Room. Luckily the occasion was entirely peaceful. But the Friends were puzzled why Louisa Jacob was not with us. Just as I had slipped out to prepare lunch for the group, Brenda answered a phone call, reporting that an American lady had been run over by a motor bike. Would I come at once. I discovered poor Louisa had a 10 cm wound in her leg, and injuries to

her arm. I went with her to the nursing home and stayed until she was comfortably in bed. She was kept there for six weeks, but said she felt cherished by visits from her many Nuremberg friends.

Summer Visit to England

At the end of June Mary and I left for England. We made the usual visits to family and friends, but the highlight of the holiday took place in Peterborough where Granny, Sarah Tupholme, celebrated her 80th birthday. There was a feast of strawberries and a magnificent iced cake. Seventeen of her children and grandchildren were present. Aunt Kate Russell came from Missouri, and shared her distress about the marital problems of their sister Jennie Falconer in St. Louis. The brothers and sisters in Peterborough decided to contribute a monthly allowance for Jennie to help look after her four small children.

On 2nd July Mary heard from Leonhard that despite hoping for a last minute reprieve from losing his job, he was now unemployed. Mary wrote in her diary:

> We have no prospects of getting any insurance benefit until all our savings are exhausted, so I am encouraging Leonhard to come to England as soon as he can to prevent him from getting too depressed. We have shared what we had with others in the past, now we must share their poverty too. I talked these problems over with my brother Bert and his wife Amy Tupholme in Sheffield, who advised me to visit the American Consul to explore emigration to America. However when we heard this could not be contemplated unless we had several thousand pounds for settling-in costs, we pursued the idea no further. This was a disappointment.

When Leonhard had arrived, Bert took us for a lovely drive to Derbyshire to visit Hardwick Hall. After which we went to Dorking to stay with Helen Dixon. On one of the days we came up to London, for a visit to the Natural History and Science Museums in South Kensington, we caught a glimpse of King George V's garden party at Buckingham Palace from the top of a bus.

A few days later we took the train from Waterloo to Glastonbury. The three tickets cost £2. We were met by Morton, the footman of Roger and Hilda Clark and were taken to stay at their home at Millfield. We had the west room with an adjoining dressing room. It was all in a style we were not accustomed to, but we enjoyed it.

Roger Clark was the Managing Director of C & J Clark, the shoe factory, where Mary had been the first industrial welfare worker in 1922. The three of us were fitted with new shoes during our stay.

On 30th July the Clarks arranged for us to join the factory staff at their annual holiday camp at the seaside near Weymouth. Mary still knew some of the hundred staff members who were there with their families, and she helped with the First Aid post. A large bell tent was provided for our family, equipped with three iron bedsteads. We returned to Germany via Holland and arrived for our first visit to Bad Pyrmont on 24th August, to attend the Yearly Meeting which was to be held in the Kur Hotel there.

Yearly Meeting at Bad Pyrmont

Bad Pyrmont was a small country spa town of some 8,000 inhabitants, 40 miles south-west of Hanover. It is set in an open valley of rich agricultural land, surrounded by wooded hillsides. Four different types of healing waters were found in local springs, along with hot mud which is still recommended for treating rheumatism. In the 17th century the area had been developed as a spa by the Prince of Waldeck, who designed a park around his moated castle and planted a remarkable avenue of trees leading from his castle up the hill to the Bomberg observation tower. Today, lovely Georgian buildings surrounding the main square give the town a graceful character.

This was my first visit to Pyrmont when I was aged nine. I loved the warm, sunny weather and the freedom to roam along the streets, through parks and on footpaths into the woods with other children. We stayed as paying-guests with the Schoendorf family, who were Jewish. Their new house and garden in the Moltkestrasse was 10 minutes walk from the main Kur-Hotel where the Yearly Meeting sessions were held.

During the first few days Mary was ill and in bed. A Quaker, Dr Otto Buchinger senior, came to see if he could help and prescribed some belladonna, which soon got her on her feet again. He became one of Leonhard and Mary's lifetime friends.

Friends arrived at Yearly Meeting with heavy hearts as the growth of Hitlerism impinged on their lives. The need to be discreet in expressing their opposition to it was equally depressing. Several Quaker teachers had already lost their jobs and others were under pressure. There were also Quakers who had Jewish family members and realised things could only get worse for them. How could Friends best support them? Many of the Quakers were unemployed and very short of money. Two Friends from Nuremberg, Hans Exmer and Michael Werner, had walked 200 miles to Pyrmont and then walked back again. German Friends were greatly encouraged by the many visitors who had come from abroad and especially welcomed Henri van Etten from France and the 17 young Friends who came with him. One Friend remarked on the easy understanding which developed with their French visitors, who said it actually seemed easier talking with them, than with the more reserved British Friends whom they had known so long.

Rebuilding the Quakerhouse

The development of a small Quaker community in Germany had begun with the visit of William Ames in 1656 who found small groups of seekers receptive to the Quaker message. This was followed by visits of George Fox, William Penn and Robert Barclay. Prince Waldeck made land available in Friedenstahl for the Quakers who were being persecuted elsewhere, to open a boarding school and to follow their occupations in weaving and cutlery.

The original Meeting House in Bad Pyrmont had been erected in 1800, with the help of English Friends, for the Quaker community at Friedensthal, a hamlet in a small wooded valley two miles away. They chose to build the Meeting House beside the Bomberg Allee where it might attract the attention of the many visitors to the town as they strolled up and down the famous avenue. In 1893, after many of the Friedensthal Friends had emigrated to America to avoid conscription or had died, the Meeting House was sold to a Friedrich Voelker. The burial ground still bears a plaque declaring it to be the property of English Friends.

Voelker did little with the building, and eventually sold it to the Catholic nursing nuns at Georg's Villa. The descendants of the Voelker family lived in the blue-tiled house opposite the Friedrich's flat and became friendly neighbours to Mary. The nuns let the Quakerhouse out as a riding stable and later leased it to a man who kept donkeys there to give rides to children in the Allee. The 1928 Yearly Meeting had been held in nearby Bueckeberg, and a number of Friends who had attended remembered an excursion they made to Friedensthal and Pyrmont and talked of their dream to buy the property and to rebuild on the foundation of an earlier generation of German Friends.[2]

In the threatening political climate of 1932 this dream had a more practical value because Friends saw the need to have their own Meeting House away from the political limelight of the cities. They realised the importance of having control over the building in which they met to ensure a greater degree of security for free speech. Pyrmont was also reasonably accessible by rail to many parts of Germany.

In April 1932 Emma Raeydt (1873-1947), the last survivor of the Friedensthal Friends and a member of the peace movement and the Social Democrats, alerted the Executive Committee to the intention of the Catholic nuns to demolish the old Quakerhouse to make more garden space. This gave Friends the opportunity to purchase the dilapidated structure as building material for £40. Hans Albrecht and the Executive Committee arranged the purchase quickly and the Pyrmont planning department agreed to lease an adjoining piece of land for buildings beside the old cemetery. The exterior of the new Quakerhouse was to look as near as possible like the old one, reusing old building materials such as the oak beams and stone roofing slabs. The interior retained the lovely proportions of the main Meeting Room, but included a semi-basement to provide a kitchen, dining room, toilets and warden's accommodation. It cost 42,000 marks to complete the building, which was raised over a number of years from Friends both in Germany and abroad.[3]

During Yearly Meeting at the end of August Hans Albrecht led a dedication ceremony in the shell of the new Quakerhouse. It was traditional to celebrate a *Richtfest* with the builders when the roof timbers were raised and the roof was crowned with a wreath of fir from which the flags of 11 overseas contributing Quaker Yearly Meetings were hung. Hans Schoendorf, the son of the family we were staying with, presented a bouquet to Joan Mary Fry (1862-1955), a British Quaker, thanking her for the Quaker child-feeding programmes which followed the First World War and expressing the hopes of young Friends for the future. He was supported by three young girls crowned in wild flowers, including myself (illustrations 9 and 10).

Leonhard and Mary were very impressed with the potential for Quakerism to grow from Bad Pyrmont, and asked Hans Albrecht if they might be considered as wardens for the new premises. Mary also raised the possibility of Leonhard taking over the responsibility for the Quaker publishing business, which might also solve their employment problem. However, she realised that the residential accommodation would be inadequate for a family and hoped they might be able to find a flat nearby. A move to Bad Pyrmont would fulfil Mary's long-held desire to live in rural surroundings, whilst still continuing in Quaker work, which meant so much to them both.

Return to Nuremberg

In September we were glad to be home again in Nuremberg, after such a long absence, and Mary was grateful to find a cheque for £50 from Helen Dixon at Friends Service Council, for 'family maintenance'. I was happy to be at school, but to Mary's distress, came home with head lice.

Leonhard, who now had no job, went to the Meeting Rooms most days to deal with the accounts for the Quaker publishing enterprise which was badly in arrears. He did this in his capacity as Treasurer to the Yearly Meeting. The fact that Leonhard had something to do outside the home must have been a life-saver for both of them. During this year Mary frequently referred to marital disagreements, a common difficulty among the unemployed. Mary also had recurrent health problems. The many days she spent in bed cannot have been easy for Leonhard to understand.

9 and 10. *The original Pyrmont Meeting House built 1800, situated between Georg's Villa and Quaker cemetery, and the shell of the new structure being re-built with salvaged building materials.*

Mary was still producing reports on social conditions in Nuremberg, and now wrote additional letters of appeal for the new Quakerhouse in Bad Pyrmont.

Notes from the Minute Book of Nuremberg Friends

There were now so many Friends visiting Nuremberg that a committee was set up to look after them and show them the sights of the old city. Some visitors also gave talks at the Meeting:

Louisa Jacob	Geneva Disarmament Conference
Frl. Ranoch	Fridtjof Nansen
Hans Exmer	China and Japan
Alvana Goddard	Ramallah
Gertrud Jacob	Palestine and Syria
	India
Louisa Jacob	Quaker Worship
Richard Cary	Problems in Czechoslovakia
Leonhard Friedrich	John Woolman
Alfred Garret	An American on Evangelism
Wilhelm Mensching	Gandhi

In July a party of 33 French Friends on a peace and reconciliation visit were entertained to a meal at the Meeting Rooms. This was arranged by Gerhard Halle, a Berlin Friend who had served in France as a German officer during the First World War, where the retreating German army had devastated the Pas-de-Calais district. After becoming a Friend and pacifist his conscience troubled him, and he returned to the area to organise reconciliation activities, such as holiday exchanges of schoolchildren.

On 27th November the Nuremberg Meeting celebrated it's 10th anniversary. The older members were honoured and it was a chance to reflect on the sense of fellowship which was so important to all of them. Leonhard and Mary were presented with a leather writing case as founders of the Meeting. It meant a great deal to both of them to feel so much appreciated at this time.

Christmas of 1932 was a rather muted affair for the adults, despite the Meeting parties and nativity play. Mary invited a number of Friends to a Christmas meal of roast pork. The greatest thrill for me was to receive a pair of ice skates and to discover the pleasure and beauty of skating on a nearby frozen lake.

CHAPTER III

Hitler Becomes Chancellor 1933

Nuremberg

BRITISH FRIENDS BEGAN PUBLISHING Quaker literature in Germany in 1922, in order to spread the Quaker message of peace and reconciliation. In 1933 the Quaker *Verlag*, or publishing business, was moved to the Meeting Rooms at 13 Theresien Strasse, Nuremberg, and became Leonhard's responsibility. He was given expenses and a small retainer while he considered how to cut publishing costs and increase sales. He could earn a small commission if German Friends ordered their books through him as a bookseller. He persuaded Friends Service Council in London to cancel a long-standing £50 debt for printing George Fox's Journal in German and generally enjoyed the challenge of being a publisher.

Despite the small retainer Leonhard received from the *Verlag*, our family was among the increasing number of unemployed Friends in the Meeting. One afternoon a week they met in the warm Meeting Rooms to exchange children's clothing and to mend garments and enjoy a bread and cheese supper together. There were times when Leonhard's welfare payments failed to come through for several weeks and I worried about how I would feel if I should have to receive a clothing hand-out at school.

During January Mary heard that her mother was seriously ill in Peterborough. Mary was the only one in the family who had nursing experience and longed to go home to make her mother comfortable, but it was a difficult time to leave us. Sarah Tupholme died on 25th February at the age of 80. Coming home from school the day Mary heard the news, I found my mother, whom I had never seen crying, in tears. Her diary entry says:

> I had been planning to leave for England the next day. When Brenda came home her face went red, then she climbed on my lap and rubbed her face against mine and said 'now I haven't got a Granny any more'. Then she sensibly got on with her homework and fetched her friend Ella and played at dressing-up.

After her mother's death Mary's nine brothers and sisters seemed to become of greater importance in her life. The fearful atmosphere in which she lived in Germany made her long for the security of her family, who lived comparatively normal lives. There had always been a strong sense of responsibility for the family among all the brothers and sisters. This began in 1894 when the older children looked after their mother and the younger children at the time when their father became obsessed with what Mary described as 'religious mania' and quite suddenly left his well-paid engineering work, ignoring the financial needs of his large family. Five of the siblings emigrated to North America, but all of them came back with their children to visit Granny and Aunt Margaret, the youngest sister, who looked after their mother in Peterborough. There were often family consultations about how this sister or that brother could be supported through hard times. Mary did all she could to help and also relied on them to support her.

Mary's close family ties, which partly accounted for her lengthy visits to England every summer, must have been trying for Leonhard. His own father had died when he was a child and his undemanding mother died when he was 21. His only close relative was his brother, Bernhard, who had lived in Pennsylvania since 1913. When Leonhard visited the Tupholme family, they were always friendly, but I think he felt an odd man out, though I never heard him say so.

Berlin: Political Events

The four elections held in 1932 culminated in a fifth held on 30th January 1933, when Hitler became Chancellor in a coalition government with von Papen. This event was marked in Berlin by a triumphant torchlight procession of thousands of singing SA in their uniforms, presided over by Hitler. This struck all the Quakers with foreboding and fear as they considered the effect it would have on their lives. Even the radio newscaster announcing the election results seemed to speak in a different voice.[1]

Hitler now had control of the power base of the state, and his next aim was to replace the coalition with a National Socialist government. Goering assisted by purging the Prussian police to make way for loyal Nazis. The final election was planned for 5th March and was preceeded by a campaign of street violence in all the cities, particularly against Communists and Jews.

A few days before the election, the country was stunned to hear that the *Reichstag* (parliament) was on fire. Even while the fire engines were fighting the blaze, the Communists were named as the perpetrators and this gave the pretext for action against all prominent Communist leaders.

Rumours of plots to burn down a number of other public buildings abounded. Many ordinary people were now too frightened to vote for the Communists, who lost a million votes in the elections. Mary wrote in her diary: 'I voted Social Democrat, but was really tempted to vote Communist, to support their strong opposition to Hitler.'

Bruening of the Centre Party could make no impact on the media, and President Hindenburg kept silent in the run-up to the elections. The election gave 44% of the votes to Hitler, with the Social Democrats coming second. The right-wing Nationalists won 50 seats in the Reichstag, and declared their willingness to serve in a Nazi coalition.

On 15th March Leonhard went to town to attend the Quaker youth group at the Meeting Rooms and was shaken when one of the members shouted 'Heil Hitler'. The streets outside were full of rowdy people creating all kinds of mayhem. Edith Straus, who was Jewish, lived in town between the main railway and tramway stations. She phoned Mary to say that the Youth House, whose activities were financially supported by Quakers, was being forcibly occupied by uniformed gun-carrying youths. Flags of the 1848 Revolution and the 1918 Republic were dipped in petrol and burnt in the streets.

Corder Catchpool in Berlin

Corder Catchpool (1883-1952) had many contacts among German and international peace organisations in Berlin. Some of their leaders were already in trouble, but Corder decided to go ahead with organising a peace meeting, to be addressed by the visiting French Friend, Gilbert Lessage, on 17th March. Eight policemen came into the meeting, although there was no disturbance. Quakers decided to avoid the word 'pacifist' and described themselves as 'Friends of Peace', because the Nazis assumed that pacifism demonstrated a political involvement with the Communists, who were regarded as traitors.

Nuremberg

The Nazi's powerful propaganda was hypnotic. As a nine-year-old, I was quite desperate to have a flag hanging from our fourth floor window, like every other family. I was overjoyed when Leonhard decided we could hang the Nuremberg flag from our window. Mary got out the sewing machine and produced a magnificent red and white flag, with a red tassel at the pointed end.

The following Sunday, on 19th March, David Hodgkin came to Meeting, he was 18 years old and six-foot-three inches tall. He was the son of Edward Hodgkin, a Quaker painter and businessman from Darlington. Mary wrote:

> Brenda took a great fancy to him, and invited him to stay with us. He stayed a week and had all his meals with us. He only had 100 marks which were to last him for a six week trip around Germany, but he did help with the washing up!

On 21st March, both the pupils and their parents took part in a Nazi celebration at my school. We were told that Germany had 'Awakened and was united under Hindenburg and Hitler, to march towards a glorious future'. Our classroom floor was covered in straw to provide bedding for some of the thousands of SA men who came from other areas to take part in a march through the town. We were given a holiday, and went with David Hodgkin to watch the processions from the Meeting Rooms. We watched for hours as endless rows of uniformed men with swastika arm bands marched by, singing Nazi songs and giving the raised right arm-salute. The perfectly-drilled columns of marching men and the rhythmic sound of their feet and drums were very exciting for me, but I knew my parents and the Friends were watching with dread and foreboding and I had to control my urge to cheer with those on the streets. The greeting of 'Heil Hitler' was replacing the customary south German *'Gruess Gott'* (Greetings to God), which Friends were determined not to give up.

After we had tired of watching the parade we went to visit Edith Straus, who was very upset and crying because she had heard of the many acts of violence against Nuremberg Jews. As we walked home through the town and the lovely old Marketplace, then renamed Adolf Hitler Platz, we saw illuminations and torchlights everywhere. Mary said she had not seen so much hysteria since Mafeking night in Piccadilly Circus in 1902.

'Gleichschaltung' (The Enabling Act)

The last vestiges of parliamentary government came to an end on 23rd March when Hitler, with the votes of the 50 Nationalist coalition MPs, obtained Reichstag approval for the 'Enabling Act'. He proclaimed the consolidation of the 'National Revolution' which would tolerate no opposition and give the government all statutory powers for the next four years. They could now issue decrees without reference to the Reichstag or the electorate.

For Edith this was the final signal to leave. On 28th March we went to the station to see her off for London, her husband Willi was to follow a few weeks later. Mary was very sad, knowing how much she would miss such a good friend. In her diary she wrote:

I wished I could have gone too. But I am comforted by my happy little Brenda, who plays with her dolls, saying they are her children. She enjoys helping me to look after visitors, but is equally happy spending the day with other people when I am busy.

The Jewish Boycott 1st April

The evening before the boycott, Willi Straus visited us in great distress, having heard about the decrees issued against the Jews. It was a terrible experience for people who felt themselves to be more German than Jewish suddenly to find that they were spurned and unable to earn a living. The next day Willi expected to have the medieval yellow circle and a notice pasted on his doctor's surgery brass plaque warning people against contacting him, with a sentry posted at the door to enforce the order.

Mary decided this was the day for us both to walk through the town to visit Willi and all the small Jewish shopkeepers *en route*. She ignored the warning signs, simply telling the guards she needed to speak to the shop-owner and walked through any doors that were open to talk to the frightened people inside. No doubt Mary's English accent must have indicated that she was a foreigner and afforded some protection. News camera crews were on the streets to record the events of the day. One of the Quakers went to a cinema that evening and saw us both on newsreel, talking to a guard and then walking past him into a Jewish shop. Friends in Meeting the next day were very perturbed and felt Mary had taken a great risk, particularly as she was a German citizen by marriage.

Corder and Gwen Catchpool, the British Quaker Representatives in Berlin, had paid similar visits to Jewish shops during the boycott. Two days later, early in the morning, their house was searched and the family held under arrest. Corder was taken off to the Alexander Platz Gestapo HQ for interrogation about his contacts, though released 36 hours later. The Nazis were skilled at skimming through papers to search for 'disloyal elements'. Whilst this was extremely unpleasant for the Catchpools and their children, it gave great anxiety to the individuals who were being helped by them. Corder was the first Briton to be arrested by the Nazis and Major Clement Attlee MP, raised a question about his safety in the House of Commons. It suited the Nazis to try to frighten Corder without actually hurting him. When, under questioning, Corder claimed to 'be a friend of Germany', the Gestapo responded by saying he had made insufficient effort to interpret 'our great National Revolution'. This appeared to challenge him to arrange more meetings and contacts with hard line Nazis, in order to feel that he was not avoiding the most difficult contacts. It was, of course, uncongenial to attempt to establish

11. *Corder and Gwen Catchpool in Berlin 1933 with their children, Neave, Jean, Annette and Pleasaunce.*

personal contacts with leading Nazis, and yet how can one try to understand their motivation for joining the movement without establishing dialogue at a personal level? This coincided with the Quaker belief that there is 'that of God in everyone'.[2]

There was some embarrassment among the German Friends when they heard of Corder's contacts with Nazi officials. They felt that as a Briton, Corder might not understand what use was being made of his goodwill. After the SS interrogation, the Friends Service Council appointed William Hughes to support Corder as a travelling case-worker to deal with the sensitive contacts, leaving Corder to work in more visible roles.

Fundamental Policy Decision of German Friends

The Quaker Executive Committee met on 8-9th April in Frankfurt, only a few days after the Jewish boycott. Every Friend was worried about the 'Enabling Act' which undermined the democratic state and Hans Albrecht, Clerk to the Yearly Meeting, feared it could lead to the closure of the Society of Friends. He lived in Hamburg, where the Gestapo had closely questioned him about the activities of Friends. He now shared his views with an extended Executive Committee.[3] Bertha Bracey from Friends Service Council was also present and wrote:

> I have never felt the strength and depth of German Friends so strongly though there were differences of opinions about the conclusions we arrived at. But throughout the weekend there was a dignity, restraint and quietness which made me realise afresh that every ordeal and every moment of critical decision is also a moment of witness to the spirit of true religion. No one can foresee what may happen in the next few weeks and months, but Quakerism in its strength and simplicity lives in Germany today, and will live, come what may.

She recorded some of the decisions in English:

> As members of the German Yearly Meeting we must now put aside our feelings of anxiety, to fill our hearts and spirit with positive responsibilities. We need to identify the basic and essential tasks laid on us as Friends . . . We are not merely a peace society, or a humanitarian/welfare organisation. The Religious Society of Friends is a community of men and women who are striving to express in their lives their Faith in the direct relationship of man to God . . . There can be no gap between our religious conviction and our actions. Others need us, and have faith in us.
>
> As a religious society politics are not our concern, because no decisive moral regeneration can be brought about by the State . . . The

path of non-violence is not one of weakness, it demands courage, direction and the utmost personal sacrifice. Our unchanging task is to work through non-violent means for international understanding and to remove the causes of war . . . We ask our members to live in the spirit which accepts 'there is one God who dwells in all mankind, all men are brothers'. We exhort all of our members to proclaim in word and deed the spirit of non-violence and friendship. Each of us in our own circles will find the right opportunities for action.

However we beg our members to think calmly and carefully before taking action. Actions inevitably have consequences which must be considered responsibly by each member. Do not feel that you have to bear witness as Quakers, nor that as a Quaker you should shoulder burdens that are greater than you have strength to carry on your own.

We warmly advise Friends to turn to the two Books of Discipline at this time, and ask each of you to reconsider and test your inner position. If you feel any doubt about these things, you may decide to resign from the Society into the outer circle of the friends of the Friends.[4]

Reading this statement 60 years later, I am astonished that Friends appear to have retreated to their inner beings, detaching themselves from worldly responsibilities and the daily challenges they were encountering. Hans Albrecht had persuaded the Executive Committee that this was the only way their Society of 200 members would survive. He was worried that the witnessing actions of some Friends could endanger others. He also hoped that some of the weaker or more exposed Friends might decide to leave. From this point on, Friends were individually aware of the need to make their own choices about their relationship with the Nazi system without depending on the support of other Friends. Most decided to avoid co-operation with the Nazis as far as they dared. For some it was to avoid contributing to the Nazi charities, or to avoid the Nazi salute. For others even this minor form of resistance was too risky. A number of Friends courageously supported Jews they knew and sometimes offered to hide them. We who were not there cannot understand the personal pressure of having no one to trust.

The April Executive Committee reported that a number of Friends were already suffering under the new regime:

Heinrich Becker lost his job some months ago. In recent weeks the following have also lost theirs: Emil Fuchs, Herta Kraus, August Jacob and Walter Schadow. Rudolf Schlosser was held in prison. We agree to recommend that those overseas Friends who wish to give financial help, might contribute to the maintenance of Heinrich Becker, Herta Kraus and Emil Fuchs.

When Bertha Bracey reported the weekend Meeting to British Friends she said:

> How deeply discouraging it was for those in Germany who had struggled after the First World War to create a more open and liberal society. The suffering and hunger people had endured seemed to have given birth to the poison of anti-Semitism. Jewish doctors, teachers, lawyers and social workers had suddenly become the pariahs and were cut off from society.[4]

Bertha Bracey (1893-1989) had come to Germany for Quaker relief work in 1924 and worked with young people in Nuremberg. Between 1926 and 1929 she did similar work in Berlin, after which she was called back to Friends House in London to administer Quaker Centres and other related work in Europe. As the persecution of the Jews increased she became the central figure in a large network of people who helped the refugees settle in Britain, providing hostels, language training and employment projects. She had been a frequent visitor to our home in Nuremberg and in the last years of her life she was a valuable interpreter of events for me, when I was beginning this research. (Illustration 12)

May Day

Leonhard, Mary and I went to Luitpoldheim Stadium to watch the May Day procession. It took five hours for 100,000 people to march past

12. *Bertha Bracey.*

the podium. Many people had been ordered to attend and wear the Nazi arm bands. The entire day was organised to humiliate the trade unions and the next day all trade union offices were occupied and their funds confiscated. Many of the union leaders were arrested and taken to the first concentration camps. A few days later Mary had to look after our neighbour who had tried to kill herself with an overdose of aspirin because her husband, a postman, had been forced to join the SA in order to keep his job.

'Gleichschaltung' (Elimination of Opposition)

On 27th May Mary attended a meeting called by the committee of allotment holders, to which our garden belonged. Members of organisations like these were asked to sign a loyalty oath promising to support the 'Great National Revolution'. The oath was publicly confirmed with a special handclasp. Mary openly refused, saying she could not give the oath because Quakers did not swear and she also disapproved of the Nazi treatment of the Jews. She left the meeting implying she did not understand what they were saying and would have to ask her husband. Leonhard, who happened to be at home, went in her place and made the required gesture. Mary was very sad about this, because she felt they should be ready to suffer for their beliefs. Leonhard, having attended the Frankfurt Executive Committee Meeting in April, said this was not the occasion on which to demonstrate his opposition.

A few days later Mary received an intimidating phone call. She had been in the garden repairing the summerhouse and when she got back to the flat someone purporting to be a policeman rang her complaining about the noise of the hammering. 'Such behaviour had to stop, or else she would be taken into custody!' Having heard of the house search which the Catchpools endured, Leonhard and Mary decided to take some of their private papers to their friends the Wiesners, for safe keeping.

On 28th May Willi Straus left for England and we all went to the station to see him off. Leonhard and Mary agreed to arrange for the packing and transportation of most of the family's household possessions, which eventually arrived safely in London. Willi was unable to sell the practice, or to take any money with him, so they became entirely dependant on Edith's mother in Britain. (Illustrations 13 and 14)

Interview with Ernst Roehm

Elsie Howard was a Quaker Committee member from London who came to stay with us from 3-6 June to hear what was happening in Germany. Mary took her to visit Rabbi Heilbron and the Jewish Welfare Committee and they also visited the Mayor, Herr Liebel, to discuss welfare needs in the town. During this visit Elsie and Mary asked to visit Ernst Roehm, one of Hitler's long-standing henchmen who was Commander of the SA Brownshirts. The violent activities of his men had ensured Hitler's victory at the elections. Elsie Howard and Mary saw him at his office in the Braunhaus, the national headquarters of the SA in Nuremberg. They were received courteously for 45 minutes and Elsie wrote the following account of the visit in her book *Across Barriers*:[5]

> I went to stay in Nuremberg with an English Friend, married to a German, both Quakers. Their little flat in a working-class quarter of the town was a centre of kindness and sympathy.
>
> Mary and I took our courage in both hands and went to the Braunhaus, having made an appointment with Roehm, the highest official there. We were handed on from one young Brownshirt to another into the august presence. It was a magnificent house confiscated from Faber, the Jewish pencil factory magnate. Roehm was very friendly when I explained we were English Quakers and deeply interested in the welfare of Germany and that we would be grateful to be enlightened on the new Revolution and its aims.
>
> He said they were trying to clean things up and doing a great deal to provide employment. Already a million more men were in work since March. They were encouraging the farmers and peasants so that everyone should feel they had a stake in the country, and if possible a bit of land. They were trying to even up the wage and salary scales, so that manual workers got a decent wage, and officials were not overpaid. So far I agreed this was good. Then a few questions. In England there was interest in the current methods of suppressing all opponents, even those on the Right. Roehm said: 'Well of course, in one way or another all the other political parties have betrayed the Fatherland, and can no longer be allowed to endanger its safety'. Then I asked: 'Then how about the Jews? Was it not a loss for Germany that so much scientific and other professional knowledge should no longer be available?' He replied: 'Christians have just as much knowledge as the Jews, but they were crowded out of the professions by Jews, now they have a chance. No German woman must ever be treated again by a Jewish doctor, they have misused them too much'. I asked: 'What about those who are only a quarter Jewish and feel themselves so entirely German?' He replied: 'We can make no exceptions'. We spoke about peace and asked why pacifists were so suspect. Is it really treachery to one's country to work for peace?
>
> At this point the phone rang, and he spoke to the caller saying:

III HITLER BECOMES CHANCELLOR 1933 45

13. *Dr Willi and Edith Straus, safely in London, 1933.*

14. *Elizabeth Fox Howard.*

'Yes of course, call in the police, and occupy the house, and bring him here. We shall know how to deal with him!' Then turning back to us he said: 'Yes of course we all want peace' . . . We were relieved to be able to leave the building and to get back into the sunshine.

It later transpired that Ernst Roehm was bitterly disappointed by Hitler's lack of confidence in him as a possible Commander of the Army. Roehm had expected that on gaining power, Hitler would integrate the SA with the Army. But the Generals were loath to accept co-ordination with such an ill-disciplined force as the SA. Hitler may also have feared that with their three million members, Roehm would be capable of starting a social revolution if he became impatient with the leadership.

Concentration Camps

The first concentration camps were created in 1933 when the prisons were already overcrowded. They were mainly run by the SA in remote places, where their brutality would be less visible. Some political suspects and influential Jews were detained for only a few weeks, but others remained there until they died. Acts of bestiality and sadism were common, though not as routinely organised in the early years as later on. The isolated gravel pits and disused factory buildings at Dachau near Munich were typical sites, but 30 other concentration camps were opened in various parts of Germany, though all were generally referred to as Dachau. In the camps torture and degrading punishment were used not only to humiliate and extract money or information, but also to intimidate opposition in the outside community. Some wealthy Jews were able to purchase their release and to obtain exit visas to leave the country.

Hearing of these horrors, British Friends tried to visit concentration camps in the spirit in which earlier generations of Friends, like Elizabeth Fry, had visited prisons in many countries. Approaches were made in Berlin, and the Nuremberg Meeting also considered whether it should try to visit prisoners.

A few of the German Friends were uneasy about possible repercussions such visits might have for them, but they were also grateful to British Friends for undertaking it. In October Friends Service Council sent William Hughes and Corder Catchpool to see how the number of visits could be increased. William spent about 20 months visiting families of the victims all over Germany. He was able to offer small sums of money to meet pressing needs and assessed the possibilities of emigration for each case. Younger people able to undertake domestic or agricultural labour were easier to place overseas. William Hughes was open with the German police about his movements, enabling them to watch him if they chose to do so. But he avoided interviews on Quaker premises or in the houses of Friends with whom he stayed. But it was agreed for security reasons, that very few Friends would know the details of his activities.

William Hughes, and Corder Catchpool, visited many of the concentration camps, asking to see particular prisoners. Their reports convey their uneasiness, and describe the evil they sensed. They were unable to speak to prisoners alone. When they asked to see the punishment cells, they were shown unoccupied 'dark cubicles equipped with heavy leg irons'. However they found that after some time, there was a considerable improvement in the circumstances of some of the prisoners about whom they had enquired by name. William and Corder considered speaking openly about their findings in England, but realised regretfully this would cut off the possibility of further visits. They also wanted to avoid re-awakening the intense hatred of Germany which had developed in Britain during the First World War. It was a difficult decision for the committee in London over whether to speak out or to continue helping individuals. They chose to keep quiet to maintain access for prison visits. In 1945 when the first Friends Relief Service team entered Belsen, Bertha Bracey pondered: 'Did we make the wrong decision not to speak out, when so many appalling details had lain in the files at Friends House?'[6]

Friedrich Family Decisions

The Nazi Party doctrines and scurrilous methods of enforcing compliance reached like tentacles into all aspects of life. Since Nuremberg was the city of the Nazi Party's headquarters, it may have been felt more strongly there. Leonhard and Mary were aware that they might suddenly find themselves victims, and were particularly worried about my future. In March they obtained a British passport for me, which was quite easy since I had been born in Peterborough. It was not, however, until July that Mary made enquiries about my going to a British Quaker school.

Children were now being indoctrinated with Nazi beliefs and behaviour patterns. At my school Jewish children and teachers were being picked on and bullied. My teacher confided to Mary how deeply she felt against this, but if she were to protect Jewish children, she herself would be set upon. The intimidation was formidable and Mary and Leonhard now urgently wanted to get me away from all this. The Friends at Street Meeting agreed to help with my school fees at Sidcot School in Somerset, though Mary also contributed from her savings. There were now only a few weeks left in which to teach me about pounds, shillings and pence and to write in English. At such short notice there was no vacancy at Sidcot for the September intake class, but a place was found for me at the

Saffron Walden Junior House. I took my dolls with me and looked forward to this new adventure, but was sad to leave my playmates.

Leonhard and Mary were invited for the autumn term at Woodbrooke, the Quaker College in Birmingham. But they decided that Mary needed to stay on in Nuremberg to look after the various Quaker responsibilities and Leonhard went by himself. This was an exciting opportunity for him. He hoped it would give him a better grounding in Quaker theology and be of help in his publishing work.

Yearly Meeting 1933

On the journey from Nuremberg to Yearly Meeting in Pyrmont, Leonhard lost his spectacles whilst leaning out of the train window. Since he was very short-sighted it was extremely frustrating to be without them. There had been some doubt as to whether it would be possible to hold Yearly Meeting at all, because of the Nazis, but in the end 150 Friends came, of whom 25 were foreigners. Everyone was overjoyed to be able to hold the Meetings in the Quakerhouse, although the building was incomplete and meals had to be taken elsewhere.

As a result of the difficult policy decisions of the April Executive Committee, 27 resignations from membership were received, mainly people who felt their identification as Quakers could compromise their jobs or other aspects of their lives. At the same time 23 others made a commitment to join. Emil Fuchs, a Lutheran pastor who had been held in custody and interrogated several times, decided to become a full member and others who joined included Margarethe Lachmund, Gerhard Halle, Kati Lotz, Elise Herzog, Heinrich Otto and Marie Edert. There were now almost 200 members of the Yearly Meeting; 16 members had already lost their jobs and others had their pensions withheld.

The Yearly Meeting set up a relief committee to deal with the financial and other problems of members, from which some real income sharing resulted. The relief work of the Berlin office involved Herta Kraus, Emil Fuchs, Leonhard Friedrich, Olga Halle and Lotte Hoffman, who co-ordinated with Bertha Bracey in London about the selection of German Friends who had been under stress, for 'short stay' hospitality in England; starting the Ommen Quaker school in Holland; establishment of an agricultural settlement at Perpignan in the South of France, for people who were in difficulties with the regime, and the co-ordination of British and American visitors to Germany.

Friends returning home from the Yearly Meeting felt less isolated and strengthened, having shared each others' problems. Friends loved the relaxed atmosphere of the new Quakerhouse and the links with earlier generations of Friends that it conjured up. The Young Friends group provided the practical help needed to hold the Meetings, a service also given by some young English Friends whose German was not really up to listening to Yearly Meeting sessions. Leonhard and Mary, who were hoping to move to Pyrmont, were able to exchange ideas with many Friends about the vision of what they hoped to do. They also explored possible flats to rent should they be selected as wardens.

Autumn in Nuremberg

On 11th September Leonhard and I left Mary behind on the Nuremberg railway platform, waving goodbye as the train pulled out of the station on our 30-hour journey to London. We were met at Victoria by dear Edith Straus. Leonhard took me to Saffron Walden, where I was to be a boarder in the Junior House, before he went on to Woodbrooke. Mary must have found our flat very empty, but she said the neighbours were kind and attentive, and she was quickly caught up in Quaker activities. The first visitor was Howard Yarnell, an American Friend, whom she said: 'looked pale and thin, but showed great interest in the problems here'.

On 19th September, when Mary was on her own in the Meeting Rooms attending to the publishing business, Herr Gehringer, the husband of a member of the British Wives Club, came in wearing his SA uniform. He was very angry and called her a 'dirty Jew', furious about the support she had given his wife and children during their court hearing for a divorce and the help she had given the family to try to return to England. He threatened to get the SA to 'do her over'. Mary went to the Welfare Office and asked for protection for Mrs Gehringer and her children. After many difficulties and several changes of plan, the family left for England from Fuerth railway station to avoid a possible confrontation with her husband at Nuremberg station. On the drive to Fuerth they were protected by a police motorcycle escort. All went well, and Edith met the family at Victoria, having found a flat for them in Kilburn. She kept in touch with them for years and her mother gave the children tuition to help them settle into English schools.

A few weeks later Mary was summoned to the police station to be questioned on the way Leonhard at Woodbrooke was describing conditions in Germany. She must have been very shaken by this experience. From this time on, Mary made fewer diary entries. When Leonhard heard about the interrogation on his return home, he was convinced that a German studying English at Woodbrooke must have been an informer. It would not at the time have been difficult for the Nazis to place an agent there as a language student, if they wanted to find out more about the Society of Friends activities in Germany.

On 14th October Hitler announced that Germany was leaving the Lausanne Disarmament Conference and the League of Nations. Hitler blamed the League for the international community's unequal treatment of Germany regarding permitted levels of armaments and he refused to continue submitting to the conditions of the Versailles Treaty. Referring to this event in an article in *The Friend*, Corder Catchpool wrote:

> I feel drawn to the German people, and believe in their peaceful nature. It would have been dishonest of Germany to have remained as a member of the Disarmament Conference, in the present atmosphere of war fever.[7]

Death of Richard Cary

Richard Cary (1886-1933) the American Friends Service Committee representative in Berlin, lived there with his wife Mary and their two children. He shared the Quaker office in Berlin with Corder Catchpool, working closely together with representatives of German Friends. Cary had been part of the AFSC relief work in Germany after the First World War and on his return to America worked on the *Baltimore Sun*. When he returned to Germany in 1931 he covered political events for the newspaper and was also chairman of the American Chamber of Commerce in Berlin, as well as carrying out Quaker duties. The family came to Nuremberg from time to time and my parents felt very close to them. I enjoyed the company of their children John and Ellen. During the summer of 1933, they had gone back to America and spent six weeks on a tour, speaking to Quaker audiences, Rotary Clubs, universities and on the radio. Richard came back to Germany exhausted and died shortly afterwards, aged 47. It was a devastating shock for his family and the Friends. A hundred people attended the memorial service in Berlin. He was greatly respected as a quiet person with a marvellous sense of humour who thought deeply before taking action. He was the first Friend to be buried in the recently re-acquired burial ground at Bad Pyrmont. The annual Germany Yearly Meeting lecture is named after Richard Cary. His wife, Mary, stayed on for almost a year to continue their work.

Leonhard came home from Woodbrooke at Christmas, looking relaxed and well, and having been stimulated by H. G. Wood's Bible study classes and having enjoyed the social life. This is reflected in an entry of the Woodbrooke Log Book for the autumn term:

> The tennis tournament began with Leonhard Friedrich wearing a Bavarian blue linen jacket and George's tennis shoes, playing with much zest; his teutonic giggles of mirth made good, for any lack of court craft.

He had never been on a tennis court before.

CHAPTER IV

The Move to Bad Pyrmont in 1934

ON NEW YEARS EVE 1933, Mary reflected on the past year with her sense of realistic Quakerly concern. Writing in her diary:

After 12 years in Germany Leonhard and I are still working for peace in a society which seems more disturbed than ever. I am very relieved to have Leonhard back from Woodbrooke, where he has enjoyed his studies and the escape from the tensions of our life here.

On 26th February 1934 Mary organised the first of many tea meetings she was to hold for Jewish women. She was helped by Mary Cary, the American Friend, who was on a visit from the Berlin Quaker Centre.

Visit to England

Mary had missed her trip to England the previous summer and decided to go early this time. She left on 22nd March in order to be with me for the Easter school holiday. We made the usual family visits to Peterborough and Sheffield, and also saw Mrs Lilian Birt in Liverpool, who had been in charge of the Children's Sheltering Homes, where Mary had worked before the First World War for a remarkable child emigration programme to Canada. During that war Mary stayed on in Liverpool as a volunteer to nurse wounded soldiers.

Mary visited the editor of the *Manchester Guardian* to talk about conditions in Germany. She was a regular reader of the weekly edition which, although it was banned in Germany, arrived safely when posted in a plain wrapper.

A Talk to Saffron Walden School

Whilst visiting me at Saffron Walden Friends School, Mary was invited to speak about Germany to the Old Scholars Association. She told them about food shortages, that people regularly greeted each other saying '*Heil Hitler*' instead of 'good morning', and of the pressures to join the Hitler

Youth or the League of German Girls. She also said that families were expected to forego their Sunday joint for a single casserole dish and to contribute the money saved to the Winter Aid Fund, supposedly for the welfare of the unemployed who had to survive on 30 pfennigs a day.

Mary explained that the Winter Aid Fund also encompassed 'voluntary' wage deductions to boost industrial production. For instance, in order to increase the profitability of cars made at the Volkswagen factory, every worker had five marks deducted from his regular wage packet. Weekly door-to-door collections were made by women of the Nazi Party. Many of them were 'volunteered' by their husbands, who were under pressure for their wives to make the collections. After a while it became generally known that these collections were not confined to charitable purposes, but were used to bolster the national budget or buy another Messerschmitt fighter plane.

Political Developments

The Versailles Treaty of 1919 had separated East Prussia from Germany by creating the Polish Corridor, giving Posen and Silesia to Poland. Hitler, of course, had ambitions to get back these territories. In preparation for this, he tried to weaken the Polish/French alliance by declaring a non-aggression pact with Poland on 26th January.

In January there was a severe crisis in the Protestant churches. Pastors were asked to exclude from their congregations any people of Jewish origin who had become members of the church. Pastors who were unwilling to join the Nazi Party were threatened with dismissal from their posts. Ludwig Mueller, an army chaplain and Nazi official, was imposed on the Church as their leading State Bishop in a newly-created Ministry for Ecclesiastical Affairs. Twenty-eight Lutheran and Reformed churches were amalgamated under his control, which effectively silenced much of the church opposition to the Nazi state. As a final affront, the Old Testament was deleted from new editions of the German Bible because it recounted the history of the Jews.

After this, open resistance from the churches came mainly from Dietrich Bonhoeffer and Martin Niemoeller, who represented a minority 'Confessional' church. The Bishop of Chichester and many foreign church leaders protested, but to no avail. Hitler then began a campaign against the trade unions, following a march of 100,000 workers in Berlin who threatened to strike if he were to become Chancellor. These repressive measures created increasing disquiet.

Hitler was now prepared to install himself as Hindenburg's successor. On 16th May at Bad Nauheim he obtained the support of the army generals, on condition that he would not permit Roehm or the SA to interfere with the army because the SA were undependable and ill-disciplined. Early in June there were rumours of an imminent putsch, prompting Hitler to curb Roehm's ambitions. Hitler felt disquiet when he met with Roehm and insisted that the entire SA be sent on holiday.

The Vice-Chancellor von Papen spoke at a meeting in Marburg on 17th June to express the strong middle-class disquiet at the decline of the freedom of the press, the public burning of books, the banning of Jewish musicians and the absence of what had hitherto been regarded as normal honourable behaviour. Von Papen was deeply hurt to find his speech was unreported and denied publicity. He gave up the struggle with Hitler and resigned his cabinet post. A few weeks later Hitler appointed him ambassador to Austria, to get him out of the way.

The Night of the Long Knives, 30th June

After his recent conversations with Roehm, Hitler finally decided that his former colleague was now a danger to his own future plans. He drove to Bad Wiesee where Roehm and most of the SA leadership were on vacation and gave orders to have the high-ranking officers arrested and shot at dawn. Roehm was taken away separately and given the choice of suicide, but preferred to be shot for the cause he believed in. The German people were dumbfounded and frightened to learn Hitler had ordered the cold-blooded shooting of Roehm, an early Nazi Party member who had done more than anyone else to ensure Hitler's rise to power.[1]

On 13th July Hitler informed the Reichstag that 77 persons had been shot in the SA purge, but after the war it transpired that over a thousand people had lost their lives. As a reward to Himmler and the SS for their loyal support, the SS were given their distinctive black uniforms and were directly responsible to Himmler. This highly-disciplined force grew to 50,000 men, while the SA became rather irrelevant although they continued to exist.

On 25th July, the public were shocked to hear that Dr Dolfuss, the Chancellor of Austria, had been murdered by soldiers of the Austrian army. It later transpired the assault had been by SS men dressed in Austrian army uniforms. However, Hitler's planned putsch had failed because the Austrian forces led by Kurt von Schuschnigg regained control and forced the Germans back over the border.[2]

The Friedrichs' Departure from Nuremberg

Leonhard and Mary were asked to move hurriedly to Bad Pyrmont, because the Nazi Youth of Pyrmont had asked that the new building be requisitioned for them. Mary returned to Nuremberg on 19th June, with only 10 days in which to pack up all the family possessions for the removal.

It must have been an emotional upheaval for Leonhard to move from the city where he had grown up, although he expected to return for visits. The Nuremberg Meeting Minute Book records that:

> It is with heavy hearts that we say farewell to Leonhard, Mary and Brenda. Mary's patience and sustaining love constantly renewed our hope. We thank them deeply for having started this Meeting and for their service with us. We will now have to share among those of us who remain the many tasks which the Friedrichs and the sisters Therese and Elise Herzog, who are also moving to Pyrmont, undertook for the Meeting.

At this time the Nuremberg Quaker group numbered 60 persons, though fewer were in actual membership. There were about 25 people attending Sunday Meetings. The Quaker youth group had been closed because a Nazi edict said that all boys had to join the Hitler Youth and girls were to join the League of German Girls. All church-led youth groups and even the Scouts and Guides, eventually closed down.

Leonhard and Mary had an emotional send-off at the railway station when they left on the evening of the 30th June. There were neighbours and Friends and Leonhard's cousin Kaetchen, who came laden with bunches of flowers and boxes of chocolates. But everyone was talking excitedly about the sensational story of Roehm's death, which the newsvendors of the evening papers were calling out.

Leonhard and Mary spent the same night at Kassell with Heinrich Otto and arrived in Bad Pyrmont early next morning. The furniture van was already there and by evening they were safely installed in their new home on the top floor of Villa Harmonie, which still stands a hundred yards up the Bomberg Allee from the Quakerhouse. The flat had a large west-facing sheltered balcony where Leonhard and Mary enjoyed many summer evenings watching the sun set over the fields and hills, restoring a much-needed sense of tranquillity.

Moving to Bad Pyrmont from Nuremberg must have been rather like moving from Bristol to Buxton. They missed the bustle of a busy city, but loved the rural surroundings of a small town. There were also Friends to welcome them to Pyrmont: Therese and Elise Herzog, retired teachers who had moved from Nuremberg a few weeks earlier, and the elderly Friend Emma Raeydt, whose enthusiasm had led to the rebuilding of the Quakerhouse. Emma lived with her friend Frau Schuettemeier, who was connected with one of the Friedensthal Quaker families.

After settling themselves into their flat and establishing the office in the Quakerhouse, Leonhard and Mary made arrangements for welcoming the 150 people who were expected for the Yearly Meeting on 1-6 August. I was also due to arrive from England on my first visit to our new home. I travelled to Germany with Joan Mary Fry, who had given so much help in Germany since the First World War.

The Death of Hindenburg, 2nd August

Hindenburg died at the age of 86, giving Hitler the opportunity to achieve his ambition of becoming President as well as Chancellor. Following the secret agreement Hitler had already made with the Generals, he issued a decree through the Reichstag saying that the office of President and Chancellor would in future be combined and that the armed forces would swear unconditional obedience to him as Head of State. The people reacted in astonishment at such audacity, but no one challenged him.

On 19th August the country went to the polls to approve Hitler's actions and to confirm his assumption of power. Hitler was now 45 years old and had set the scene to implement his territorial ambitions to acquire more *'Lebensraum'* (living-space) in Europe, and to compensate for the loss of Germany's African empire after the Versailles Treaty of 1919.

Yearly Meeting 1934

There were slightly fewer Friends at Yearly Meeting this year, although 30 overseas Friends attended. The closing Epistle reflected how powerless and concerned they felt about the problems of their country. The theme of the Meeting was 'Where is Christ leading us today?' Introductions to sessions were given by Alfred Garrett, the theologian Friend from Philadelphia, and Emil Fuchs and Alfons Paquet. (Illustration 15)

The major event was a report of the opening of the Ommen Quaker school in Holland, which Dutch Friends and Bertha Bracey of the Friends Service Council had worked so hard to establish. The staffing was largely made up of Quaker teachers from Germany whose educational philosophy sprang from a combination of the German experiments in the 'Country School Movement' and from Quaker educational experience. Most of the pupils were from German Jewish families, although a few came from Britain and elsewhere, and a number of Dutch day scholars attended.

Other issues which were discussed included the care of the Pyrmont Quaker cemetery, which was to retain a simple natural appearance without further headstones. The improving finances of the Quaker publishing were noted. Mary Cary, who was returning to America with her children John and Ellen, received tributes for her work and courage. Emma Raeydt and Mary Friedrich were thanked for the provision of refreshments from the kitchen, although there was still no proper cooker or floor

15. *Alfred Garrett, Alfons Paquet, Leonhard Friedrich, Manfred Pollatz. Yearly Meeting, 1934.*

to the dining room. The young Friends camped in any available space in the building and garden, bringing their own equipment. Overcoming the challenges posed by the limited facilities of the unfinished building engendered a good team spirit.

First Summer in Bad Pyrmont

The warm sunny weather was delightful. After the Yearly Meeting Friends had left, Mary and I enjoyed exploring our new surroundings. The Quakerhouse garden had some heavily-laden apple trees ready to be picked. There were beautiful parks and lovely walks and an excellent open-air swimming pool beside the River Emmer. I was, however, disconcerted to find that after nine months in England I seemed to have forgotten how to speak German. The problem was made worse by the 'High German' spoken in the Hanover district. I felt like a Glaswegian trying to make herself understood in London, and missed my Nuremberg playmates.

Leonhard was finding out more about the past use of the burial ground. We discovered two or three small headstones lying under years of uncut grass and overgrown bushes. Leonhard borrowed a 5 ft iron rod with which he prodded deep into the ground to discover the outline of graves which had sunk below the surface. Eventually he was able to draw a chart marking the locations of several graves where the Friedensthal Friends had been buried in the 19th century, when there had been some twenty Quaker families in the area. The earliest grave we found was that of John Pemberton, a Quaker visitor from the United States who was buried in Pyrmont in 1795 aged 68.

The Beauty of the Quakerhouse

Therese Herzog, who had recently moved to Pyrmont, wrote the following:[3]

> Since our arrival in midsummer our love for this beautiful place has kept growing. The streets of Pyrmont are filled with the fragrance of roses and lime trees, and now we enjoy the mellow September days. We are deeply thankful for the spiritual home we have found in the Quakerhouse. We have discovered a deep and restful feeling, which many other German Friends also experienced during our family gathering and at the Yearly Meeting. When we meet on Sundays for worship, the vacant rows of seats still seem to be filled with the Friends who were with us a few weeks ago. On my first Sunday, alone with Emma Raeydt, the two of us seemed to fill the Meeting House on our own. Since then our numbers have increased a little, and now and then there is a visiting Friend or a passer-by who may have been attracted by the notice on the entrance gate.
>
> We love our Quakerhouse at all times of day and night, in the bright morning sunlight the shadows of the trees play over the walls, in the cool of the evening, hushed and quiet against the glowing tints of the sunset, or when it stands white and solemn in the moonlight. Our 'doorkeeper', the giant Canadian poplar tree in the front garden is alive with music, rustling happy melodies in the fresh morning, or whispering mysteriously in blue summer nights when the many bright stars seem to hang from its branches. At other times we rest on the white garden seat in the small grassy burial ground, looking up to the clear summer sky and the wooded mountain, or we see through the sweeping branches of the weeping willow tree which shades the graves of the early Friends, and also that of Richard Cary who died recently. We enjoy the ivy covered walls, the fine elder trees, and the old apple trees whose fruit Brenda has carefully gathered from the dewy morning grass, to share with us.

Autumn

In September I had to leave Pyrmont for school in England. I was now 11 years old and very proud to be allowed to make the long but familiar 30 hour train-and-boat journey on my own. I was met at Victoria by Edith Straus, who prepared my school trunk for Sidcot Friends School, Somerset, which had a vacancy for me.

Louisa Jacob, who had spent the summer term acting as Headmistress of Friends Girls School, Ramallah in Palestine, spent an enjoyable week in Pyrmont with Mary before returning to Nuremberg. Mary's health had not improved since her move to Pyrmont, where she became a patient of Dr Gustav Sturmthal, a respected Jewish family doctor. In early October she was well enough to feed and look after 50 Friends who came for Quarterly Meeting at the Quakerhouse. By now sufficient money had been collected to complete the dining-room floor and buy a cooker.

Mary made contact with Martha Seebohm, the great-niece of Ludwig Seebohm, the founder of the earlier Quaker community in Friedensthal. The family had married into the Rowntrees of York and produced Seebohm Rowntree, the social reformer. Martha was a single lady living in one of the grand Georgian style houses in a square in the centre of the town. Martha was interested in the connections of her family with Friends, and had lively memories of the old Quakerhouse and kept pictures and documents about the Quaker settlement. She felt the cutlery and weaving manufactures undertaken by the Friends in Friedensthal were probably not of good enough quality to market successfully. She deplored the

16. *Seebohm family house, Kirchenweg, Pyrmont.*

fact that the loyalty oath to the state had prevented the early Friends from studying at university or entering public service. Martha occasionally attended Meetings at the Quakerhouse, though she never considered joining them. (Illustration 16)

The 'Rest Home' at St Joseph's House

The 'Rest Home' was opened in Falkenstein-am-Taunus in November 1933 by Friends Service Council, to provide a few weeks of recuperation for political and racial Nazi victims who had been driven to the limit of their mental and physical endurance. The idea had come from Herta Kraus, a German Friend, who felt that people discharged from concentration camps or who had suffered in other ways could be helped to regain their strength and morale through a retreat with understanding English and German Quaker hosts.

Since the Pyrmont Quakerhouse was now open, the Rest Home was transferred from Falkenstein to St Joseph's House, run by American Catholic nuns in Pyrmont. The American nuns understood why these guests needed complete privacy for their recovery and supported the Quaker objectives. As Americans, they were under less pressure to comply with anti-Semitic rules. Mary and Leonhard often took part in the group activities and in discussions as advisors. Visiting Friends and their guests frequently joined in weekly Meeting for Worship. The Rest Home was run in Pyrmont during the spring and autumn months for five years until 1939, during which time it offered recuperation to some 800 people.[4]

In the autumn Leonhard and Mary visited Nuremberg to catch up with their old friends and concerns. Whilst there, they heard of the insidious Nazification of all aspects of life and the decline of trade union power, making it impossible for workers to resist compulsory wage cuts. Schools were being turned into Nazi training grounds. Teachers had to become party members and children were taught to tell tales about their parents if they noticed any anti-Nazi attitudes at home.

Germany was being put on a war footing. The military forces were being augmented and money was taken out of the economy to pay for weapons. The numbers of unemployed were falling because of lavish public works programmes, such as sports stadia and *autobahns*. The first European motorway system was being created to facilitate rapid military movement.

CHAPTER V

Consolidation of Nazi Regime 1935

ON SUNNY DAYS EARLY IN the New Year Leonhard and Mary enjoyed hill walks in the sparkling snow. They also had to cope with frozen pipes in the Quakerhouse, which had been badly installed and caused problems every winter. They were drawn into the activities of the Rest Home. Early in January and again at the end of March, Mary catered for the Executive Committee, a task she enjoyed. This time Leonhard reported that the sale of books had increased three-fold, and that there were now 430 subscribers to the journal *Der Quaker*, although only 250 people were in membership.

Mary's Visit to England

At the end of March, Mary left with Louisa Jacob, the American Friend who lived among Nuremberg Friends, to visit the Ommen Quaker School in Holland. Mary had taken part in the preliminary discussions on the establishment of the school and was keen to see how it was working out. Mary and Louisa went on to Haarlem to visit Manfred and Lily Pollatz's family school, which was doing well. Mary then visited Miep Lieftink in Amsterdam, who took her to see the Rembrandt collection at the Rijksmuseum. On the way she was disturbed to see a procession of 60,000 fascist demonstrators.

On 1st April Mary arrived in London, where we were both looked after by Edith Straus. We spent the Easter holidays together visiting relatives. At the end of the month Mary saw me off to school at Paddington Station and then enjoyed a walk through central London to the Charing Cross Road bookshops. She admired the street decorations for King George's silver jubilee festivities. Mary attended London Yearly Meeting as a representative of German Friends. She stayed with Helen Dixon, the Chairman of the Germany Emergency Committee, and was taken to the Chelsea Flower Show.

Ernst Reuter (1889-1953)

Mary visited Elsie Fox Howard in Buckhurst Hill, where she again met Ernst Reuter, whom she had met at the Rest Home earlier in the year. He had been a Social Democrat member of the Reichstag, imprisoned by the Nazis. Elsie Howard had struggled for months to achieve his release from a second term in a concentration camp. Her appeal had been through Dr Hanfstaengl, a confidant of Hitler and head of Foreign Press Section, part of the Ministry of Propaganda. Quakers had helped Reuter to emigrate to Britain. In 1948 he became internationally known as the first post-war Mayor of Berlin. His political leadership helped Berliners to withstand the pressures of the Soviet Union during the Berlin airlift.

After Elsie Howard had succeeded in getting Reuter's release, Hanfstaengl jokingly said to her: 'If I am ever in trouble, I hope I shall find as faithful a friend as Ernst Reuter has in you'. Elsie replied: 'If you are ever in a concentration camp, I'll do my best for you'. In December 1939 she discovered that Hanfstaengl was in a British internment camp. He had sought refuge in Britain in 1937, having fallen out of favour with Hitler. Elsie Howard sent him a Christmas card, but decided to do nothing more because she considered he was probably better off there than anywhere else.[1]

My Guardians

Before returning to Germany, Mary wrote her will and set up a trust and guardians to care for me until I reached the age of 25, in case both she and Leonhard were arrested. Edith Straus was to look after me, Julia Whitworth, now wife of Roger Carter, was to provide Quakerly care, and my cousin Norman Tupholme was to have financial and legal responsibility. This arrangement gave me a sense of security. Mary came to see me at Sidcot School in Somerset for a few days before returning to Germany on 22nd June.

Quaker Reactions to Saarland Plebiscite

The League of Nations, which had been given trust responsibilities for Saarland under the Versailles Treaty, held a plebiscite in January for its largely German population living under French administration. Ninety per cent voted for a return to Germany. Members of the peace movement knew that many of the ethnic Germans feared the Nazis and that it would lead to another wave of emigration to France. Horace Alexander, a British Friend who went to observe the plebiscite for British Friends, reported:

> During the fierce excitement of the plebiscite, when many people joined the Nazi Party and hung swastika flags from their homes, I met frightened folk who were cowering behind the noisy crowds.

After the resounding response of the electorate, British Friends regretfully decided there was no point in continuing their involvement in the situation.[2]

Re-arming Europe

On 4th March Sir John Simon, Britain's Foreign Secretary, announced plans to re-arm because Germany was now exceeding the arms limitations set by the Versailles Treaty. Hitler responded to this challenge by announcing the establishment of a German Air Force. A few days later France increased the size of their army and doubled the time served by conscripts. On 16th March Hitler re-introduced conscription.[3]

The escalation of the arms race created alarm in Britain and there were references in the press for the need of air raid precautions. The peace movement organised hundreds of meetings all over the country, which attracted the attendance of Communist Party members. Bertram Pickard (1892-1973), the Quaker observer at the League of Nations in Geneva, reported unanimity against the German flouting of the Versailles Treaty. The United States, never a member of the League, felt this was a 'European threat to peace' and not their business. The Soviet Union had joined the League in January of that year and felt much the same.

In April 1935 Corder Catchpool wrote a surprising letter to *The Friend* from Berlin defending Hitler's declaration of peaceful intentions, saying there was no choice but to take them at face value. The article provided another reference to the different German Quaker usages of the words *'Pazifist'* and *'Friedens Freund'* (friend of peace), terms which were also used by Leonhard during his Gestapo interrogation in 1942.

National Honour.

The German ex-soldiers' associations are permeated with the desire for peace, as is the British Legion, though in both countries their members would willingly march again at the command of King or Fuehrer. Herein lies the distinction between 'Friedensfreund' and 'Pazifist', a difference unstressed, or even unknown in England; but of importance for understanding the situation here. The destruction of pacifism may be regarded more as part of a political revolution from democracy to dictatorship, than as a symptom of a will-to-war. Danger to international peace is more likely to become acute as a result of violent Nazi reaction from some supposed slights to national honour, than to arise from the inherent features of Nazi ideology. 'Authority' of the Nazi brand, and the blind obedience it claims, naturally arouse profound distrust abroad; yet I am for faith in Germany's peace pronouncements. I do not see how radical 'friends of peace' can act on any other principle. It is, however, a mistake to be over-optimistic and credulous. My purpose is rather to temper with hope the prevailing pessimism, and so to lead to positive action.[3]

Conscription

Hans Albrecht was warned that the dissolution of the Society of Friends in Germany was under consideration at the highest Nazi levels, as part of the structural changes which had been forced on other Protestant churches. Following the Government decree to introduce conscription, Hans Albrecht decided on the 4th April to send a letter to the Government on behalf of the Quakers, explaining the problems of conscience that conscription would create for those adhering to the Quaker peace testimony. He outlined our historic reasons for refusing to take part in any war and the positive peace work undertaken by British and American Friends in Germany. He explained how the Society of Friends allows its members to determine for themselves how they will respond to call-up. Whilst some members will see it as their duty to serve, others may decide they cannot support war and will be prepared to submit to any personal suffering rather than take part in the armed services. However, all Quakers are committed to serve their country in other ways, regardless of what sacrifice this may entail. This peace testimony has remained unchanged for the last 300 years as an integral part of the religious life and service of Quakers.

The Minister quickly replied saying no exceptions to military service could be made for Quakers, although service in the medical corps might be considered as an alternative.[4]

On 21st May Hitler made a speech in the Reichstag which was quite different from his usual pronouncements. He spoke of the futility of all the wars which had been fought, and even expressed goodwill toward peace-makers.

London Yearly Meeting, which was in session a few days later, was surprised by the tone of this speech, but also distressed by Hitler's rearmament and revoking of the Versailles Treaty. Friends had used their influence to have the treaty moderated for Germany through raising public awareness about the problems. They urged the British Government to respond positively to Hitler's accommodating speech of 21st May, whilst also recognising that each of his propositions needed to be considered carefully. Friends seemed to agree with Corder Catchpool that they had to accept Hitler's words, though some were doubtful of his sincerity.

Mary's Visit to a Women's Prison

That summer Elsie Howard was again the hostess at the Pyrmont Rest Home. She experienced particular difficulties in integrating the diverse group who had little in common but the need to recuperate from their Nazi persecution. There was an ex-president of a province, a well-known trade union leader, a former newspaper editor and a couple of elderly Communists who did not mix well with Social Democrats or Quakers.

During this period Elsie was asked by American Friends, to visit a woman doctor who had fallen ill in prison. She invited Mary and me, now aged 12, to accompany her on the long drive through beautiful countryside to a small town where a wing of the local prison was being used as a concentration camp for political and Jewish women prisoners. The prison Governor received us saying he found these prisoners behaved very differently from the ordinary criminals. He invited Elsie and Mary to tour the wing and to shake hands and talk with the women, some of whom were Jehovah's Witnesses. I was entertained in the garden by the governor's son while Elsie and Mary talked with the woman doctor in her cell, but they emerged feeling that they had been of little help. However, a year later Elsie had a letter from her from America, saying that a few weeks after our visit, she had been released to go abroad.[5]

The conditions and treatment of the women in this prison appeared to be more humane than Elsie had seen elsewhere. This very privileged visit was followed by tea in the governor's private family apartment. Mary pleaded that the women be allowed to do some handicrafts during their long hours in the cells, to which the governor agreed if Quakers would provide materials. Mary later arranged for the women to make several dozen sea-grass hassocks for the Quakerhouse, a few of which still survive. This useful contact with the governor continued for a number of years. (See Chapter 8, 1938.)

Tenth Anniversary Yearly Meeting in Germany

Julia Whitworth came to stay a few weeks before the Yearly Meeting in order to help with the practical arrangements. Julia recently told me how much the experience had meant to her. She was then in her early twenties, and realised that she had led a very protected life in England. Corder Catchpool thought it necessary to advise Quaker visitors from Britain to come with sufficient funds so as not to be a burden on German Friends.

Yearly Meeting was attended by 220 participants, including many overseas Friends. Never before had so many German Friends met together under their own roof. Accommodation was booked by Leonhard in hotels and guest houses all over town, paying attention to the special needs of those who could only walk short distances and those who required the cheapest accommodation.

For the first time all the catering was provided at the Quakerhouse, though meals were taken in three shifts because space in the dining room was very limited. Everyone helped with peeling potatoes, preparing salads and washing-up. Many foreign Friends whose German was not fluent retreated gratefully to these domestic tasks.

The topics for discussion were: Heinz and Else Kappes, who spoke about the need for a Quaker centre in Jerusalem to promote Jewish/Arab understanding; Emil Fuchs, on social conditions in ancient Palestine; and Joan Mary Fry, on the value of vegetable growing and allotment holding for the unemployed in Britain. This was also the first year that Heinrich Otto, who later wrote the history of Quakerism in Germany, arranged a special children's group. There were 15 of us school-age children. We had a wonderful time walking in the woods, stopping for discussions and hearing the traditional Quaker stories on the way. I wrote the report on the children's gathering for the Yearly Meeting.

After the Yearly Meeting Mary received a letter from Julius Ursell of Attendorn, who described himself as a non-believing Jew and not a Quaker:

> I was so surprised to find how much I had enjoyed the Yearly Meeting, I felt happy like a little child. I had brought all sorts of anxieties with me, but in the safe and loving care of Friends I found new strength growing out of the powerful silent Quaker worship. Ideas from the lectures we heard stay clearly in my mind and have given me courage.

When Elsie Howard was leaving Germany in August, she was taken off the train at the frontier and brought back to Berlin for questioning. Her address book and letters she was carrying to avoid censorship were taken from her, which may have had serious consequences for those she was trying to help.[6] A few days later Corder Catchpool was again called to the Prinz Albrecht Strasse Gestapo HQ in Berlin and questioned about his activities. He was told: 'You are deliberately undermining the purposes of the punishment we are directing against those who do not support the State'. William Hughes was also taken in for questioning and advised not to return to Germany again.

These incidents warned the Germany Emergency Committee in London of the need to take great care and maintain a very low profile for their rescue work. They risked expulsion from Germany and might become a threat to the continued existence of the German Society of Friends. Most German Friends wanted the Quaker rescue work for Jews and political dissidents to continue, but it now seemed safer for it to be administered solely by foreign Friends. Meanwhile more requests from individuals in need arrived at the Berlin office every day. Much of the work was handled by Olga Halle and Martha Roehm among other German Friends who were willing to risk continuing to work with the AFSC and FSC Representatives.

The Nuremberg Laws Against the Jews

On 15th September the Reichstag held a special session in Nuremberg to pass laws against the Jews, which deprived them of citizenship, forbade marriage to non-Jews and employment of Aryan servants. The intention was to frighten the Jews into exile and deprive them of their wealth and possessions as they left the country. Quaker workers in Berlin, London and Paris all reported a great increase in refugees needing help. In early 1933 there had been 525,000 practising Jews in Germany. After the Nuremberg Laws anyone having a Jewish grandparent was also classified as a Jew, even if they had had no religious affiliation. These laws led to a large increase in the numbers of people being classified for exploitation as Jews.[7]

Corder Catchpool Visits German Prisoners in Lithuania

In the autumn of 1935 reports circulated in Berlin about the mistreatment of German Nazi prisoners in Memelland, a fifteen mile-wide strip of territory within Lithuania which had been part of East Prussia before the First World War. Some of its ethnic German population were Nazi followers, demanding union with Germany. This led to an armed revolt, which was put down by the Lithuanian police, followed by the Kovnov treason trial in March 1935, 83 ethnic German revolutionaries were condemned to prison. The incident attracted great interest in Germany. Corder was asked to visit Kovnov by relatives of the prisoners. He decided to consider the request, since it accorded with the Quaker principle of helping sufferers regardless of race or creed. He may also have felt that by performing this service for the Nazis, they might be disposed to give more help to Quaker efforts on behalf of anti-Nazi prisoners in Germany. Corder arrived in Memel on 5th November and was closely watched by the suspicious Lithuanian authorities, but he eventually managed to visit the prisoners. He reported there was no ill-treatment, although the conditions in which the prisoners were kept were primitive and unhealthy.[8,9]

During this visit the Lithuanian authorities agreed to release those prisoners asking for a pardon. Corder communicated this to the prisoners' families and six months later they were indeed set free. This episode seemed to reinforce the Quaker belief that it is worthwhile approaching political leaders, who are often more open to enquiries from foreigners than from their own nationals. This incident also became a subject of Leonhard's interrogation in 1942.

Friedrich Family Christmas

This year there was a Christmas party at the Quakerhouse attended by 37 people. Having spent the previous two Christmases in England with Edith Straus, I was happy to be going home. Mary wrote in her diary that I arrived home looking very pale; she may not have realised how affected I had been by an incident on my journey. It had been arranged that I should travel from England in the company of Mrs Werner, a member of the British Wives Group which Mary had formed in Nuremberg. We did not really know each other, but it felt good to have someone to talk to. When we reached the German frontier and the customs men came to the carriage, I declared a jar of marmite and a packet of tea. Mrs Werner maintained she had nothing to declare, although she had already told me of her joint of pork, pounds of butter, tea and bars of chocolate. I was horrified when she had to open her large case. She was very upset and quite hysterical and was taken off the train by the police. I did not know what to do, but she had told me to sit still and look after the rest of our belongings. She was detained for a long time and the train was delayed. Eventually she returned to our carriage sobbing her heart out. I never discovered what had happened to her until some weeks later, but Mary heard that when she got to Nuremberg the police were waiting for her and the poor lady committed suicide. Her crime had been to try to hide the food she was bringing for her family, items that were not available under the austere 'guns before butter' policy.

CHAPTER VI

Bad Pyrmont 1936

IT HAD BEEN A COLD WINTER, and the Quakerhouse taps had frozen. In early January Emil Fuchs, who had been travelling all over the country to minister to the needs of Quakers, came to speak to the Quarterly Meeting about 'lighting a candle in the darkness'. This was the first Meeting attended by Otto Buchinger senior, who had just moved his fasting clinic from Witzenhausen to Bad Pyrmont. He was already a Friend at this time and added strength to the Pyrmont Quaker group with his ministry.

Occupation of the Rhineland

On 7th March 1936 Hitler directed a surprise troop movement to re-occupy the demilitarised Rhineland at Aachen, Trier and Saarbrucken. These were territories with largely German populations which had been handed to French administration by the Locarno Pacts 1925 and the Versailles Treaty 1919. The reluctant acceptance of this *fait accompli* by the international community was a significant victory for Hitler. It was also satisfying to the astonished German people, who felt very emotional about the return of this part of the Rhineland.

Mary's Visit to England

This year Mary came in April and rented a cottage for the Easter holidays on the sand dunes at Bream, on the Bristol Channel, not far from Sidcot. I was nearly 13 years old and enjoyed bracing walks on the beach. Various friends and relations came to stay including Edith and Willi Straus and Edgar, their adult son.

After I had returned to Sidcot, Mary spent a further six weeks visiting relatives and attending Yearly Meeting and Quaker committees. In Sheffield she saw the three new houses which her brother Bert had bought for her, as a better investment than the Post Office for her savings. The cost of the three houses was £900, which she covered with £300 and a mortgage to be paid off by the tenants' weekly seven shillings rental payments.

Mary attended Meeting for Sufferings, the executive body of the Society of Friends in Britain, where Bertha Bracey reported on German Quaker activities and suggested that British Friends might offer a few weeks holiday to German Friends in need of respite or who wanted to consider emigration. Bertha spoke of the urgent need for funds to help more non-Aryans to get away. Emigration without passports to South America, was possible for those who could pay the costs. She also reported that there were 2,000 German Jewish refugees in France whom the Paris Quaker Centre was trying to help.

British Friends were disturbed to note the growing influence in East London of Mosley's Fascist Party and its anti-Jewish demonstrations. Friends Peace Committee was considering whether to advise Quakers not to participate in building air-raid shelters. They also noted that the build-up of the armaments industry was reducing unemployment.

At this same Meeting Bertha Bracey reported on the distress experienced by a German minority in the Bohemian part of Czechoslovakia. These were mainly unemployed glass and musical instrument workers whose children were under-nourished. A German charitable body had collected relief funds for them and through Corder Catchpool they asked Friends Service Council to act as a channel. After months of negotiations, and with the help of a Czech Friend, Dr Jaroslav Kose, 21,000 school-children in Bohemia received a hot school lunch during the winter months. An extended programme was repeated in the winter of 1936-7. This minority group later formed the Sudeten German Party under the Nazi-style leadership of Konrad Henlein.[1]

The Catchpool Family Leaves Berlin

In July the Catchpool family returned to England, when their five-year term of service ended. The risks Corder was taking incurred the displeasure of the Gestapo and worried Gwen and their four children. It was time for the two elder daughters to join me at Sidcot School. After the family had settled at 49 Parliament Hill Fields in Hampstead, a timely legacy freed Corder from having to take full-time employment. He therefore continued his commitment to German issues, visiting Europe frequently, while Gwen kept open-house for many guests from Germany.

The Catchpools were quite unique in the warmth and friendship they offered to people they met. At a time when everyone in Germany was extremely cautious, people looked over their shoulder to cast a '*Deutscher Blick*' to ensure they were not being overheard.[2] Corder and Gwen inspired individuals whom they met with a remarkable feeling of caring and confidence. To Germans at this time, it seemed truly amazing that such love for other people could exist. The circle of Catchpool friends and acquaintances who came to their Berlin Sunday afternoon 'at homes' was ever widening. Whilst German Friends loved them for this generous attitude, they also understood the need to be more discriminating about their fellow Germans, particularly when this open hospitality introduced individuals who might not be trusted to the Quaker circles.

Long after the Second World War, when English Friends went to Germany, they were likely to be approached by a stranger who would say 'I am a friend of Corder Catchpool', hoping to find the same kind of personal warmth, or to receive help.

Bad Pyrmont Yearly Meeting

The peak period of Leonhard and Mary's work was the Yearly Meeting held annually at the end of July. This was the fifth annual gathering in Pyrmont and they were now reasonably confident about the arrangements that had to be made to receive over 200 guests.

Hans Albrecht, the Clerk, opened the Meeting by advising Friends not to be seduced by the relaxed atmosphere at Quakerhouse into expressing unguarded opinions too freely. He cited the arrest of Rudolf Wieding, who was now in prison because he had been too open with someone who had come with the Berlin Young Friends Group in 1934. Hans warned that plain-clothes Gestapo officials were sometimes present in Berlin Quaker Meetings and might also attend this Meeting.[3]

Hans Albrecht had talked with Leonhard about this before the Meeting and arranged for him to be the 'look-out' doorkeeper, because he knew everyone. They agreed that if any unrecognised stranger joined the Meeting, Leonhard would make a sign to the Clerk. Hans had earlier explained to the Meeting that if he were to move the Minute Book from the table to the lectern, this was a signal to exercise particular caution. A short while later a Gestapo official, whom Leonhard had personally met, arrived after the session had begun. Once he was seated, Leonhard sent a whispered message around the room saying 'the Gestapo is here, pass it on'. He saw the Clerk move the Minute Book to the lectern. Leonhard watched the message being whispered along the rows of seats around the room, and felt quite tense as he saw it reach the row where the Gestapo official sat. When the message reached the official, he simply said 'Yes, I know', and luckily did nothing more about it.

Kati Lotz moved to Pyrmont in 1936 on her retirement. She had been a headteacher for many years and was very interested in more liberal educational methods. Her presence added strength to the small group and relieved Leonhard from local group clerking responsibilities. Hans Albrecht was criticised for taking too many decisions on his own, without reference to the Executive Committee. During the Nazi period it was not advisable to involve too many Friends in the usual democratic Quaker decision-making processes, nor to record detailed Minutes, but Kati Lotz, who had a fine intellect was appointed as an advisor to Hans Albrecht. (Illustrations 17 and 18)

17. *1936 Yearly Meeting catering group, Gertrud Graf and Mary Friedrich seated, Paul Helms behind them.*

18. *Heinrich Otto with his daughter Dietgart and Brenda.*

CHAPTER VII

Mary's Commitment to the Jews 1937

MARY HAD ENJOYED HER LAST visit to Nuremberg so much that she decided to take me there for a few days after Christmas. I was excited about going back to see the young friends I had grown up with, but I found that after a four year absence we children had grown apart. We had a party for my school and neighbourhood friends at the Meeting Rooms. I was 13 and think this visit imprinted Nuremberg strongly on my mind, so that I seem always to remember walking on the cobble-stones through the castle tunnel and down the steep hill past the Albrecht Duerer House to the Meeting Rooms and the town.

Bad Pyrmont

Pyrmont looked beautiful under a blanket of clean white snow, but soon after we got back I had to leave for England. That January Leonhard fell down the icy Quakerhouse steps and broke two fingers. Mary settled down to a lot of letter writing. In April she noted in her diary that she had an acute abdominal pain, suspected to be appendicitis. Three days later, on 23rd April she wrote:

> I had a horrid visit from three Gestapo men from Hanover questioning me about a Herr Kaufman. After they had left I decided it would be wise to leave the next day for Holland. But unfortunately I got into the wrong train at Hamelin. I had a really splitting headache and decided to return to Pyrmont, as I had missed the connecting trains to The Hook of Holland. When I reached home, I found a beautiful coverlet waiting for me, sent by Frau Kaufman, who had heard of the visit by the Gestapo. Quaker friends, Anne-Marie Cohen and her husband came for the weekend, enabling me to ask their advice about how to help Rudolf Wieding, who is in prison.

Such changes of plan may seem confusing to us, but it is not untypical of the kind of unforeseen events which occurred in Mary's life. She was frequently let down by her own health, and often interrupted her own plans to help someone who turned up on her doorstep.

Mary's Visit to England

Mary left a week later, resting for a few days in Holland with her Dutch industrial welfare colleague Ru Schulemann. She went on to London where she stayed with Edith Straus and met me when I returned from a language study course in Paris, and put me on the train to Sidcot. Mary visited various friends and was in England for the coronation of King George VI. She later came to stay at a guest house near Sidcot for a few weeks and attended the Yearly Meeting which was in Bristol that year. She reported that Hugh Doncaster, then aged 23, spoke with great inspiration about the Meeting for Worship being the centre of Quaker life. Hugh became a leading Quaker thinker.

During the Meetings Mary heard of a sinister questionnaire which Germans wishing to return home had to complete after an unsatisfactory attempt to emigrate. There were 38 questions, including one asking: 'Are you in a position to give the names of any Germans abroad who speak disloyally about the State?'

Mary had arranged for Hans Buchinger to come to Sidcot School as a German teacher, starting in the summer term in 1937. Hans was the first of many refugees for whom Mary arranged sponsors abroad. Dr Otto Buchinger's wife Elsbet was of half-Jewish parentage, so their children could be discriminated against as being quarter-Jewish, making a teaching career impossible for Hans. She later helped him find a post at the Quaker college of Earlham in Indiana.

In June Mary again visited her brother Bert Tupholme and his wife Amy who lived at 210 Abbeyfield Road in Sheffield. They drove her to Lincolnshire to visit the 11th century Tupholme Abbey, near Newark. Mary's Tupholme ancestors could be traced back to that area in the 16th century. They also drove to see the cottage called Cranesgate, Whaplode Street, Fen End, Holbeach, Lincolnshire, where their father Beeston Tupholme had been born on 31st January 1851.

Bad Pyrmont

Mary returned home in the middle of June feeling remarkably well. Soon afterwards she and Leonhard went for a five-hour walk to Hohenstolle. They both loved the beautiful Pyrmont countryside. A few days later they were sad to hear that the husband of a Quakerhouse cleaning lady had disappeared. He was found after 10 days, having hanged himself in the quarry, because he had been victimised by the Nazis.

One morning in early July Mary was walking the few steps from their flat to the Quakerhouse, thinking about the arrangements for receiving the 200 people coming to Yearly Meeting, when she saw a poster on the billboard beside the small Jewish cemetery opposite the Quakerhouse entrance. This board generally displayed posters for the tourists about Pyrmont's attractions. But this new one carried a strongly anti-Semitic message. Mary was shocked and outraged at the desecration of this beautiful place, where Friends from all over Germany and abroad would soon be coming to pray and worship.

Leonhard had left early that day for business in Hamelin so there was no one to talk it over with. Mary decided she would remove the poster. She took a scraping implement from the kitchen drawer, and found she could quite easily remove the newly-glued poster. She must have known the risks she was taking in broad daylight. With the shreds of the poster in her hand she walked the short distance to the town hall and went into the Burgermeister's Office. Placing the torn poster on the Burgermeister's desk, she voiced astonishment that he would permit such lurid anti-semitic posters to be displayed beside the Jewish cemetery in full view of the Quakerhouse. After all, he did his best to attract and welcome visitors, on whom the prosperity of the town depended. Could he imagine the dismay of the many foreign visitors who would soon be arriving for Yearly Meeting? After delivering her tirade she left the office and never heard anything further. The usual tourist poster appeared again the next morning. Mary was 55 years old and had all the assurance of an outraged Britisher. She was, however, a German citizen and by no means as secure as the British Friends visiting Germany.

Yearly Meeting, 28th July to 2nd August

There were now 15 Quaker Meetings in different cities of Germany with a membership of 256. Of these 230 people came to the Yearly Meeting. Mary as usual planned the hospitality, although Gertrud Graf did the cooking. Heinrich Otto ran the children's group, which I greatly enjoyed. This was the first year when the morning worship periods were preceeded by songs and music on the entrance steps of the Quakerhouse. The children led the singing of a most beautiful hymn of praise, '*Aus Frommer Morgen Stille*' by Alfons Paquet. It has remained one of the best loved songs by succeeding generations of Quakers, because it evokes a feeling of closeness to God on an early summer morning in Pyrmont.[1]

After the Yearly Meeting visitors had left I enjoyed the Pyrmont swimming pool and adjoining boating lake. However my friend Elga, the daughter of Dr Gustav Sturmthal, could not come with me because Jews were forbidden entry. Instead we went together to swim in a small lake at Holzhausen. I had just discovered the joys of rowing a boat on the Gandelteich, a gravel pit beside the swimming pool. One day I persuaded my reluctant mother to let me row her out. Mary was quite unaccustomed to getting in and out of small boats, and had not realised how easily the boat could drift into the lake while her hands were still gripping the landing. There was no one at hand to help her and to my horror she slowly fell into the water fully-clothed. A man dressed in SA uniform suddenly appeared to pull her out. Unfortunately he was extremely abusive and created an unpleasant scene. Mary retreated to a dressing cubicle feeling undignified, whilst I hurried home for a dry set of clothes. That night there was an air raid practice 'black-out' all over Germany.

Leonhard at the Second Friends World Conference

In mid August Leonhard was one of a group of six German Friends who attended the second Friends World Conference in Swarthmore, Pennsylvania, the first having been in Britain in 1920. The group sailed on the *Queen Mary* from Hamburg, and were joined by British Friends at Southampton, making up a party of 49. This journey was one of the highlights of Leonhard's life. When the European Friends arrived in Philadelphia they received a warm welcome. There were 700 American delegates and 300 overseas Friends representing 24 nationalities. Open evening sessions were attended by 4,000 Friends. Leonhard was happy to find people he already knew among this large gathering. There was Joan Mary Fry, who opened the conference and Howard and Anna Elkington and other Friends who had visited them in Germany. Whilst the conference was taking place, Mary and a group of Pyrmont Friends were able to listen to Rufus Jones' keynote address on the BBC overseas programme.

Afterwards Leonhard was invited to visit Friends in the Mid-West to tell them about conditions in Germany. He was a staunch pipe-smoker, which posed problems when visiting the conservative non-drinking, non-smoking Friends. He later enjoyed recounting the story of being a house guest in such a Quaker family. After the meal was over he asked if he might light up his pipe. His hostess replied: 'Friend, if thee really needs to sin, thee may go and do it in the garden'.

An extra pleasure for Leonhard was visiting his only brother Bernhard, whom he had not seen since he had emigrated to Pennsylvania from Liverpool in 1913. He had married Dora Kluge, also of German origin. Bernhard worked in the offices of the Kayser Bond knitwear factory and had two children, Martin and Hildegard. (Illustrations 19 and 20)

19. Friends World Committee Conference, Swarthmore 1937.
Leonhard, Fred Tritton, unknown.

20. Leonhard's brother Bernhard and son Martin in America.

Leonhard did not return to Pyrmont until 21st November. He found it difficult to pick up the threads of his work again, although Mary had kept things going. He may have felt that the good times he had experienced in America contrasted with his own situation in Germany. In the weeks that followed Mary made several diary references to Leonhard's short temper, which had been especially embarrassing during a Quaker business meeting. He was known for occasionally blowing his top, and spoke his mind freely in a Bavarian worker's style which north Germans often felt was unacceptable.

Hitler's Ambitions

During 1937 Hitler became more convinced of his mission to make Germany the world's most powerful nation. Following the successful seizure of the Rhineland in the previous year and Mussolini's partnership in the Berlin-Rome Axis Treaty, the armaments industry was given highest priority and jobs became easier to find. There were, however, problems in obtaining raw materials such as rubber. The chemical industry was challenged to find substitutes for this and many other materials. These ingenious materials were talked of with pride in Germany, but with derision in England.

Shortages of raw materials, which other European countries obtained from their colonies, led the Nazis to plead for more territory. This was the main thrust of an important secret speech Hitler made on 5th November to an inner circle of the Nazi Party and the military. He called for the need of raw materials and territory for the expanding Aryan race. If Britain or France showed signs of weakness, Germany would seize Czechoslovakia and Austria. A regulation was also issued at this meeting requiring all Jews to have their passport stamped with a red 'J', making it impossible for them to leave the country without giving up all their possessions.

CHAPTER VIII

Annexation of Austria and the Munich Crisis 1938

I CAME HOME FOR CHRISTMAS again in 1937 and found Pyrmont blanketed in deep layers of pure white snow. Twenty Quakers gathered for Quarterly Meeting held in early January. Leonhard Friedrich and Alfons Paquet reported on the significance of the Friends' World Conference held at Swarthmore, Pennsylvania.[1] Dietgard Otto, whose company I had enjoyed over several summers, had come with her father Heinrich Otto, and we both had a wonderful time tobogganing down the Bomberg Allee.

A few days later Mary's sewing lady came to stay for several days. She lived in Hanover, but travelled around the area working for a few days for each of her regular families. She was settled into my bedroom with the treadle sewing machine and mended the sheets, made pillowcases, turned the collars and cuffs on Leonhard's shirts, altered Mary's dresses and made clothes for me. Mary took trouble to look well-dressed. She always wore a hat to Meeting on Sundays, though few Pyrmont Quakers did so. She did this so that any visitor coming to Meeting wearing a hat, would not feel over-dressed. She regularly took her hats to a shop where they were re-modelled to meet the current fashions.

Mary and Leonhard heard that the first-floor flat in the Knierim House at 37 Bismarckstrasse was vacant. They had often looked down longingly on this modern well-built house from their fourth floor balcony of Villa Harmonie and were delighted when they were accepted as tenants. It had wonderful views of the hills and fields from all the windows and an enclosed balcony where we could eat meals in the summer.

In mid-January, after I had returned to school, Mary was visited by her 32-year-old nephew, Charlie Tupholme, who came from Sheffield on an exchange programme with a large engineering firm in Krefeld. The company, Deutsche Edelstahl must have been of strategic importance to the armaments industry because they employed 7,000 workers to make stainless steel wire and sheeting. His weekend visits brought a breath of

78

fresh air to Leonhard and Mary. On 1st May 1991 Charlie wrote the following account for me:

The experience was professionally very useful for me. I found my German workmates very friendly and helpful. I must have visited Leonhard and Mary every month. Leonhard and I had a memorable walking holiday in the Black Forest.

On one of my visits to Pyrmont, they said we were going to visit a local church. But we really went to hear clergymen from several districts relate their experiences of the Gestapo: how they were dragged from their beds in the night and taken to the police station for interrogation and rough treatment. It was exciting and frightening for me. During the meeting there were people on 'look-out' duty to check whether the meeting had been observed. I was quite glad when we returned home safely.

Another time Mary and Leonhard took me to visit a Friend who had just been released from prison. My German was not good enough to follow the conversation, but I remember we sat in a room with the curtains drawn.

Leonhard and Mary often walked with me in the beautiful Pyrmont parks and I was surprised how many people stopped to greet them. It was quite noticeable that they never gave the Nazi salute. Neither did I.

On one occasion when I returned to my lodgings from work, I was told by an excited maid that the police had been to look through my papers and belongings. They had found many copies of the *Manchester Guardian*, which my cousin Margaret Tupholme used to send me. I was ordered to report to the police the next day, and told in no uncertain manner that I must not receive banned newspapers. After this I felt I was being watched and became very cautious about responding to friendly approaches from strangers. Though there was some stress in my time there, I was young enough to value the experience and the understanding it gave me.[2]

Annexation of Austria

The events leading up to the annexation of Austria were very disturbing to Leonhard and Mary. Throughout the winter of 1937-8 Hitler had strengthened the Nazi presence in Austria, aiming to destabilise and terrorise the country.

On 12th February, von Papen, then the German Ambassador in Vienna, arranged a meeting at Berchtesgaden between Hitler and the Austrian Chancellor Kurt von Schuschnigg. But when Schuschnigg arrived, he found Hitler was demanding complete surrender of Austria to Germany. Hitler gave Schuschnigg three days to return to Vienna and obtain the consent of the Austrian President to annexation, while simultaneously ordering the mobilisation of the German army.

On 20th February, Hitler told the Reichstag that the 10 million ethnic Germans living in Austria and Czechoslovakia should no longer be deprived of their right to be governed by the Reich. This speech produced massive pro-German street demonstrations in Vienna. There was economic panic and withdrawal of foreign funds, and foreign tourists fled home. Schuschnigg reacted by announcing a plebiscite on 13th March for the people to vote 'yes' or 'no' to annexation. This infuriated Hitler, who hastened the invasion. Orders went out to the Austrian pro-Nazi groups to riot in the streets and make the country ungovernable. At midnight on 11th March both Schuschnigg and President Miklas capitulated to Nazi pressure and cancelled the plebiscite.

On 12th March Hitler drove into Austria, receiving tumultuous applause from the villages through which he passed. Now aged 50, he was returning to his native land in triumph.[3]

In the next few days, under Himmler's orders, Austria was purged of Social Democrats and opponents of annexation, thousands of whom were imprisoned. When Hitler held a referendum in Austria on 10th April he obtained a 98% vote in favour of joining Germany. The name of Austria disappeared from the map and Vienna was plundered of assets.

A pogrom against the Jews followed. Elderly men and women, including well-known doctors, lawyers and shopkeepers, were forced onto their hands and knees to scrub the pavements and clean the latrines in barracks occupied by German soldiers, who taunted them. They were put into prison and their belongings stolen. Some of the wealthier Jews managed to buy their freedom to emigrate by handing over their property to the Nazis.

During this period Corder Catchpool visited the Quaker Centre in Vienna. Travelling by train through Germany he saw railway wagons and truck-loads of guns travelling towards Vienna. He found enthusiasm for the annexation among the youth, but silent acceptance from the adults. At the Quaker Centre he heard that the prisons were overflowing with Jews and prominent Catholics. The Jewish community had lost all means of livelihood and were paralysed with fear. Hundreds were taking their own lives. There was immense pressure at the Quaker Centre to assist emigration.[4]

Bad Pyrmont

Mary returned home from her visit to Britain on 6th June, having heard much more about events in Austria than she would have done from the German news services. Leonhard was very pleased to see her, and they enjoyed making their new flat more comfortable. As it was somewhat larger, she bought some more carpets and curtains and several lovely old pieces of furniture.

In July, the Berlin Quaker youth group, which included a number of children from Jewish families, came for a camping holiday at Friedensthal. Mary had 12 youngsters to supper twice that week. At the end of the month I came home again, this time with my Sidcot school friends, Barbara Walker, Rosalind Barkas (Priestman) and Jean (Greaves) and Pleasaunce Catchpool (Holtum).

Thirteenth Yearly Meeting

The Quaker membership rose to 271 and now included nine Austrian Friends from the Vienna Meeting. Many Friends were suffering under the Nazis, both at home and at work and they cherished the opportunity of being together. By this time no Friend was unaware of the evil that was being perpetrated by Hitler and his followers, though many Germans seemed to shut their minds to it. Some Friends felt helpless and withdrew into prayer. Visiting Quakers from abroad were very anxious about the evidence of German re-armament and the dictatorial trends they observed. They went away to renew their campaigns for 'peace through the League of Nations'. They deeply sympathised with the unemployed, the persecuted and those in prison, or those who had to become refugees. There seemed to be no way to stop Hitler's evil progress.

The American Friend Thomas Kelly gave the annual Richard Cary lecture. Leonhard published his book *Testament of Devotion* in German, which had a profound impact on Friends at this time.[5]

Pyrmont, which in those days had about 8,000 inhabitants, had always put on a splendid welcome for the Yearly Meeting, because the overseas visitors were thought to be good for business. Yearly Meeting ended on 'Golden Sunday' when the town mounted a fairy-tale display of lanterns and lights hiding in the trees, in the park and the main shopping street.

Quakers Help Emigration of Jews

Mary devoted much of her time during the next 12 months trying to arrange emigration for Jews, and 'non-Aryans', as people with Jewish ancestry were known. Most of the people she helped no longer identified with the Jewish community. Some were married to non-Jews, or had no religious affiliation, but according to the Nuremberg Laws of genealogy they were classified as Jews. These 'lapsed' Jews, or those who were not born of a Jewish mother, were given no help from official Jewish organisations. The offices of the Friends Centres in Berlin, Vienna,

Frankfurt, Paris and London, gave priority to helping those who had no organisation to turn to. No records were kept in the small Berlin Quaker office for security reasons and we therefore have no statistics about the numbers of people who were assisted. The case material from the work done in Friends House in London was also destroyed in 1947 after Bloomsbury House, the centre for assistance for Jewish refugees, was closed. Roger Carter, who was the last British Quaker representative in Berlin from 1938-9, estimates the Berlin office is unlikely to have helped more than a few hundred to emigrate between 1933-9, though many hundreds more were sympathetically advised and referred to relevant agencies.[6]

In Berlin an office to assist non-Aryan Christians was set up by Pastor Heinrich Gruber of the Confessional Church. This was given moral support from England by Bishop Bell of Chichester. His sister-in-law, Laura Livingstone, set up a Berlin advisory centre, which later combined with the Buro Gruber to operate on a larger scale. They worked closely with Friends, particularly when Herta Israel from the Berlin Quaker office was seconded to them. Pastor Gruber's principal partner in Britain was Bertha Bracey, working for the Friends Germany Emergency Committee in London. She found settlement opportunities in other countries for 2,000 refugees who had arrived in Britain on temporary visas.

Up to 1937 the staff and volunteers in the London office were never more than nine people. The work escalated after the invasion of Austria, so that by the end of 1938 the numbers of case workers employed had risen to 59. The stream of refugees needing help at Friends House swelled so much that the two grand staircases became more or less permanently blocked by queues of people waiting to be attended to. Interviews had to be conducted in corridors when the offices were overflowing. A few months later, in February 1939, the work moved to Bloomsbury House. At this time a staff of 80 case workers moved out of Friends House along with 14,000 case records. The expansion of the work for Jewish refugees from Germany, Austria and Czechoslovakia led to the formation of a co-ordinating body known as the Inter-Church Council for German Refugees. Bertha Bracey was the Secretary of this body, whilst still employed by Friends Service Council as Secretary to the Friends Committee on Refugees and Aliens.[7]

Mary's Emigration Work from Pyrmont

The anxiety of the Jewish community reached panic level. Our family doctor, Gustav Sturmthal, who was much loved in Pyrmont, had hoped he might survive with the help and support of his patients. But after the annexation of Austria, and the subsequent pressures in Czechoslovakia, he reluctantly realised that even in the quiet backwater of Pyrmont, his family existence was threatened. Following Kristallnacht in November 1938 no Jewish physician was allowed to practice. He then asked Mary's help to emigrate to England and urged that his daughters be got away as soon as possible.

During her annual visits to England Mary had spoken to many Friends about the problems of living in Nazi Germany. She now turned to them for help and also conferred with the Jewish Refugee Aid Committee, set up by the Jewish Board of Guardians at Woburn House and with Bertha Bracey and Helen Dixon at Friends House and subsequently at Bloomsbury House, to keep abreast of changing immigration regulations. It was comparatively simple to find guarantors for children and adaptable young people, but extremely difficult to help whole families like the Sturmthals, who had elderly parents to care for. British immigration regulations required that each refugee had an affidavit from a property-owning adult who was willing to guarantee that the refugee would not become a public liability.

Quaker Publishing Transferred to Leonhard Friedrich Verlag

On 21st September, following a state decree which prohibited religious bodies from publishing literature, Leonhard bought the business from the Friends and carried on in his own name. He was still advised by the Quaker Literature Committee, but welcomed the freedom to publish non-Quaker literature, such as health books written by his friend Dr Otto Buchinger senior.

After the transaction had taken place Leonhard received a letter from the National Association of Booksellers, saying:

Under regulation 7 of 15.9.34, you are required to submit your family tree, to demonstrate your Aryan lineage at least as far as your great-grandparents, by means of certified documents. Similarly the person to whom you are married, must also submit documents showing her antecedents. A stamped and addressed envelope is enclosed for the return of the certificates. Please reply in a two week period.

After a visit to Marktbreit, where he looked up parish records, Leonhard was able to provide information back to his great-grandparents with dates of birth, baptism, marriage and death. Fortunately no names such as Sarah or Solomon occurred in the family and Leonhard breathed a sigh of relief. His relatives were all from the rural area of Marktbreit. Some had been fishermen on the River Main, others had owned vineyards or grew flax. Lutherans and Catholics had for generations inter-married happily in his family.

Leonhard Received a Warning

The following incident happened while I was still at home for the summer. One day in early August Leonhard was on his own in the Quakerhouse office when a stranger walked in, saying he had an important message, but was unable to say who had sent him. The message was to ask Leonhard to walk down to the Kur-park on Wednesday at 1.30 pm. When passing the Strawberry Temple there, he would notice a man standing under the beech tree. Leonhard should speak with him for a moment and then pass quickly on. He would be given important information.

This threw Leonhard and Mary into considerable anxiety. If he kept the appointment he might be walking into a trap. After careful thought he decided to go to the designated place and was surprised to recognise the governor of the women's prison with whom he and Mary had kept in touch since her visit there with Elsie Howard in 1935. The governor warned that Leonhard had been named in the regional Gestapo group as a disloyal person who was to be roughed up. He advised Leonhard to leave Pyrmont for a few weeks, because he thought the problem would blow over.

Leonhard and Mary made an immediate decision that we should go to a friend's holiday cottage at Holm-Seppensen. We then went on to Timmendorf on the Baltic coast for a week by the sea. It was unusual for both my parents to leave their Pyrmont responsibilities to be away from home together. When we returned Leonhard was relieved to find all was well, but to allow more time for the threat to settle, he went off again to Holland for the following week. He returned home for a couple of days while his cousin, Babette Rupp, came from Marktbreit for a visit, then left once more for meetings at the Vienna Quaker Centre. By the time he returned the Gestapo obviously had more serious matters occupying them.

Dr Otto Buchinger – 'The Scandal of Bad Pyrmont'

A brief article entitled as above appeared in *Der Stuermer*, the official Nazi newspaper on 19th October 1938:

Bad Pyrmont does not wish to accept any more Jewish Kur-guests, but Dr Buchinger who is director of a clinic there and is a Quaker, regrets this fact and recently sent the following letter to a Jewish patient:

'Dear Dr Tucher,

For the last several months I have been obliged to use a rubber stamp on all my correspondence, stating that Jewish patients cannot be accepted. As the director of this clinic I was not in a position to oppose this measure. However as a human being and a physician I regret the necessity to do so.

With best wishes, Respectfully yours,

Otto Buchinger.'

It is a scandal and an insult to the entire German people that a leading German doctor should still manage after six years of a National Socialist Government to regret measures that are taken to protect our society against the Jews! We are also outraged that a German doctor should end his letter with, 'best wishes, and Respectfully yours', to a Jew! Many thousands of German doctors are glad to live under National Socialism and support the policy of anti-Semitism. A man of Dr Buchinger's type should have no place among the German medical profession.

Czechoslovakia – Munich, 29th September

Throughout the summer tension mounted and Hitler was pressing his generals to speed up preparations for the invasion of Czechoslovakia. In Britain the Sudeten problems were at first regarded as an unimportant issue about a German minority and Chamberlain advised Czech President Benes to make concessions for the sake of peace. As Benes won no other support for the Czech cause, he invited Henlein, leader of the Sudeten German Party to Prague on 4th September in order to discuss their demands, but there was no response. On 12th September, at a Nuremberg party rally, Hitler made another aggressive speech about Sudetenland to the cheering Nazi audience in the stadium. This was broadcast around the world as the signal for Henlein to start the Sudeten uprising. President Benes' security forces were, however, prepared and reacted speedily, causing Henlein and several thousand of his supporters to flee to Germany.

Prime Minister Daladier of France, a signatory with Britain to the defence pact with Czechoslovakia, then appealed to Chamberlain to intervene. On 15th September Chamberlain flew to Berchtesgaden. Hitler was flattered and agreed to Chamberlain's proposal for a plebiscite, to determine whether Sudetenland should be annexed by Germany. The Czech army mobilised a million men. In Berlin a division of the German army rumbled through the streets, past the Chancellery for Hitler's approval. The troop movements towards Czechoslovakia created gloom all over Europe, recalling vivid memories of the First World War.

Chamberlain appealed to Hitler to ask him for a final effort to achieve a peaceful solution. The resulting conference held in Munich was badly organised, without adequate translation, ended in the German decision to amputate the Sudeten areas from Czechoslovakia. Hitler had obtained Sudetenland without war and concluded that Britain wanted peace at any price. Chamberlain returned to a cheering London with a piece of paper signed by Hitler, which he claimed guaranteed 'Peace in our time'.

On 1st October the German army marched into Sudetenland, gaining 11,000 square miles of territory and much industrial capability. They acquired the sophisticated defensive installations which had been built along the Bohemian mountains to protect Czechoslovakia from Germany. President Benes was exiled and the country was divided. Six months later, on 15th March, the German army took Prague and the rest of the country.

Peace in our Time

After Chamberlain's return from Munich, the peace movement was greatly relieved that an outbreak of war in Europe had been avoided. But the first feelings of relief gave way to uneasy and conscience-stricken feelings about the price paid by Czechoslovakia, which had been sacrificed. These views were reflected in a statement by a group of Friends which included Roger Wilson, who met at Ratcliff Meeting House in East London:

> In the present crisis we appreciate the determination of those who feel war must be avoided at all cost, but also of those who believe that we should never seek to save ourselves at the expense of others. It is our belief that the only way out of the dilemma is to attempt a wider solution of the problems which threaten peace, through an international settlement.[8]

Corder Catchpool who was in Prague, wrote to *The Friend*:

> It was peace, but peace without honour. After all the nervous tension we have been through, most of us have got off scot-free, while Czechoslovakia pays the full price . . . including the plight of 31,000 registered Jewish and political refugees from Sudetenland who are in Prague. The British government should be persuaded to pay the Czechs substantial compensation, since we have avoided the expense of war.[9]

Corder Catchpool and Roger Carter, the Berlin Quaker Representative, had spent the last few days before the German annexation with the Quaker group in Prague who had for some years been helping refugees from Germany. Roger Carter mingled with the demonstrating crowds in the streets. On 27th September, two days before the Munich Agreement, Roger sent a report from Prague to Friends Service Council:

> When the defection of Britain and France was announced there was anguish and despair, bitter to behold. There was no rowdyism, no disorder; but both men and women stood silently in the streets and wept.

That evening demonstrations began and went on all night, marching to the Presidential Palace. On the following day thousands demonstrated outside the Parliament and Communist symbols were seen. Later on when Hitler's insatiable demands were understood, a determination to fight to the last breath became apparent.[10]

Last Minute Help by Friends in Prague

Six months later on 15th March 1939 Hitler also took Prague. Tessa Rowntree, a young British Friend (later married to the American Quaker, Jack Cadbury), had been in Prague since early 1938 assisting Quaker refugee work. On 15th March, the day of the German troops entry into Prague, she brought out 66 refugees by train en route to Britain. Tessa Cadbury wrote me a letter about this, dated 2nd January 1991:

I spent a hectic few months from October 1938 onwards, working closely with a few Friends in Prague and the Germany Emergency Committee in London. We co-operated with a diverse group which included Margaret Layton of the *Daily News* and Barbara Duncan Harris, a Friend and member of the Women's International League for Peace and Freedom. We all generally followed the leadership of Doreen Warriner who had a quite unique ability in getting disparate people to work together.

Besides interviewing refugees who had fled to Czechoslovakia from Germany, we had good contacts with the leadership of Czech groups who would be threatened by a Nazi invasion. Some of these groups were eventually settled together along the Peace River in British Columbia.

Doreen Warriner persuaded one or two of us who were British passport holders to help convoy train-loads of refugees out of the country. I took two convoys consisting mainly of German Labour leaders who had escaped from the Nazis to Prague, and were considered in such danger that their wives and families were left behind. We travelled across Poland by night train. The Polish guard locked me in the guard's van on my own, while the already frightened refugees were crowded into other carriages. We knew a boat was waiting for the group at Gydnia, but our train was running very late and near panic set in among our group. We finally had to hire a bus, which seemed to lose its way. When we arrived at the dock-side the boat was just about to pull away. However, it waited for our party, and I was very thankful when the last refugee set foot on board before the gang-plank went up. I led a second such party a few days later.

In those last months as war drew nearer we seemed to lead double lives. There was so much tension and near panic on the part of those who felt trapped by the Nazi invaders and we felt frustrated by our own inability to find solutions. Some people we knew, were bravely determined to stand firm and would not consider escaping. One such person was Peter Zenkel, the Mayor of Prague, who later survived a concentration camp, and whom I met again after the war. There were also two stalwart members of the Prague Friends Meeting who died in German concentration camps.[11]

CHAPTER IX

Kristallnacht 1938

MARY AND LEONHARD ANXIOUSLY followed the Sudeten crisis, listening to the BBC or Radio Luxembourg, or reading the weekly *Manchester Guardian*. All these sources had been declared illegal in Germany. They became more worried when they read that the reserves of the British Army had been called up. The crisis atmosphere meant cancelling their visit to Bueckeberg, to Pastor Wilhelm Mensching, who was travelling secretary of the Fellowship of Reconciliation in Germany. This was a great disappointment to Clarence Pickett, the General Secretary of the American Friends Service Committee (AFSC) and his wife Lily, who were staying with the Friedrichs while on a peace mission in Germany. Pastor Mensching (1887-1964) had been associated with Friends since the 1920s, but waited until after the war to become a member. In 1949 he set up the 'Freundschafts Heim' under the auspices of the International Fellowship of Reconciliation.

Kristallnacht Pogrom, 9-10 November 1938

A few weeks after the Munich Agreement on Sudetenland Hitler instigated a pogrom against the Jews. No one in Germany or abroad could now fail to understand the intentions of the Nazi regime.

On 7th November 1938 a Jewish boy, called Hershel Grynszpan, entered the German Embassy in Paris and shot a diplomat. News of this incident reached Hitler on the night of 9th November, whilst attending the annual celebrations of the Munich Beer Hall Putsch. This incident was an opportunity to punish the Jews.

Goebbels ordered 'spontaneous demonstrations' that night in every city, town and village. A thousand synagogues were burnt down, 7,500 Jewish homes and businesses were smashed and looted. The police did not intervene and as many Jews as possible, especially the wealthy ones, were arrested.[1]

This resulted in severe destruction and suffering and thousands of shattered shop windows on the city streets. Homes, offices and shops were destroyed and looted that night, though incidents continued for the rest of the week. Information from Buchenwald shows that 9,815 Jews were admitted to the concentration camp immediately afterwards and 30,000 Jews were sent to other camps.

The German insurance companies feared bankruptcy, but soon discovered there was no liability to compensate Jewish claimants. Jews were themselves compelled to clear the streets of glass and rubble. The Gestapo had made advance preparations for such a pogrom and had alerted youth units, even providing them with firemen's hatchets and the addresses of Jewish homes and businesses.[2]

Kristallnacht in Pyrmont

Pyrmont was a small, quiet place, our home was among a few widely-spaced houses on the edge of town. Normally all that could be heard at night was the hooting of an owl. But on 9th November Mary, who was on her own, was awakened by sounds which seemed to be coming from the Quakerhouse. She looked out from her bedroom window and was relieved she could see nothing unusual. But next morning she found the gravestones in the Jewish cemetery had been smashed. The Jewish cemetery was a small triangular-shaped area between two roads, which used to look neglected and overgrown. On the other side of the road was the equally small but well-kept Friends burial ground, which had been left undisturbed.

Marlies, the wife of young Dr Ott Buchinger jnr. remembers how that night Nazis had smashed the Abrahams' umbrella shop window in the Brunnenstrasse, creating fear among the Jewish community.

Elga Isom (née Sturmthal) wrote to me, on 4th December 1990:

> Nicholaus Sturmthal, my grandfather, who lived on the ground floor of our house in Kirchstrasse, close to the Brunnen Platz, had the shop window of his 'Gentlemen's Outfitter' smashed that night. All Jewish men were taken to the police station. The next day the police asked us to take food to our men. I sat in the graffiti-covered cell with my father and grandfather, while they ate the food we had brought. I was 14 years old at this time. Later in the day the police allowed us to return to say goodbye to our menfolk, before they were taken to Hanover by bus. In the early hours of the next morning my father and grandfather, then aged 75, mercifully returned home. We believe their release was due to the intervention of Friedel Wiedel, the chemist, who was also deputy Mayor at that time. He had been an old school friend of my father's, though they had been unable to socialise for some years. It doubtless took a good deal of courage for Herr Wiedel

to intervene, because having a Jewish grandmother, he himself was vulnerable.[3]

Mary records in her diary that over the next 10 days she visited all the Jewish families she knew in the area. She did this to express the shame and compassion that many others also felt, but few dared to show. She saw the destruction of Jewish property and heard about the brutality and who had been injured or taken away. Her efforts to find sponsors abroad for at least the younger members of Jewish families became more urgent.

In the summer of 1989 I visited Hilde Sturmthal, the widow of Dr Gustav Sturmthal, in Letchworth, Herts. Mary had helped their family reach England just before the war. Hilde was then an alert 91-year-old widow living close to her daughter, Elga. She told me that after Kristallnacht her husband was visited by a council workman who said: 'Don't worry Herr Doktor, I made sure that your mother's grave [Lina Sturmthal 1919] was not smashed up, I covered it with a good layer of earth so that no one could know it was there'. After talking with her mother, Elga wrote more about Kristallnacht:

We knew about two of the deaths which followed Kristallnacht. One was Solly Abraham, aged 65, who suffered from an enlarged prostate which needed frequent catheterisation, the only treatment known in those days. He must have suffered a very painful two weeks before his death, at Buchenwald on 25th November 1938.

We also heard of the death of Adolf Salamon, a retired violinist, aged 79. He was not related to the other Pyrmont Salomons. When he retired from the Hamburg Orchestra, he came back to Bad Pyrmont where his wife had died and been buried during a visit some years earlier. It was said that on Kristallnacht when a guard tried to hurry Adolf Salamon along, the old man suddenly turned around and hit him. For this he got a severe beating from which he did not recover. He also died in Buchenwald on 13th November 1938.[3]

After the war the Jewish cemetery was pleasantly landscaped as part of Bad Pyrmont's park and bears a memorial stone inscribed 'In memory of their Jewish fellow citizens, erected by the Town of Bad Pyrmont'. The park layout was sensitively supervised by Walter Fink, then the town planner. He took care to replace the gravestones in their original positions, which he had earlier recorded with photographs.

At the Bad Pyrmont Yearly Meeting of 1988, the 50th anniversary of Kristallnacht, the Friends held a Meeting for Worship by candlelight on this symbolic site. Until two years earlier the grave of Adolf Salamon had been tended and planted with flowers, as is customary for Christian graves. This had mystified the local Friends, who had enquired about surviving relatives in the town, but came to the conclusion the grave may have been

21. *Pyrmont Street Sign: 'Dr Gustav Sturmthal, a Jewish doctor who rendered great service in this town.'*
Hilde Sturmthal, Gerda, Elga and Dr G. Sturmthal.

looked after by the family of his former Christian landlady. One of the most painful feelings for survivors of the holocaust is to have no personal grave where their relatives can be mourned. Now at least any surviving members of the historic Pyrmont Jewish families can find graves of their forbears when they visit the town.

Walter Fink, the Pyrmont archivist, told me that none of the Jews who survived the war now live in Pyrmont, though several have visited from abroad. The town planning office had already closed the cemetery for further burials in 1928 in order to preserve the purity of the water of the nearby spring. For this reason the Quaker burial ground is only permitted to receive cremations encased in copper urns. Fink claims that the decision in 1938 to level the Jewish graves was made earlier and had nothing to do with Kristallnacht. The work just happened to be undertaken in November 1938. Most of the gravestones were broken up and used as hard-core for a footpath in the Goslingerstrasse, as is customary in Germany. He said that the civic authority's mistake had been in not realising that Jewish graves had an exceptional right to remain in perpetuity, beyond the usual 30 year period allowed in Germany. A new Jewish cemetery was at that time already in use on a nearby hillside.

Fink may have been mistaken when he said it was coincidence that the Jewish gravestones were removed at the time of Kristallnacht, particularly as after I had told him Mary had been woken up by unusual noises in the night, he then remembered that a story had circulated about a nun on night duty at Georgs Villa, having also heard a disturbance at the cemetery on 9th November. Heinrich Otto, author of *Quakertum*[4], described the desecration of the cemetery which he saw a few days after the event on a visit to Pyrmont.

Walter Fink collected a file of material about the cemetery, which can be seen at the Pyrmont Amts-gericht reference library. His particular study has been on the origin of the Pyrmont street names and it was he who suggested that a street be named after Dr Sturmthal. The street sign bears the additional information, *'Dr Gustav Sturmthal, Juedischer Artz mit grossen Verdiensten um Bad Pyrmont'* A Jewish Doctor who rendered great service to our town. (Illustration 21)

Fink went on to tell me a story, which Marlies Buchinger also remembers. Before the war, it may have been 1937, there was a brawl between the SA and the SS in the Haupt Allee outside the Rasmussens Cafe. In the course of the fight, one man had part of his nose bitten off. Someone picked up the piece of flesh and wrapped it in a piece of butter paper and took the injured man with the fleshy fragment to Dr Sturmthal's surgery close by. This skilful doctor managed to stitch it back on, an operation which seems an extraordinary accomplishment considering the minimal equipment a general practitioner would in 1938 have had in his surgery. Elga also added:

> Both my mother and I remember this incident. The vital factor in the operation was the speed with which it was performed. The tissues had no time to die before being re-united.[3]

Rudolf Wieding Returns from Prison

Over the weekend of 22-24 November, a fortnight after Kristallnacht, two Quaker couples, Manfred and Lily Pollatz from Holland and Rudolf and Martha Wieding from Hanover, came to stay. Rudolf, who had recently been released from prison told about his interrogation and subsequent imprisonment. His troubles originated because he had been a member of the Social Democrats and the German Peace Society. During the Yearly Meeting of 1934 he had spoken too openly with Franz Wempen, a young unemployed man whom Corder Catchpool had helped and encouraged to come to Yearly Meeting with the Berlin Young Friends group.[4]

After the 1934 Yearly Meeting, Franz Wempen had visited Rudolf in Hanover where they happened to talk about the recent Roehm affair. Rudolf showed Wempen an article describing this event, published in a journal regarded as seditious by the Nazis. Some time later Wempen, perhaps under pressure from the Nazis, denounced Rudolf Wieding, who was arrested by Berlin Gestapo officials on 17th February 1936, interrogated for 11 months and found guilty of 'preparations for treason'. After serving a sentence of two years and four months he was released on 17th June 1938.

List of 'Trusted Friends', (*Vertrauensleute*)

A confidential list of 22 Friends who, like Leonhard and Mary, were willing to help Jews and others suffering persecution in different areas of Germany, was compiled in the Berlin Quaker office. The list was held by Roger Carter, the Berlin Friends Service Council representative. In June 1939 Hans Albrecht agreed that Roger should share these names with Otto Hirsch, who was head of a rescue organisation known as the Central Jewish Organisation. Such Jewish organisations were for a time permitted to exist, because they assisted emigration, but Otto Hirsch himself perished in a concentration camp in 1941. The Quakers listed as 'Trusted Friends' were as follows: Edwin Bernhardt, Friedrich Christiansen, Rudolf and Anne-Marie Cohen, John Davis, Paul Durrbeck, August Fricke, Leonhard and Mary Friedrich, Gusti Fuchs, Josef Gingerich, Carl and Eva Hermann, Margarethe Lachmund, Martha Legatis, Henny Ludwig, Lydia Neubrand, Marie Pleissner, Johanna Rieber, Kurt Richter, Erna Rosier, Rudolf Schlosser, Ludwig Siebert and Jangeorg Specht. These Friends did not organise together, but they certainly knew each other and exchanged experiences when they occasionally met at Quaker gatherings. Friends were not the only people helping the persecuted, I am sure other undocumented networks existed.[4]

Kindertransporte 1938-9

Kristallnacht had caused panic throughout the Jewish community in Germany, whole families committed suicide together. Leadership was again shown by the Jewish businessman Wilfrid Israel (1899-1943), the director of Tietz the department store in Nuremberg. He had close ties with the Jewish community in Britain (see Chapter 1). Wilfrid contacted the London Council for German Jewry, insisting that extraordinary measures must now be taken to save at least the children. He had kept in touch with Bertha Bracey since her stay in Nuremberg in 1923-5 and now asked that some British Quakers visit Germany to report to the British Government on what was happening. Bertha wrote to me about this on 10th March 1986:

> When the Jewish Refugee Committee could not risk sending a Jewish delegation, we sent five Quaker workers to Berlin to confer with Wilfrid Israel, who directed them to different areas to work alongside the Jewish women doing welfare work, and helping the younger people for whom emigration possibilities still existed. On one of my visits at this time I had intended to avoid the Quaker office at Prinz Louis Ferdinand strasse because our committee considered it was then unfair to risk the involvement of German Friends, or for them even to know of our rescue plans. However there was no chance of disguising the fact that I was in Berlin when I ran into Emil Fuchs in the underground station. Ben Greene, who was one of the five people in the Quaker mission, came back to London after a few days, and went with me to talk to Lord Samuel and the Home Secretary. Parliament sitting that night, authorised emergency permits to admit 10,000 children. Most of them were Jewish, but a small group of less than 20 were Christian non-Aryans, these were put into the care of Minna Specht and her deputy.[5]

Minna Specht was one of a number of non-Aryan German Quaker refugees in Britain who helped to care for the sudden but welcome arrival of a large group of children. They set up hostels all over the country to allow more time to find suitable family care for individual children. Many children were taken into Quaker families, but the heaviest burden was born by the Jewish relief organisations.

50th Anniversary of *Kindertransporte* 1989

Fifty years later Jewish groups organised large-scale anniversary reunions in London at the Festival Hall and elsewhere. Several thousand people who had left Germany on the *Kindertransporte* came together from all over Britain and abroad, bringing sons and daughters and grandchildren with them. Most were now in their 60s and 70s, but many still felt the emotional scars of their hasty separation from families who subsequently perished in concentration camps. Some of them had as children repressed their feelings in order to adapt more quickly to life in their host community. They had now reached a stage where they reflected on their life experiences, and wanted to discover aspects of their early years which one normally hears of from parents' accounts. Some had come as very young children and had no memory of their families or how they had arrived in Britain, or even the people who first cared for them. Many first believed their parents would follow a few weeks later, but after the difficult war years, most had to accept that their family had not survived. Some of them dare not face the trauma of a return visit to Germany, but others have been back to explore the towns and villages where they were born, and have discovered cultural roots. Many German civic bodies have offered hospitality to visiting Jews. Some who accepted the invitation found it had been a healing experience for themselves and their German hosts, particularly to discuss the Nazi times with young people in schools. A number of Jews who never adjusted to exile, have returned to settle in Germany. I attended this reunion to represent the Society of Friends, and wished Bertha Bracey who died a few months earlier could have been with me.

CHAPTER X

War Becomes Inevitable 1939

Bad Pyrmont

I HAD BEEN HOME AGAIN for another beautiful white Christmas, with crisp deep snow all round. I did not know it was to be my last one in Pyrmont, although I felt my parent's deep anxiety for the Jewish community. Much had happened since the summer holidays and I was anxious for my parents' safety. I was 15 and reading the *News Chronicle* at school, which had covered the events of Kristallnacht. But I now learned what had occurred in Pyrmont and how people I knew had been affected. Just before Christmas, Mary took me to visit several Jewish families and deliver the Christmas *stollen* cake she had baked for them.

The usual hardy Friends came for the January Quarterly Meeting, despite the freezing winter conditions. They stayed in chilly guest-houses, where a few rooms were kept open for out-of-season visitors. This year the Quaker representative in Berlin, Roger Carter, then aged 27, addressed them on 'Quakerism in our Time'. The report in *Der Quaker* posed the question: How can we renew our spiritual strength? It will not be through earthquake, wind and fire, but in listening for the still small voice of Love, working through the hearts of people, to drive out fear and overcome evil.[1]

Mary Helps Jews to Escape

Mary began to see some results from her work. She personally found guarantors abroad for 38 people. Departure dates:

5. 3.37   Hans BUCHINGER, a Pyrmont non-Aryan Quaker left to teach at Sidcot School and subsequently at Earlham College in the USA. Ingrid, his wife and two daughters did not follow until after the war. After Hans died in the 1970's Ingrid and their daughter Beate returned to live in Germany, where Beate worked as a physician.

18.12.38	Lisa and Margarethe URSELL, teenagers connected with the Friends Meeting. From Berlin to the Retreat in York, where they trained as nurses.
20.12.38	Dr Ellen SALOMON, dentist from Pyrmont, to Paraguay.
20.12.38	Hans KRAMER of Minden left for Paraguay. He was the nephew of Henny Israelsohn, who lived together with the much older Ellen Salomon. Hans and Ellen separated before reaching Paraguay.
21.12.38	My friend Elga STURMTHAL, age 12, to Sidcot School. Quaker boarding schools in Britain provided free places for 100 refugee children.
25. 1.39	Her parents Dr Gustav STURMTHAL, his wife Hilde and their younger daughter Gerda were sponsored by Dr Henry Gillett in Oxford. They sailed via Hamburg to Southampton and Leonhard accompanied them to the port. Their first job in England was to run the newly-opened Friends hostel for German refugees at 122 Westbourne Terrace, near Paddington Station, which was short-stay accommodation for 40 residents. Sturmthal later settled as a GP in Letchworth, where he and Hilde joined the Quaker Meeting.
1.39	Rudi HEYMAN, adopted son of Israel and Anna Heyman, who ran the drapery shop selling fine embroidery in Pyrmont. He went first to Leeds and then sailed to Australia. His parents were taken to Warsaw 28.3.42. Rudi visited Pyrmont in 1949.
9. 2.39	Hans and Edith ABRAHAMS, Pyrmont umbrella-makers to stay with Edith Bigland at Jordans in Buckinghamshire. Hans worked for many years at Lyons Corner House and took the name of Harry Anderson. His sister also lived in north London, her married name was Linton.
18. 2.39	Ingrid SEUTEMANN, 10-year-old daughter of Cilli and Hans, members of the Pyrmont Meeting, left on her own and was received by Henry Gillett of Oxford. On finishing school she became a nursing sister and after the war often visited her mother in Pyrmont. Cilli died in 1989.
2. 3.39	Frau Margarethe de HAAS, her daughter Marianne and grandmother Tilly de HAAS, then aged 85, left Pyrmont for Sweden, where they were received by Swedish Quakers. They later travelled on to the USA, but Tilly died during the journey.

3.39 Max de HAAS and his daughter Charlotte, aged 17, also left within a few days. Max was an Elder of the Pyrmont Synagogue. In 1952 Mary visited the United States and met some of the de HAAS family in New York. Her diary entry: 'Max and Charlotte were both so excited to see me. Max has become a landscape gardener. Marianne is a qualified nurse: she has married a German Jew who changed his name to Gordon, and works as a gardener. Margarethe has married a tailor, but their mother has died'.

21. 7.39 Ilse HERBECK, a non-Aryan Quaker, to London.

21. 7.39 Erich URSELL, an attender of the Berlin Friends Meeting, brother of Lisa and Margarethe, who left earlier. In 1949 Roger Carter, formerly Quaker representative in Berlin, 1938-9 met him in Washington, where he ran an exclusive ethnic craft shop.

3. 8.39 Ilse and Marion LOWENSTEIN of Steinheim, near Pyrmont, to Sheffield. Also Dinah LOWENSTEIN, mother of Hilde Sturmthal.

3. 8.39 Otto HOCHEIMER, a writer from Steinheim, to South America.

10. 8.39 Nicholas STURMTHAL, from Pyrmont, the father of Gustav STURMTHAL, with his housekeeper, Henny ISRAELSOHN, left for Oxford.

10. 8.39 Hans SCHOENDORF left Pyrmont for England. He occasionally still visits his sister Annemarie Blanke, who remained in Pyrmont and became a Quaker. His name was changed to STANSFIELD.

8.39 Gertrud and Richard STEIN, a young couple, from Luegde to Oxford.

Date ? Kurt STEIN, a child from Paderborn, to Marjorie and Roger Wilson in Britain.

" Sigmund and Rosel NEUMANN, a Nuremberg journalist and wife, to Chicago. Mary also visited this family in 1952 and wrote in her diary: 'Sigmund now works in a hospital laboratory, and occasionally does some freelance writing. He has diabetes and looks unwell, but Rosel seems fine. Their son Walter works in a garden centre. When they first arrived in London, their hostess could not collect them until the next day. They spent hours waiting in the Friends House garden wondering what to do. The Quaker refugee hostel was full and eventually they went to a shabby Euston hotel, using all their money. Next day they were met by their hostess. Some time later they got to New York, where their son was able to help, but life was not easy. They attend the Quaker Meeting at Riverside'.

Date ? Max ISRAELSOHN, nephew of Henny Israelsohn.
" Margot, Giesela and Kurt MEYER, children from Pyrmont to England.
" Kurt LANDESMANN, aged 12, nephew of de HAAS family in Sweden, from Pyrmont to Birmingham.
" Herr and Frau SPARGENTHAL from Pyrmont area to Lucy Gillett, Oxford.

The Refugee Reception Camp at Richborough, Kent

Wilfrid Israel, the Nuremberg Jewish leader, provided information for the British refugee organisations to persuade the Government to permit the establishment of temporary refugee camps in England. Refugees were held in these camps while their requests for settlement in the UK or elsewhere were being negotiated. Ultimate emigration to South America was easier.

Eventually in January 1939 the first such refugee camp was opened at Richborough, Kent, in an old refurbished army camp. Passport and visa requirements were temporarily waived for 2,500 young people, as they had been for the *Kindertransporte*. Many of them had been released directly from concentration camps on payment of a fee to the Nazis. Some 8,000 young people passed through the Richborough camp before the outbreak of war. Many of the men joined the Pioneer Corps of the British Army or volunteered for farm work before they were able to leave for Palestine. An appeal to lift the immigrant quota for the USA did not succeed.[2]

I was then a 15-year-old schoolgirl at Sidcot Friends School in Somerset. My friend Freda Pearce and I read a newspaper story about the primitive conditions at the Richborough camp. We sympathised with the young people not even having enough money to buy a stamp to write a letter home. We decided to send them our weekly pocket-money. The Council for German Jewry, responsible for the camp, released our letter to the press in order to strengthen their appeal for funds needed. Our letter was then picked up by *The Friend*, whereupon we quite unexpectedly received many small sums from the readers, enabling us to increase our contributions.

No headmaster likes to open a newspaper to read about his pupils. Consequently Freda and I were called to George Hutchinson's study and told we had been foolish to act on our own. He then really frightened me by pointing out that I had been quoted as saying 'my parents are at present in Germany helping the Jews'. If this were picked up by the Nazis, it could be quite enough to get my parents arrested.

Eastern Europe

Throughout the winter of 1938-9 the German Government encouraged subversive activities in Poland, and among the Slovaks in Czechoslovakia. This culminated in the triumphant entry into Prague of the German army on 15th March. Hitler took up residence in the hilltop Hradcany Castle which dominates the city, annexing the whole country and acquired valuable opportunities for the economic exploitation of Czech industry. A week later he forced Lithuania to cede Memelland.

Hitler presumed that Britain and France would not intervene, but the turning point in British foreign policy was reached when it became clear that Hitler's expansion in Europe had destroyed Czechoslovakia and that German territorial ambitions must be halted. On 31st March Britain and France signed a treaty to protect the Polish Corridor, should Germany threaten an invasion. This had provided access to the Baltic for Poland after the signing of the Versailles Treaty in 1919.

At this time William Tysz, a Polish Quaker living in Katowice, a friend of Leonhard's, wrote three letters to *The Friend*, warning of the danger his country faced. He pleaded with Quakers to take a firm stance against the Nazis and deplored some articles in *The Friend*, which had suggested yet more compromises to maintain peace.

Mary's Visit to England

Mary was much affected by the death on 13th April of Helen Dixon (1865-1939), who was Chairman of the Germany Emergency Committee. Mary had sought Helen's advice ever since she first did relief work in Frankfurt in 1922; she wrote obituary articles for *Der Quaker* and *The Friend*.[3]

Mary was in frail health when she arrived in England in early May, and appreciated loving care given by Edith Straus. Together they went to see their old friend Bertha Bracey, who was now organising the refugee work from Bloomsbury House. Mary asked advice about how to help Hans Schoendorf and other non-Aryan Christians whose emigration she was trying to arrange. They also visited Woburn House, to seek the help of the Joint Jewish Refugee Aid Committee for Herr Pollack, from Cologne.

Mary then spent a week with Florence Livingstone, and Audrey Smythe in their lovely cottage near Dorking. Mary did not have much rest because she wrote 24 letters for refugees during this five-day period. She kept up this pace of writing to find sponsors throughout her visit and found a domestic agency able to offer residential domestic jobs for the Jews. Mary had some relaxation: she saw the films, *Busman's Holiday*, and *The Citadel*, based on A. J. Cronin's novel and she watched television for the first time at an exhibition. She also attended London Yearly Meeting, after which she came down to Sidcot School to be with me in June. She travelled further west to speak to Friends Meetings in Devon and Cornwall. Her itinerary included St Ives, where she saw Pendennis Castle. She said it would have been a lovely experience, had her handbag, money, railway tickets, hat and coat not been stolen.

On her return to Pyrmont in July, Mary started preparations for Yearly Meeting in Pyrmont and also visited the Jewish families she had been helping. She wanted to know how they had been managing, and to tell them about the enquiries she had made on their behalf in England. She wrote to Bloomsbury House offering to visit any applicants from the Hagen and Hanover districts. At the back of her 1939 diary there is a comprehensive list of those she helped to emigrate. Elga Sturmthal and her mother have kindly supplied additional information about people they knew.

With the help of Bloomsbury House, Mary arranged emigration for a further twenty-one people:

MOSSBERG – from Bielefeld to London.

POLLACK – from Cologne to England, c/o Woburn House.

Max LACK – to London, c/o Woburn House.

PHILLIPSOHN – from Bueckeberg to England.

Hilde FISCHER – from Bonn to England.

Doctor and Frau HECHT and daughter – from Nuremberg to England.

Karl PINO – from Hoxter to Richborough, USA.

Elizabeth ULLRICH and mother – from Nuremberg to Birmingham.

Martina WEISSELBERG – details unknown.

GRENSTEIN – details unknown.

ASCHBURGER – details unknown.

Frau MEYER – Hanover to England, August 1939, the mother of three children who left earlier.

Frau KARLE – from Hanover to England, August 1939.

Hermia MELD – details unknown.

Frau SCHARRER – details unknown.
LOEWENBAUM – details unknown.
HAHMS – details unknown.
Otto HOMER – from Paderborn to USA. He was one of the people whom Mary visited in 1952. Mary wrote: 'He asked me a lot of questions about Trudy MERGEL, the non-Aryan attender of our Meeting during the war years. Otto told me he had loved her for 20 years. I had to tell him she had taken her own life'.
Dr HENKEL – details unknown.

14th Yearly Meeting, Pyrmont, 2-6 August 1939

I had arrived a few days before the Friends gathered. Everyone felt that war was imminent, which made our time together seem very precious. For security reasons only Friends in actual membership were present this year. Altogether 259 people came, including 87 Quaker visitors from abroad. Hans Albrecht reported that some people had left the Society of Friends and that 25 new members had joined.

In 1988 Enid Huws-Jones, a British Friend, wrote to me about her experiences at this Yearly Meeting, when she was 27 years old:

Our accommodation was in a Pyrmont guest-house decorated with swastikas, and when our host began an anti-Jewish tirade, I stammered out, 'but the Jews are human beings too'. He was surprised and crumpled up and agreed with me straight away. Everyone seemed very frightened. Some young adventurous Friends wanted to invite the ever-present Gestapo guard down to our lunch room, to challenge his Nazi beliefs. Elsie Howard who happened to overhear this, explained: 'If you do that, you will ruin the relaxed atmosphere which means so much to the non-Aryan Friends amongst us'.

I particularly remember Mary Friedrich inviting the young overseas Quakers to her flat. She drew the curtains, so that neighbours would not see how many of us were there. She was concerned that some innocent young overseas Friends might carry notebooks with names and addresses around with them, and then lose them on a park bench or elsewhere. Mary told us there were very few Jewish families left in Pyrmont, whom the Nazis hoped to clear out to create a 'pure German spa'. There were several Jews at Yearly Meeting, who were forbidden to go in the park. Mary told us how she had visited the Jewish families after Kristallnacht and had left a cauliflower, given by a market gardener, with each family.

Jewish people pressed visiting Quakers to carry undeclared items back to their relatives in Britain. This created a dreadful dilemma for me as a law abiding truthful citizen. I felt I had to help them, but also that I was being pressurised by 'powers of evil'. Eventually I brought back a ring hidden on a chain around my neck and a huge suitcase of winter coats for the Sturmthal family. I shall never forget the surprise and rapture of seeing it slide down the ramp at Victoria Station, and of getting into a taxi to take it to the hostel where they lived near Paddington Station.[4]

Carl Heath gave the Richard Cary Lecture with the title 'Life is Prayer' and Emil Fuchs spoke about the 'Inner Light', saying that so long as we live we must serve others. He felt a God-given mission to weaken injustice and the class system.

Emil Fuchs and his Family

Emil's eldest son, Klaus Fuchs, later became a renowned physicist. He is remembered in the West as a traitor who disclosed the secrets of the atomic bomb to the Russians.

Yearly Meeting in 1939 ended with a personal tragedy for Emil Fuchs when his 30-year-old daughter, Elizabeth Kittowski, committed suicide by jumping out of a moving railway carriage soon after the train had left the Pyrmont station. Emil had been holding her by the hand because he knew she was very depressed. The train was very crowded and they walked along the carriage to look for a seat. The train jolted, he lost his balance and let go of her hand. In an instant she had opened the carriage door and had thrown herself out. The train was stopped and Emil and Friends who were with him, brought her body back to Pyrmont. Mary and Leonhard and the Pyrmont Friends supported Emil through these difficult days.

Emil Fuchs was such an inspiration to Friends and was especially close to Mary and Leonhard. He had been born in 1874 and died, aged 97, in East Germany in 1971. As a young man he had been a Lutheran Pastor, in contact with Quakers since their relief work activities in the twenties, but he did not actually join Friends until 1933. He was a short man with sparkling eyes and a small expressive moustache, and had a loving personality which drew people to him. Emil was a gifted Bible scholar, who knew how to present the old stories whilst drawing attention to contemporary problems. In 1931 he became Professor of Divinity at Kiel University. This was the year of his wife's suicide. His daughter Elizabeth, had found her mother dead on the kitchen floor and was profoundly affected by the experience.

In 1933 Emil was dismissed from his Professorship at Kiel because he had been an active Social Democrat and refused to sign the Nazi loyalty oath. He was then interrogated for five weeks and subsequently re-arrested several times. From then on he had great difficulty in earning a living. He and his four young adult children, Elizabeth, Klaus, Kristel and Gerhardt, decided to resist the Nazis through the Communist Party. For security reasons the family decided they would all be safer if they took care not to tell each other of their activities. Emil and Gerhardt supported themselves and young Klaus, Elizabeth's orphan child, by running a car hire business. This provided an income as well as being a useful means of escape for the people Gerhardt was helping. Eventually Gerhardt himself had to flee abroad.

Emil's daughter Elizabeth had married Klaus Kittowski, a Communist who at the time of the Yearly Meeting in 1939 was in prison. A number of Friends had noticed her deep depression. She had named her baby Klaus, born 1934, after her husband, but it was also the name of her brother Klaus Fuchs, who had already emigrated to Bristol, and Emil's middle name. Little Klaus was left at home while Elizabeth and Emil attended Yearly Meeting. Unfortunately the child's father died in prison, and so the orphaned child became Emil's responsibility. The other daughter, Kristel Heineman, had gone to Pendle Hill, the Quaker centre in America in 1936, and later married an American.

Not long after Elizabeth's death, Gerhardt and his wife had to go into hiding in Czechoslovakia. He eventually died of TB in a Swiss sanatorium. Emil was alone with young Klaus, without a secure home, income or employment. He was greatly helped by a Quaker family, Curt and Charlot Nuthmann, and earned some money by writing a Christian Socialist newsletter which was sent to subscribers by post. With the help of the Nuthmanns, Emil was free to undertake pastoral care among the scattered Quaker groups all over Germany and gave encouragement to those who had sorrow in their homes.[5]

Eventually Emil agreed Klaus should be evacuated from the heavy bombing of Berlin to a village in the mountains. Emil joined him there in 1943. Emil's faith remained unbroken throughout these terrible times. He experienced great sadness through the broken lives of his children, but it was his grandson, Klaus, who sustained him. After the war Emil wrote that at last the dark depression had left him, but not the pain.

Klaus Fuchs, the Atomic Spy

Emil's son Klaus Fuchs had been studying physics at the University of Goettingen, until his Communist activities made it too dangerous for him to remain in Germany. In February 1933, after the Reichstag had gone up in flames, he fled to Paris and was helped by the Quaker Refugee Centre there. He later found a home with a family in Bristol, where he resumed his Communist connections. It seemed for him the only way to fight Nazism. He was able to continue studies in physics at Bristol University, and went on to do research work for Britain's atomic weapons programme. In 1940 he was interned as an enemy alien and evacuated to Canada. In 1941, at the request of Max Born, another German physicist with Quaker connections, he was brought back to Britain to resume atomic research.

By 1943 Klaus Fuchs, who had become one of Britain's most promising scientists, was transferred to atomic research in America at Los Alamos, New Mexico. After some time there, he renewed his contacts with the Russian spy ring. Like his father, he had very high principles, and could not be bribed into betraying secrets. However, he became convinced that the world would be a safer place if the Russians also had the knowledge of how to manufacture the atomic bomb. In 1946 he was invited to return to Britain, joining the atomic research team at Harwell. In January 1950, having spent several years passing highly sensitive technical information to the Soviets, he was arrested and tried as a spy. Before this he had already begun to question his own actions, which he later described as arising from a kind of 'controlled schizophrenia'. At his trial he was found guilty of espionage and sentenced to 14 years imprisonment. On his release in 1959, at the age of 48, he was particularly distressed to discover his betrayal had deprived him of the British nationality which he prized so highly. Though a brilliant scientist, he seems to have been naive and totally misunderstood the effects of his actions. When he came out of prison he chose to go to East Germany, to live in Dresden with his father and young Klaus Kittowski.

After the war Emil lived for some years in West Germany. However at the age of 75 he was offered an attractive Professorship at Leipzig University which gave him time to follow his interests in education. As a life-long socialist he identified with Communist East Germany, and left the capitalist system of the West. He remained a Quaker to the end, though his support for his son Klaus Fuchs and the high regard of the East German government for the family may at times have caused a certain distance between him and the fifty Quakers in the GDR. Emil became a founder member of the Prague Christian Peace Conference, to which some Friends in Britain and Europe also devoted a great deal of energy during the Cold War period.[6, 7]

Last Days Before the War

In early August Mary took me to Hanover to visit two Jewish ladies, Frau Karle and Frau Meyer, about whom Bloomsbury House needed more information. The international situation was becoming very tense. On the 24th August Hitler and Stalin signed a non-aggression pact. The

British Government announced a mutual assistance treaty with Poland and ordered conscription.

Hearing all this on the radio late at night Mary and Leonhard realised war was now imminent. It was a warm moonlit night and I was sleeping on our balcony. They woke me to explain that I had to decide whether to stay with them in Germany or return to England the next day. Such a decision would be hard to make at any age, and I was barely 16. Why did Leonhard and Mary not leave at the same time? They were both German citizens, whereas I had a British passport. They would have needed entry permits and guarantees of financial support. However, I am sure they stayed on because they chose to remain with the Quaker group in Germany, having strong convictions that one does not run away from problems.

The decision was different for me. My friends were all in England. Having spent six years at school in England, I felt thoroughly British, although I never denied being half-German and became defensive when some people expected me to do so. I loved my family and would miss Pyrmont, but as a teenager short-term considerations seemed more important. I had been sitting my School Certificate examinations at the end of July. The results were not yet out and I felt I should return to school, in case any subjects had to be re-taken. My Sidcot scholarship had another year to run, and I was looking forward to being in the sixth form. Had I opted to stay in Germany, I would have been drawn into all the activities of my age group, such as the League of German Girls and other Nazi organisations, which would also have created problems for my parents. I was sad to realise that I would be unable to return home and felt divided by the emnity between Britain and Germany. I could not imagine that our separation would last more than a year or so.

I left next day, 25th August on the midday train. It was very crowded and the passengers were anxious and excited. I had no problems, Edith Straus was at Victoria to meet me in response to a telegram from my parents. The British Quaker workers from Berlin, Vienna and Prague had also left for England that day, having handed their responsibilities over to German or American Quaker colleagues wherever possible.

War was Declared, 3rd September 1939

The German secret services were staging provocative incidents in Poland to justify an invasion. On 1st September the German army moved into Poland with all guns firing. War had begun, though without the cheering crowds which Hitler had hoped for, and it was to last more than five years. On Sunday 3rd September, the House of Commons met to hear the declaration of war.

I was staying with my school friend Barbara Walker, whose parents' new house on Bream Hill near Weston-super-Mare had wonderful views over the marshlands of the Somerset Levels. Barbara's family and I listened to the Prime Minister Neville Chamberlain, announcing the war on the radio. Mrs Walker, a very beautiful young mother, turned to Barbara, her brothers and me saying: 'The war will be a very testing and challenging experience. You children must support each other through whatever may come'.

This made a deep impression on me, perhaps because as an only child I had always depended on adults. We didn't know at the time, but she had cancer and only lived about six months. When her mother died, Barbara had to leave school to look after her father. Her brother Johnnie joined the Air Force, and lost his life as a Battle of Britain pilot.

Bad Pyrmont

The day war was declared Leonhard and Mary walked over the fields and hillside above Friedenstahl to take possession of their newly-acquired garden. It had been given to them after the Sturmthal grandfather and his housekeeper left for England in July. They spent the day digging up potatoes, bringing them home in a little hand-cart. It felt good to be outdoors doing something practical whilst their minds and spirits were so low.

The letters Mary wrote after I had left were returned to her, rubber-stamped saying 'communication with enemy countries has ceased'. One of these letters she kept had been to my guardian Norman Tupholme. Mary had written on 31st August:

> We have heard on the radio about the evacuation plans for Droitwich. How terrible to think of little children leaving home with gas masks slung over their shoulders. You Norman, will also be called up . . . We here have not heard one thing about what is happening elsewhere [there had been a news embargo in Germany 27-31 August], though we have been given ration books. I am thankful that you have undertaken the guardianship responsibilities with Edith and Julia for Brenda.

Mary next tried writing to Bertram Pickard at the Geneva Quaker Centre, and was glad to hear from him that I had got safely back to school and had passed my matriculation exams.

By 18th September the motorised German army reached Danzig, the Luftwaffe having paved the way with an aerial bombardment. The Poles were overwhelmed by what came to be known as the Blitzkrieg, and the Russian army, now allied to Germany, advanced to Brest-Litovsk.

X WAR BECOMES INEVITABLE 1939 109

Emigration permits arrived too late for the following four families Mary was helping:

Meta and John JOHANNSEN. Meta was the sister of Henny Israelsohn. Her husband was not Jewish, but was in some trouble with the authorities.

Frau ISRAELSOHN, was another sister of Henny, who had a photographic studio.

Dr and Mrs Anne FRANKENBERG, friends of the Sturmthals.

Heinrich MEYER, father of the three children who had left earlier, and husband of Frau Meyer who left in August.

How devastating it must have been for these four families, and for Mary who had struggled for their emigration permits, which eventually arrived a week after the war had begun. Like many others, these people had hoped they could survive in Germany unnoticed. But after Kristallnacht, they realised they would have to leave but did not know where to turn, until they found Mary. They had put their affairs in order, had bought and packed suitcases, and given away things they couldn't take with them. Each day they had waited for the postman to deliver the permits, but when they finally arrived, the frontiers were already closed and war declared.

Some emigrants destined for countries which remained neutral when the war broke out, such as the USA or South America, could still get away through Switzerland or Scandinavia and even the Trans-Siberian railway. The Nazis did not stop the Berlin Quaker Centre from continuing to help Jews to leave Germany by these routes. Leonard Kenworthy, the American Quaker in Berlin, reported that some hundred people left in this way after the war had begun. But it did not help the non-Aryans on Mary's list. In October, Mary and Leonhard found the lack of news difficult to accept, as there was little information on the radio and few callers.[8]

On 20th October 1939 *The Friend* carried an article bringing news of Quakers in Germany, written by American Quakers Howard Elkinton and Homer Morris, who had been in Vienna, Breslau, Pyrmont and Berlin. The Berlin Quaker Centre appeared to be functioning fairly normally with the support of the resident American Quaker, Elizabeth Shipley. Elizabeth and Emilia Fogelklou Norlind, a well-known Swedish Quaker author, visited a number of German Friends in their homes and also came to Pyrmont. Emilia had brought permits with her for 100 German non-Aryan children to emigrate to Sweden, to be received into families selected by Swedish Friends. There were also some emigration opportunities arranged by Dutch and Danish Friends.

Homer and Edna Morris of the American Friends Service Committee, were in Europe at this time to explore possible Quaker relief work in occupied Poland, where some 50,000 Poles had been killed during the invasion. Homer was accompanied by two Nazi officials and was most impressed by their arrangements for emergency feeding:

By means of mobile units the German relief agency is serving 250,000 hot meals a day to the destitute of Warsaw. Although the food preparation unit is 45 miles outside the city, and meals are prepared the day before, they are stored and transported in thermos containers and arrive in Warsaw piping hot. But none of this food is available for the Jewish population, which is vast and in great need.

He then went on to raise a number of problems the AFSC would have in working with a Nazi relief organisation and concluded that they would be unable to co-operate in the relief programme.[9]

The visits of Swedish and American Friends during the early months of the war were a great solace to German Friends. Edna Morris reported in London that one young Quaker had been unable to avoid serving in the army, but that several others were in the medical corps.

Within a year of the occupation of Poland more than a million Polish citizens had been killed or deported to work as slave labour in German factories. Teachers and intellectuals and 300,000 Jews had been removed to concentration camps.[10]

Stalin took over the eastern half of Poland and the Baltic states of Lithuania, Latvia and Estonia. The Russians harassed Finland mercilessly and on 1st December began the costly 'Winter War' against that valiant country. Britain sent military support via Norway. The Friends Ambulance Unit (FAU) also sent 50 men and 10 ambulances to work with the Finnish Red Cross. The Finns held on to much of their territory until the Nazi conquest of Norway in June 1940 made their submission inevitable. Some of the FAU were taken as Prisoners of War, others got back through Sweden with the retreating British forces in May 1940.

In early December Leonhard went to Berlin for the Quaker Executive Committee. On his return, he and Mary visited some of the Jewish families in Hoxter, and prepared small Christmas gifts for many others.

CHAPTER XI

Hitler's Domination of Europe 1940

In Pyrmont

FRIENDS GATHERED FOR THE JANUARY Quarterly Meeting, in spite of particularly difficult travelling conditions. Kati Lotz, from Pyrmont, led a discussion on the life and work of Fridtjof Nansen, providing a focus for discussion on the needs of refugees and prisoners of war. Most Quakers held opinions about the war in Poland and Finland which left them feeling very isolated from colleagues at work and sometimes even from relatives at home.

After Christmas, and with the agreement of the Meeting, Mary, Berta Maas and Cilli Seutemann invited all the Jews they knew to tea at the Quakerhouse. Mary was by now in touch with some 40 Jews in the Pyrmont and Hanover district, though she also had contacts further afield in Nuremberg, Cologne, Berlin and Lueneburg. About 20 people came, simply glad of an invitation to go out to meet one another. During the year the Meeting held six such social occasions and Mary also gave weekly English classes for those who lived nearby. She felt frustrated at being able to do so little for the non-Aryans, who seemed to expect so much from her. The Berlin and Vienna Quaker Centres were organising similar gatherings for mutual support.

All the Jewish families knew by now that there was little hope of even the children getting away. Mary, sometimes accompanied by Leonhard, continued to visit families whenever she could. She was taking great personal risk and could well have been denounced simply for being seen talking with a Jew in the street.

The Friedrichs' flat was on the first floor of a villa, where the landlord's family lived on the ground floor. Herr Knierim, who kept an ironmongers shop in town, was a member of the Nazi Party. He was always hostile towards Mary and probably feared that her contacts might reflect on him. He warned that she would be reported if any Jews came to their flat, and specifically forbade their non-Aryan Friend Cilli Seutemann entry to the house. Leonhard and Mary then simply arranged to meet with Jews in the Quakerhouse, where they were thankful for privacy.

On 9th May Mary received a visit from Heinrich Meyer, the Jewish father of Margot, Giesela and Kurt, the children whom Mary had managed to get to England just before the war. His wife had also left separately as a domestic worker. Herr Meyer was very ill and said that as he did not expect to live much longer, he had come to say goodbye. He wanted to bring her the last few things he valued. The next day he went into hospital in Hanover and died there a couple of days later.

Mary, who was now 58 years old, found it difficult to manage without domestic help at the Quakerhouse where she had warden's duties. Shopping also took more time as food became scarcer. Leonhard could not offer much help because he was single-handedly running the publishing business. He spent most evenings either wrapping up small orders to send by post or running a bookstall during Dr Otto Buchinger's lectures to his fasting patients. The Yearly Meeting treasurer's responsibilities also took much of his time. Leonhard was very conscientious about chasing every pfennig in the accounts. He also undertook daily tasks at the Quakerhouse like stoking the central heating boiler, but he enjoyed talking with the people who dropped by.

Mary had just finished a series of mud baths, which are still prescribed by doctors in Pyrmont for people suffering from rheumatism. Her next problem was to get some orthopaedic shoes for her painful feet and for this she had to take the train to Hanover, 40 miles away. Sharing her compartment were some young boys who objected to travelling with an English woman. This might have created an unpleasant situation, but Mary says she 'talked them round'.

During the spring Leonhard and Mary enjoyed visits from Alice Shaffer, working from the Berlin office for the American Friends Service Committee, and Margaret Jones, from the Vienna Quaker Office. Margaret reported that emigration for Jews through Switzerland had now been stopped. Through the Vienna Quaker office the AFSC was providing financial support for 250 Jewish families, as well as assisting the Catholic Jewish Committee and the Swedish Protestant Mission Relief Committee. The management of the Berlin and Vienna Quaker Centres were now shared between AFSC and the German Yearly Meeting.[1,2]

Alice Shaffer, returned to Chicago in October and wrote to FSC in London, saying:

> To be honest, I've missed German Friends like anything, they are just some of the finest people I ever hope to meet. They try personally to apply Christian principles in a situation of very bitter reality.

A few weeks later Leonhard and Mary were visited by Howard Elkinton, an American Friend who served at the Berlin office from 1938-40. They asked if it might be possible for me to be included in the scheme for evacuating British schoolchildren, as I would be finishing school that summer and might want to study at an American Quaker college. He encouraged Mary to apply for me at Guildford College in North Carolina. In August, Leonhard received a letter from his brother Bernhard in Pennsylvania, enclosing a letter from me saying that I would love to go. Leonhard and Mary were happy to think I would soon be out of the war zone and were pleased to hear from me directly through this circuitous route.

Pum-Birn Garden

In March Mary began to cultivate the garden which had been left to them by Dr Sturmthal. It was newly-fenced and situated on a sunny hillside just below the tree-line, above the fields. Setting off at 7.30 am Mary walked there two or three times a week, across the fields to the old Quaker village of Friedensthal, and then up the woodland path above the village of Loewensen. For the Sturmthals, who had a car, the garden was ideally situated. They could escape there in 10 minutes from their town house and the doctor's incessant telephone calls. When looking for it recently, I discovered the fence had gone, and the garden had reverted to meadowland, but the *Pum-Birn* tree, an old variety of pear, was still there and the field is known as 'Jews Meadow'.

The garden provided an important source of food, as Mary could bottle and conserve the fruit and vegetables. A tin smith in the town sealed cans whenever necessary. Mary's generation had experienced food shortages in the First World War and anticipated all kinds of privations. She had already made sure we all had stout shoes, in case we became homeless and had to escape on foot. Rationing started in Germany four days before the war began, and it continued for 15 years.

British Retreat at Dunkirk

The German invasion of Holland, Belgium and France was followed by the British retreat from Dunkirk. Once the German army had accomplished the Polish campaign, it invaded Denmark and Norway on 9th April 1940. Thanks to Vidkun Quisling, whom the Reich appointed Minister President, the Norwegian forces offered little resistance to the German invaders, although the civilian population created a remarkable underground resistance. Norwegian Quakers also helped to hide people the Gestapo were looking for.

On 10th May, Mary heard on the BBC that the German forces had crossed into the Netherlands. This was one of the days that she and Cilli Seutemann walked to the Pum-Birn garden, where the two women could talk without fear of being overheard. The massive invasion of the Netherlands involved 3,000 armoured vehicles, supported by parachutists who secured bridges for the advancing army. There was a tailback of military vehicles for 50 miles along the roads. Most of the British and French forces were fighting further south from the Maginot Line underground fortifications on the German/French border. By avoiding these defences, Hitler's *Panzers* were able to invade France through Belgium and to cut off a circle of British and French forces.

The invasion of the Netherlands led to the resignation of Neville Chamberlain, the British Prime Minister. The Queen sent for Winston Churchill who was acceptable to Clement Attlee, so the Conservative and Labour parties formed a national government on 13th May. Churchill's slogan was one word, 'Victory'.

In the week between 27th May and 4th June, 338,000 British and French troops were brought back to Britain from the harbour and the beaches of Dunkirk, while RAF Spitfires cleared the Luftwaffe from the sky overhead. It was a massive withdrawal, in which the navy was assisted by hundreds of civilians with around 850 small boats. The war might have ended there had so many of these soldiers not been rescued. The battle continued in France. On 14th June Hitler's *Panzers* took Paris and the French army surrendered on 21st June after only six weeks of fighting. Hitler left the southern part of France to Marshal Petain's puppet government. In just 10 months the Germans had seized a huge amount of territory in western Europe. Mussolini now agreed to join forces with Hitler on 10th June by declaring war on Britain. In July the League of Nations, fearing a German invasion of Switzerland, suspended activities in Geneva and despatched many of their archives to the United States.

Ommen Quaker School

Just before the German invasion of the Netherlands, on 10th May 1940, hasty measures were taken to protect the Jewish children at the Ommen Quaker School. Some were helped to escape from Holland and others were sheltered by Dutch families. Sadly in 1943 nine children were discovered and sent to a concentration camp. They survived as a group keeping up their morale until just before the end of the war when they were all shot by a drunken SS guard.

Manfred and Lili Pollatz, the Quaker family who had left Germany in 1934 to start a 'home school' in Haarlem, had to keep the children under strict discipline when a neighbouring house was used by the German Occupation force.

Back in Pyrmont

On 4th July Leonhard heard that Marie Willfuer, a secondary school headteacher who lived in north Germany, was dying. As Treasurer to the Society of Friends and her executor, he immediately went to be with her. She had been a Friend since 1931 and made a will leaving her nine-roomed villa adjoining the Lueneburg Kur-park to the Quakers. This angered her brother, who was a leading member of the district Nazi Party and created problems for Leonhard.

Yearly Meeting was not held in the summer of 1940, presumably because of the tense situation on the Western Front, but also because Friends were planning to build an air raid shelter underneath the Quakerhouse dining room, a scheme which eventually proved impractical.

Battle of Britain

After Dunkirk, Britain became isolated from the continent. However, Churchill's stirring speeches in the House of Commons changed the feeling of vulnerability to a determination to defend our country. The Nuremberg trials revealed that Hitler had intended a total exploitation of Britain, as later occurred in occupied parts of the Soviet Union. During July, the Luftwaffe began an intensive bombing campaign against southern England. Hitler could not understand why public morale in Britain did not weaken and force the government to surrender. He reconsidered implementing his invasion plan, Operation Sea Lion, but was beginning to grasp what his generals were saying about the immense logistical problems of getting sufficient fighting men and supplies across the Channel.

Young Dr Ott, son of Dr Otto Buchinger from the Pyrmont Meeting, was serving in the medical corps with the German army preparing for Operation Sea Lion. He said they spent a great deal of time jumping into the sea in full battle kit and clambering back into a landing craft, in practice for landing in Britain.

In early September both sides escalated the bombing of cities. The raids made by the Luftwaffe directed at London and other large cities generally took place at night, causing many casualties. These raids were partly in revenge for RAF attacks against Berlin. Berliners had been horrified to discover that their city was vulnerable to bombing. The RAF dropped propaganda leaflets, hoping to undermine morale. The RAF became more successful in stopping daytime attacks on Britain.

Occasionally we looked up from the streets of London to see dog fights in the air. When a plane was shot down we watched anxiously among the falling wreckage for the opening parachutes of escaping pilots. A plume of smoke could then be seen drifting away in the wind while we thought of the young men dying in the sky above us.

Brenda Decides to Remain in Britain

At the end of July in 1940, I left school and went to live with Edith Straus at 8 Milverton Road in Willesden. I was in London to prepare for my journey to America. I was among a group of 20 British children being sponsored by Quaker families in the USA. The opportunity to go to college in America seemed exciting, but the procedures for leaving the country in war-time and getting a passage were drawn out and further complicated by my dual German/British nationality. The Battle of Britain was raging over London and I had time to reflect upon how lost I would feel being so far away while my contemporaries were fighting for survival. As a Quaker I felt committed to pacifism, but did not like to run away from responsibility nor from the experience of war in my homeland. Much as I would love to have gone to college in America in peacetime, I changed my mind and decided to stay in Britain.

Edith was living alone in her mother's house. Mrs Minnie Samuel had died in 1938 and the maids in starched white aprons were gone. To save trouble, Edith kept most of the house closed and covered in dust-sheets. For the first time in her life, she had no domestic help and we both had to learn to cook. We ate a lot of carrots because the Minister of Food said it would help us to see in the dark. Edith became an air raid warden, and attended training sessions where she learned how to deal with incendiary bombs. These were about the size of a milk bottle, and were dropped by the Luftwaffe in great numbers. When they landed on a roof they generally rolled off into the garden below. They could be put out with a fine spray of water carried along a hose-pipe, powered by a foot-pump which was partly immersed in a bucket of water. It was my job on a number of occasions to keep the bucket full. If one simply threw a bucket of water at the bomb it would explode, whilst a fine spray gently sizzled out the flame. (Illustrations 22 and 23)

As the bombing escalated from incendiary to explosives in mid-September, the situation became much more frightening. We slept downstairs and I felt safer under the heavy dining-room table. Edith could not sleep, but played endless games of patience on the table above me in the dim light of a green-shaded table lamp. One night her son Edgar, who had been called up in the army, was with us. He was sleeping with us downstairs on a wheeled garden sofa when a particularly heavy blast from

22 and 23. *Edith Straus wearing WVS uniform, and her son Edgar.*

a nearby bomb sent it flying across the room, smashing through the French window. Fortunately he was unhurt.

The Battle of Britain was a very frightening experience for everyone. Once I had decided not to go to America, I was very relieved when Edith suggested I should leave London. I was shattered after weeks of sleepless nights. A Friend from Street Meeting had invited me to stay with her family in Glastonbury, and had arranged for me to work at Clark Son and Morland as a filing clerk. This enabled me to earn my living while considering what I should do next. I soon discovered that for most work, or even training, one had to have reached the age of 18. So I had to be patient for another 10 months before I could join the Friends Ambulance Unit, my choice of war service.

Among German Quakers

Douglas Steere, the American Quaker theologian who spent much of his life on ecumenical and inter-faith encounters, knew German Friends well and visited them in the autumn of 1940. I have summarised his impressions:

When writing about German Friends it is important to remember that their median age is probably between 40 and 50 and that for the large majority of them this is the second world war they have experienced. This means they know they can survive, because they lived through the previous one, but they grimly expect harder days ahead. There is a calmness about them, and a sense that they are ready for what may come. The messages in their Meetings are tinged with words on the judgement of God, and on searching for a rock beneath the suffering on which they may stand. They express a sense of shame and responsibility as Germans, for what is being done in Poland to uproot and disperse this unhappy nation, as well as for the continually increasing pressure upon the Jews.

This mood is not easy for the relatively few younger Friends to understand and fully share in. They long for a lighter and more immediately positive note and there is a certain noticeable cleft between these groups. In the common tasks which they undertake however, and in the silent worship and in social functions these difficulties are overcome. The problem remains: how and on what basis, will the Society of Friends in Germany draw younger men and women into its ranks? It may be that the deeper question of how the Society can itself survive in these times eclipses the issue and postpones it for a more favourable period.

The question of conscription of course ties up with this issue for young men in Germany. There are few who dare resist the call-up, and those who do are immediately shot. The number who have paid this penalty since the war began is put by a well-informed source as around 80. Over 90 percent of these were Christians such as Jehovah's Witnesses. Friends have up to now made no outright refusals, with the exception of Gerhard Halle, whose honourable record as an officer in the previous war, before he was a Quaker, has up to now enabled a certain understanding by his fellow officers to ensure that he is not actually called up. He took the risk of a frank discussion with them about his position as a conscientious objector, but there is no assurance how long this arrangement will last. Several other young Friends have joined the medical or ambulance corps. But there is little personal choice about where they serve: they have to go where they are sent. The Yearly Meeting has left the pacifist issue to the consciences of the individual, and has promised to respect every decision sincerely made. Several Friends have helped in local civilian services.[2]

Further reference to Gerhard Halle's principled attitudes is given in *Lebensbilder Deutscher Quaker*,[3] about a letter Gerhard wrote in 1940 to the Nazi blockleader in the neighbourhood of Berlin where he lived, protesting against euthanasia of the mentally ill. Another example of this honourable man's witness came to me in a letter from Annetta Fricke, daughter of Curt and Charlotte Nuthmann, Berlin Quakers, who knew Gerhard Halle well. Annetta wrote to me in 1990:

Gerhard was an officer wounded in the First World War. He refused military service in 1939 for conscientious reasons, and his fellow officers supported him in this. However later in the war, when he heard of the misdeeds of the German soldiers in Poland and on the Russian Front, he wrote an incredibly courageous letter to Adolf Hitler offering to rejoin the army, because he hoped that as an officer he might be able to influence the men to maintain acceptable standards of behaviour. He carried the letter around for weeks, intending to post it, but eventually decided not to do so out of consideration for the consequences that would have followed for his family.

Annetta continued:

In visiting different Quaker families and Meetings during the war, I was especially impressed with the way they had kept fellowship with the Jews for whom they felt a special responsibility. Friends knew about the massive deportations of German Jews from Stettin to Poland, and of the cruel conditions of life there. Jews from the cities of Poland were deported to the poorest Jewish rural communities, where they were graciously received, though it often meant 10 people sleeping in one small room. This moved Margarethe Lachmund to organise her friends to send welfare parcels by mail. They sent packages of used clothing, which could also be sold or bartered for food or other essentials. Only Aryans were allowed to send parcels, and even they were always at risk from being reported by post office counter staff in doing so. Nevertheless Margarethe enlisted the services of some 60 Friends from all over the country, especially from the Meetings in Bad Pyrmont and Frankfurt and from Annemarie Cohen of Munich. Margarethe took all the risks involved with the full co-operation of her husband, Hans, who was a high court judge, and not a Quaker.[4]

The Last Wartime Yearly Meeting

The postponed Yearly Meeting took place in Pyrmont early in October. Some 85 Quakers managed to get there, including, for the last time, Douglas Steere, Leonard Kenworthy and Howard Elkinton, the three American Quakers, who were still in Germany. Leonard Kenworthy later wrote about this:

> The agenda had to be planned bearing in mind that the Gestapo were likely to attend all the publicly-announced sessions. The mornings were therefore given over to lengthy Meetings for Worship and Bible study. In the afternoons Friends either met in small groups in the home of Leonhard and Mary Friedrich, or went for walks together in the forest. In the evenings there was music and talks by Friends and various committees and the Executive met in the small library to transact Quaker business relating to the suffering of Friends. No official business meetings were scheduled.
>
> The Executive at this time also considered an elaborate plan on how the Society of Friends might if necessary 'go underground'. A list of Friends was drawn up for each post in that group, in case one after another were imprisoned. That plan was drawn up most reluctantly, as German Friends had tried very hard to be open in their dealings with the Nazis. No one mentioned who had drafted the plan, but we knew it had been Margarethe Lachmund.
>
> The Epistle from London Yearly Meeting that year came in the form of a 12-word Red Cross message. The main introductions were given by Alfons Paquet, Emil Fuchs and Grete Sumpf from the Vienna Quaker Centre. Many times the group settled into periods of expectant worship, times when all present sought divine guidance for the difficulties in their lives and felt the companionship of fellow seekers.[5, 6]

Mary wrote in her diary:

> The time of Yearly Meeting was a beautiful oasis in our lives.

Marie Pleissner

Friends were particularly pleased to have Marie Pleissner (1881-1983) with them again, following her release from the Ravensbrueck women's Concentration Camp. In 1934, at the age of 43, she had been forbidden to teach in Chemnitz and had to earn her living taking private pupils. These were often Jewish children, who had been forbidden to attend state schools. Marie became concerned about the plight of her Jewish friends and decided in the summer of 1939 to go to England to visit their cousins, hoping to persuade them to assist the emigration of their German relatives. The incident which led to her arrest occurred a few weeks later. Whilst giving a private lesson to a student in her home, they both heard the news of the Nazi invasion of Poland. Marie was off her guard and expressed outrage and dismay. A week later she was arrested by the Gestapo and ended up in the punishment block at Ravensbrueck, where conditions were terrible. It was a particularly harsh winter and the women were starving in freezing conditions. One day Marie fell unconscious from hypothermia. She was resuscitated by women prisoners, who bravely held off the warders' dogs while she lay on the ground. After nine months' imprisonment, her father succeeded in getting her released, though she could not return to teaching until after the war.[7] (Illustration 24)

24. *Marie Pleissner and Joan Mary Fry, 1939.*

Welfare Parcels to Concentration Camps

During Yearly Meeting the group of Friends sending welfare parcels to Jews in Poland and a concentration camp at Gurs in southern France met in Mary and Leonhard's home to exchange experiences. They also discussed sending books, games and musical instruments to Allied prisoners of war, following the tradition of British Friends in caring for POWs. German Friends worked through the YMCA, which was designated by the League of Nations convention to provide recreational materials for POWs. This work was organised by Franz and Lotte Hoffman from the Berlin Meeting, although Pyrmont and other groups contributed materials. Douglas Steere was able to visit a POW camp in Silesia in 1940, as did a Swiss Friend, Felix Ansermoz in 1943. On both occasions they saw books sent by German Quakers.

Frankfurt Friends reported to the Yearly Meeting on their efforts to send food and clothing parcels to Perpignan, in the south of France, where they had established a farm school for Jewish children in the Eastern Pyrenees just before the war.

Cilli and Hans Seutemann were well-established Friends in the Pyrmont Meeting. He was an Aryan and she came from a Jewish family, and was warned at critical times to go into hiding. Hans had a workshop where they produced craft objects, such as traditional floral-painted furniture. They also trained a number of Jews to make saleable items in their own homes, which Hans then marketed for them. Cilli, who was about forty-five at this time, was an understanding listener. She was also very practical and skilled in making attractive garments from second-hand clothing and she was central to the success of the parcels scheme. (Illustrations 25 and 26)

Gurs Concentration Camp, Pyrenees, then in 'Vichy France'

In 1989, Anni Sabine Halle, a Friend who looked after Quaker archives in Berlin, showed me a file of letters dated 1940-1 which Cilli Seutemann had entrusted to her.[8] The correspondence was mainly between Cilli in Pyrmont, Eva Hermann in Mannheim, Margarethe Lachmund in Berlin and Grete Sumpf in Vienna. The letters concerned the difficulties of obtaining materials for the welfare parcels, re-making garments and finding post offices willing to despatch them. There were also some 'thank-you' postcards from the recipients' parcels, many of whom were in concentration camps in Poland and Gurs in the south of France. The file vividly conveys the physical and spiritual strain this work entailed. At one point Cilli described the heavy heart she felt while working and thinking about the conditions of the people who would receive the garments she was sewing.

25 and 26. Cilli and her husband, Hans Seutemann, at his work-bench.

Carl Hermann (1898-1961) an eminent physicist and his wife Eva were on the Quaker list of *'Vertrauens Leute'* ('Trusted Friends') and had many contacts with the Mannheim Jewish community. Before the war, Eva had helped a number of Jews to emigrate, aided by Bertha Bracey and the Germany Emergency Committee in England. She had insisted on maintaining her friendship with Jewish schoolfriends and she had hidden a Jewish family in her flat for several weeks, although her own father was a Nazi.

The Gurs camp was originally set up by the French Government in early 1939 to receive refugees from the Spanish Civil War, but in the autumn of 1940 it was used as a concentration camp for refugees from northern France and for Jews from the Mannheim/Phalz area. Gurs is situated 1,000 metres up in the Basse-Pyrenees mountains, 50 km west of Pau. Some 60,000 people of many nationalities passed through this camp between September 1939 and 1944. Eva and Carl Hermann knew several of those who were taken there in the autumn of 1940 from Mannheim, Baden, Saarland and Pfalz. They included Dr Eugen Neter, (1878-1966), who was Jewish, though married to an Aryan, and could at this time have avoided being sent to Gurs. He volunteered to accompany those who were forced to leave. Neter wrote:

> The departing Jews behaved with great dignity. Some of them had considered driving away to Frankfurt on the night before the evacuation, but in the end they thought it better to face whatever was to happen, with the people they knew.[8]

Bernt Engelmann, author of *In Hitler's Germany* described the camp as follows:

> The landscape around Gurs was beautiful. The food and sanitary arrangements were, however horrendous, and the death rate among infants and the elderly was heavy. When you came out of the barracks in the morning, you had to be careful to stay on the plank walks or else sink deeply into a swamp, in which the barracks seemed to form little islands. The prisoners were sorted out according to sex and origin, and you needed a pass to go from one island to another.[9]

American Friends Service Committee Work at Gurs

The British Quaker support for refugee work in Paris and for the Spanish refugees in the south of France ended when the Germans captured Paris on 14th June 1940. But the AFSC were able to continue relief work in Petain's Vichy France until the winter of 1942, when the Jews in Gurs and from other camps in the region were sent to Poland. Gurs was closed in November 1942. Eleanor Slater, an AFSC relief worker wrote:

> Refugee needs have been indescribable since Paris and many other areas had to be evacuated ahead of the advancing German army. The roads we travelled on from Paris to the South of France were jammed with people sleeping by the roadside, towns were stripped bare of all provisions, frightened helpless civilians were travelling along the same road as military transport and as a result they were under constant bombardment. When people flee in this way, they seldom carry provisions, even for a few days. We brought 52 children and got them safely to our children's homes in the South at Montanban and Perpignan.[10]

The Dutch Friend Toot van Oordt, whom Cilli and Mary knew, had worked at the Paris Centre. She accompanied the AFSC team travelling south and made occasional visits to Pyrmont to share her experiences about Gurs with Friends there.

On 5th January 1941 Dr Eugen Neter wrote the following to his wife from Gurs, who passed it on to Margarethe Lachmund:

> The American Quaker group has now been installed. In these harsh surroundings it restores the spirit to watch these Friends work

quietly, without any fuss, in such practical ways. They make no announcements and no promises, but provide immediate help and comfort. People have an increasing hope of an American rescue. I keep quiet during such conversations. Why, after all, should Roosevelt bother about 10,000 Jews in Gurs, while hundreds of thousands cry for help in Poland? We now receive coffee substitute and 300 grams of bread for breakfast, a thick soup at midday, and a thinner one in the evening. There is also to be some milk for children. But many of us need more warm clothing and underwear.[8]

Dr Neter survived the war in France, managing to avoid deportation. He eventually settled in Israel where his son lived in a kibbutz.

Gurs was very overcrowded and badly run, so that many people died of neglect and harsh conditions, but it was not a labour or death camp. During the winter of 1940-1 the AFSC in Philadelphia became very concerned about the food shortages in France. Rations in occupied territories were less than in Germany. Canada and America had a surplus of grain, while children in the camps and the occupied territories were starving. The Nazi regime could only feed its own people by doing deals with the Soviet Union. Valuable coal and military equipment travelled east, while Germany imported grain and other raw materials. *The Friend* reported that as a concession, a ship carrying Red Cross supplies for the AFSC was allowed through the blockade into Marseilles, thus providing urgently-needed clothing and vitamins. The average birth weight of new-born babies in Gurs was then 5 lbs and people were sleeping on the ground without bedding.[11]

It is surprising that the Nazis could take over camps in Vichy France although it was an area where they had no administrative responsibility. The AFSC was allowed to provide supplementary feeding in these camps. There were some twenty American Friends Service Committee workers supervising thirty French and European assistants who provided extra nourishment for 25,000 people and supplied milk for 10,000 children. They were able to improve conditions to the extent that the women and children no longer had to sleep on the ground and some heating was provided in the barracks.[11]

A few young Jewish people at Gurs for whom emigration permits had been obtained reached the United States through the AFSC. The AFSC also succeeded in arranging for nearly a hundred unaccompanied children to leave. My friend Ruth Finch's brother was one of these. She herself had come to Britain in 1938 on the *Kindertransporte* and is now a member of London Yearly Meeting. Her parents and other relatives were taken to Gurs and later died in Poland.

The small group of French Quakers in southern France continued to support the AFSC welfare work in the camps. The AFSC regional organiser was Howard Kershner, who worked from an office at 29 Boulevard d'Athenes, Marseilles, but he and other American Quaker staff had to withdraw when the German army occupied the rest of France on 8th November 1940. The Danish staff member Helga Holbeck, kept the relief work going, with strong support from the remaining staff. She was given money from foreigners fleeing the country. The relief team had an enterprising quartermaster, who managed to find food supplies to purchase, until the Petain puppet government fell and the Germans occupied the whole of France.[12]

Mary's Work in Pyrmont

Mary had been concerned about the welfare of Alfred Woore, the elderly English Friend who had decided to stay in Germany when war broke out. She had written to the Swiss and American consulates in an attempt to get him back to England. Mary had also supplied him with small amounts of money to pay doctors' bills and had written to his wife in England via the Geneva Quaker Centre. When he ran out of funds, she and Leonhard invited him to live with them. They had a spare bedroom and felt it would not cost very much to feed an extra person.

Henry Rodwell, a Derby Friend, has provided some background about Alfred, who was an architect and member of Fritchley Friends Meeting. Alfred occasionally attended Derby Meeting, where Henry knew his sons. Alfred was known to be 'a bit odd', but was recognised for his gift of quoting appropriate Bible passages during Meeting.

At the outbreak of war Alfred was holidaying in Germany on his own. When war seemed imminent he was advised to return to England, but he did not want to leave. Once on the train he had second thoughts, and as the weather was lovely and everything looked so peaceful, he got off the train and returned to the guest-house at Ruhpolding where he had been staying.

On 17th November Mary visited several Jewish families in Hoxter, 20 miles from Pyrmont, travelling on two buses and spending the night there. She mentions visiting Dr and Frau Frankenberg, Frau Mehlmueller, Frau Rosenberg and Frau Hocheimer. The next week she went to visit the Lowenstein families in Steinheim, who were relatives of Hilde Sturmthal.

In December Leonhard and Mary were sorry to learn that the Nuremberg Friends could no longer afford to rent the Meeting Rooms at Theresienstrasse. They decided to meet in each other's homes, and divided up the furniture among themselves, sending some pieces to the Quakerhouse in Pyrmont.

Mary prepared little presents for everybody who attended the Christmas party at the Quakerhouse. That year about 50 people came. There was no tree, but the room was decorated with fir branches and candles. Leonhard made another trip to the house the Quakers had inherited at Lueneburg and brought back clothing which Mary washed and parcelled up for the Jews in the East. On New Year's Eve Mary wrote in her diary:

> Leonhard, Alfred and I stayed up to see the New Year in, wondering where our child was and what she was thinking. I felt gratitude for home and friends surrounded by God's gifts.

At this time there was a letter in *The Friend* saying:

> I am so thankful that the Quaker community in Germany has not felt obliged to leave the country and go 'where it would be welcome'. I know some Friends have had to emigrate; but there is still a community left in Germany to whom others, who perhaps dare not yet show their sympathy openly, look with secret admiration and hope . . .

signed: 'one of your English Friends'.[13]

CHAPTER XII

The Suffering Intensifies 1941

THE MAIN INTEREST OF THIS year's annual January Quaker gathering in Pyrmont was Leonard Kenworthy's address on George Fox, the founder of Quakerism. Leonard was the last American staff member remaining in the Berlin Quaker Centre, until the United States was drawn into the war. In her diary Mary said he was a thoughtful person, whose visits to families were much appreciated. On his return to the United States in June 1941 he wrote a book about this experience. He was in his mid-twenties and found the hardships of life in wartime Europe difficult to adapt to, but he valued the experience.[1]

In early February Leonhard went to Berlin for the Executive Committee Meeting and heard Grete Sumpf of the Vienna Quaker Centre, reporting that a train was being prepared for the exile of 1,000 Jews to Lublin in Poland on the 15th February. The Meeting discussed the welfare packages which Friends were sending to the Jews in the East and the books in English and musical instruments being sent to POW's in Germany. Mary eventually parted with 600 of her English books, trying to snatch time to re-read her favourites before parcelling them up. One of the Friends Ambulance Unit members taken as a POW in Finland, and released in 1943 from Stalag VIIIB in Silesia, wrote an article in *The Friend* saying:

> Our only contact with German Friends was the presence in our library of a number of books which had been sent by the Berlin Quaker Centre.[2]

While Leonhard was in Berlin, Emil Fuchs told him of the difficulties Friends with Jewish family connections had in attending the Meeting for Worship. The Gestapo sometimes posted sentries outside the building to see who came and on one occasion a non-Aryan Friend had to escape through the lavatory window at the back.

During the spring Mary records a number of visits to Jews in and around Bad Pyrmont, either alone or with Cilli Seutemann or Berta Maas.

She was anxious about Trudy Mergel, who was in hospital with broken ribs. She was a non-Aryan lady who attended the Pyrmont Meeting and occasionally helped Leonhard with office work. Mary also mentions a Jewish family called Lichtenstein, whose mother, Laura, aged 80, lived with her three unmarried adult children. Mary sometimes did their shopping, because Jews were no longer served when trying to buy the meagre rations to which they were entitled.

The Vienna Quaker Centre

The file of letters which Cilli Seutemann, a member of the Pyrmont Meeting, entrusted to Anna Sabine Halle,[3] provides a vivid account of the help Grete Sumpf gave to Jewish families in Vienna, many of whom were forced out of their homes for Nazi officials arriving from Germany. Grete Sumpf took over the management of the Vienna Quaker Centre after she lost her teaching job.

On 28th February Grete Sumpf told the Executive Committee of a Nazi plan to deport 60,000 Austrian Jews to Poland. The first to go were the frail and the elderly and those who occupied apartments the Nazis wanted for themselves. Jews married to Aryans were at first given 'protected status' and were not victimised until the others had been taken. Families were given two days notice before they had to go to the reception centres. They were advised to take a small suitcase of food and clothing and encouraged to take as much cash and jewellery as they could. Just before boarding the train they were forced to change their money into Polish currency and regardless of how much cash they had handed over, were given back just 400 zlotys per person. Their valuables were removed from their suitcases and they had to sign a form giving all their possessions to the State. The men travelled in cattle trucks, while the women and children were provided with seated railway compartments.

Grete had heard from an acquaintance who had left in the first train to Opale, south-west of Lublin. The woman said a brave Jewish family in a Polish village had offered her a bed in a room where eight people slept. She asked Grete to send her some bed linen.

Grete started a clothing store in the Vienna Centre to help meet the basic warm clothing needed by Jews leaving for Poland. Since 1939 Jews had not been allowed clothing coupons, and most of them had been unemployed since the annexation in 1938. Grete reported how happy she was to have found some good boots for a nine-year-old girl whose feet were already swollen with chilblains. She organised a sewing room, where volunteers made rucksacks and hessian bags which could be filled with straw to provide crude mattresses to sleep on when they arrived in Poland.

In March, Grete wrote to the Pyrmont sewing group to thank them for four boxes of clothing and thermos flasks. She said:

> How encouraging it is to have received 36 useful packages from German Quakers, who also sent money amounting to 917 Marks. Sometimes a warm coat, a blanket, or de-lousing powder may make the difference between life and death. Many of the people who come to see me are already wretched with fear and anxiety. Others show an amazing dignity, feeling they must bear their suffering as the will of God. Such people are an inspiration to us all, especially for our volunteer workers, many of whom have Jewish family members. There is so much need that we cannot meet, we have to select those for whom we can really be helpful. For example, one lady enquired: 'I have not come to ask for welfare items, but I need your advice to discover ways in which I might help others, if I am sent to Poland. I don't have many practical skills, but I am musical and might be able to be of solace with my flute'.

Grete invited some of the Jews attending the Vienna Quaker Centre to a worship and study evening with the Friends. They found strength in talking through their problems together:

> Experience shows that our efforts can sometimes make a striking difference to the frame of mind in which some people leave. If we can only help a few to retain their remarkable personal dignity, as they face a terrible fate, they will surely also help others. We hear of the special difficulties of the Jewish converts to Christianity who are ostracised among the orthodox Polish Jewish communities they live in.[3]

On 17th March Grete reported that after six train-loads had left, a notice had come round postponing further deportations until September. This gave Grete an opportunity to take a much-needed break, after which she expected to return to Vienna. However, in September her residence permit was not renewed and the Quaker work came to an end.

Back in Pyrmont

Mary and other Friends in the Pyrmont sewing group had worked hard to send many parcels to Jewish people in Poland. Margarethe Lachmund's letter of 26.6.41[3] throws light on their work:

> Dear Cilli, I am sending you some of the old clothes that were given to me, but which I can't think how to use. Your sewing group may perhaps lovingly produce something useful from them. I have already thrown out moth-eaten materials, but perhaps there is enough good stuff to make some lined trousers for little boys. If some of the

moth-holes were cut out of this dress, it might do for a thinner girl! I hope you will not be cross about my sending rubbish? My felt hat unfortunately got caught in the lawn mower, but I feel sure you will create something lovely from it! My thoughts go out constantly to those in the war-zone, but I am delighted when we hear of the safe arrival of our packages. My loving thoughts are also with you, and with Mary and Leonhard.

In late March Mary invited Almuth Niemann from Bremen to stay with them for a break from the heavy RAF bombing. This was the first of many visits by Almuth and her elderly mother. In August Almuth made the following entry in Mary's visitors book:

In times of desperate need I found sanctuary here in March, May and July. In these hard times when hospitality is seldom offered, I found peace and rest from nightly air raids, and meals prepared without any requests for food coupons. One day our hostess managed to prepare a meal for 10 people, instead of the usual three, and we all ate our fill. I contributed the many mushrooms I had gathered in the forest to this meal. It was actually all that I could give, because my heart was sad and my head hung down. My old mother also spent a month in this household, where she appreciated many an encouraging word, much care and many satisfying meals.

Alfred Woore

Alfred had been living with Leonhard and Mary since the previous November. They may not yet have realised that he was in the early stages of senility, although they must have realised that he was a difficult person to live with, despite a certain charm. He would gossip in the small Quaker group about the problems of living with the Friedrichs. On 31st May, Alfred decided at 10.30 pm to move in with another Quaker, Anna Goetze. Mary and Leonhard helped him carry his suitcase and a box of food there, but they were surprised when he returned the next day to have his lunch and to spend the day with them. A week later, on 7th June, Mary wrote in her diary:

Alfred rang our doorbell at 11 pm, after we had gone to bed and said he wanted to return to live with us again. So we took him back. Alfred was contrite and did what he could to help me with the garden.

Edith Alexander was an Englishwoman living at 6 Hafen strasse, Hamelin and became a friend to Mary. Edith was born in England in 1912, and was almost half Mary's age when they met in 1941. She was married, with two children, and had lived in Kent. She had German grandparents and came to visit her relations in Germany in the thirties, when she fell in love with her married cousin, Reinhold Korte. Just before the war, in August 1939, she suddenly decided to visit him and his wife in Hamelin, abandoning her children and husband.

In 1989, Camilla, Edith Alexander's daughter who now lives in Sissinghurst, Kent, told me that her mother admired Mary's ingenuity in overcoming her shortage of money. In 1942, while Leonhard was held for interrogation in Hanover, Mary often stopped off in Hamelin to visit Edith and she in turn came to spend several weekends with Mary in Pyrmont.

Events of the War

While the German army was extending its occupation of Europe in 1940, Stalin tried to legitimise his seizure of Lithuania, Estonia and Latvia by holding elections there. Hitler objected, and Stalin responded by requesting the withdrawal of German diplomats. Angered by such defiance, Hitler secretly ordered the Wehrmacht and Luftwaffe to pursue the detailed planning for Operation Barbarossa for early 1941. He had already proposed the invasion of the Soviet Union in his book *Mein Kampf* and now decreed that the Russian campaign be supported by Gestapo civilian control to terrorise the population into submission and direct Soviet economic and food resources towards Germany.

Hitler had little confidence in Mussolini's army in North Africa, so he sent General Rommel with German troops to lead the attack against Egypt. The aim was to gain the Suez Canal and to prevent British trading with India. However Rommel was stranded with insufficient men and resources, whilst all efforts were suddenly re-directed towards the Eastern Front.

One of the most mysterious episodes of the war occurred on 10th May, when Hitler's Deputy, Rudolf Hess, flew to Scotland to make peace proposals to Britain through the Duke of Hamilton, an RAF officer. Hess conveyed the message that whilst Hitler had every intention of destroying Britain, he offered to renounce actions against the Empire if Britain would cease to interfere in Europe. The British Government rejected this peace initiative, and imprisoned Hess. After the war he was tried at Nuremberg, and incarcerated in Berlin's Spandau Prison where he died in 1989, aged 90.

On 22nd June 1941 Hitler launched a widespread attack on the Russian army between the Baltic and the Black Sea. Despite German advances, the United States remained cautious about involvement in a second European war, although great sympathy existed for Britain. In July 1940 the US had signed the Lend Lease agreement, whereby the Americans funded the cost of shipping war materials to Britain in return for use of British military bases. The alliance was cemented on 12th August

1941 when Roosevelt and Churchill met at sea off the coast of Newfoundland to sign the Atlantic Charter.

On 6-7 October the first of the long winter snowstorms fell on the Eastern Front. The Wehrmacht command had failed to provide snowboots and heavy winter clothing which the soldiers needed. On 30th November the divisions charged with capturing Moscow only had about 30 kilometres to go, but the extremely cold conditions rendered their vehicles immobile. The Russian general, Zhukov, then launched a fierce attack, forcing the German army to withdraw, suffering great loss of life.

The families of the German soldiers were horrified when the news gradually filtered home about the conditions their men were enduring at the front. Hitler stubbornly refused to permit retreat. By the end of the winter thousands of German soldiers had died of frost-bite and hypothermia. Russian civilians were suffering even more severely, but it was the strength of the Russian defence of their homeland, rather than the freezing winter conditions, which forced the German retreat.

On the 7th December the Japanese forces in the Pacific attacked the American base at Pearl Harbour, forcing the United States to enter what now became the Second World War. During a visit in March 1941 by the Japanese Foreign Minister Matsuoka to Berlin, Hitler had tried to involve Japan in the war against Britain, but he found that Japan was far more concerned about the activities of the United States in the Pacific. On his return Matsuoka broke his journey in Moscow to sign a non-aggression pact with the Soviet Union, and then plotted how to draw the United States into the war. After Pearl Harbour, Hitler declared war against the USA on 11th December.

Back in Bad-Pyrmont

In July, Mary and Leonhard were relieved to receive a Red Cross message from me saying I had joined the Friends Ambulance Unit. Mary was working very hard in the Pum-Birn garden to raise a good crop of fruit and vegetables. She recorded having sent five marks to several needy people.

Yearly Meeting in Pyrmont was cancelled again this year and was not resumed until after the war. At the end of August Leonhard went to the Executive Committee in Berlin and then took a much-needed walking holiday in the Black Forest with Emil Fuchs, who was living with his grandson Klaus in the heavily-bombed Berlin. Leonhard was away for three weeks, leaving Mary to look after the publishing business and pack up the 17 parcels of books which had been ordered, to manage the bookstall during the lectures at Buchingers' sanatorium and be available at the Quakerhouse during office hours.

From November until Christmas Mary was very busy visiting the local Jewish families. On one occasion she went with Cilli to Detmold, to visit the Kanders family and a Jewish school, where they helped to set up a sewing group. Since Jews could not purchase clothing, they un-picked and re-made adults garments for children. Mary and Cilli encouraged people to use their duvets to make down-filled waistcoats, mittens, caps and leggings. They were aware of the harsh conditions of travel and life in Poland which Pyrmont Jews were expecting to face.

On 5th December Mary went to Fuerstenau to visit *Pension Judenberg*, which she said was extremely sad. It may have been a collecting centre for Jews about to be transported to Poland. On 7th December, in the pouring rain, she took her cabin trunk from the attic on a small hand-cart to give to the Stein family in Luegde, three miles away. The Steins were the parents of Kurt, whom Mary had managed to get to England in 1939. Three days later, she learned that they were taken to Warsaw. The next day Mary went to Luegde again to visit Frau Meyer, the invalid sister of Gertrud Stein who had emigrated to Oxford just before the war. She was very unwell and died a few weeks later. Mary was able to send a 25-word Red Cross message to England to inform the relatives.

There was little mention of Christmas in the diary this year. Disturbing news about conditions on the Eastern Front was filtering back and the fears of friends who lived in the cities was ever present in their minds. Most distressing was their inability to prevent the elimination and break-up of the Jewish community in their midst. At this time Leonhard and Mary would have expected that the Jews would be made to work in Poland. They had heard something about the degrading treatment people endured in the concentration camps, but did not know of the policy to exterminate the Jews.

CHAPTER XIII

Expulsion of the Jews 1942

GERMAN MILITARY ACTIVITY ALMOST ceased on the Russian front during the bitter winter weather, forcing them to retreat. The men were demoralised by the appalling conditions and when the snows began to melt in March, they were exhausted and their vehicles were immobilised in mud. But Hitler was determined to renew the offensive to take Stalingrad and gain access to the Caucasian oilfields.

A secret Nazi conference was organised at Wannsee in Berlin on 20th January 1942 for an inner circle of the Nazi leadership by Himmler, head of the Gestapo, and his assistant Heinrich Heydrich. They explained how they planned to rid Germany of the Jews. It was agreed to construct gas chambers in certain concentration camps for the elimination of Jews, Gypsies and other races classified as 'sub-human'. This policy of genocide was referred to as 'the final solution'.

Back in Pyrmont

The January Quarterly Meeting was held in Pyrmont as usual and two weeks later Leonhard went to Berlin for the Executive Committee, which was attended by fewer members, due to the difficulties of war-time travel. Leonhard was pleased that August Fricke (1880-1965), editor of *Der Quaker*, was to be Hans Albrecht's deputy, as too many decisions had been left entirely to Hans.

While Leonhard was away, the Quakerhouse boiler fire had gone out, resulting in a freeze-up of the pipes, and the basement awash with water. On his return journey RAF bombing of the railways delayed his train by five hours, he had a dreadful cold and a bout of lumbago. One of the letters Mary wrote at this time reached Elsie Howard via the Quaker office in Geneva and was published in the FSC European News Sheet 14,[1] dated 26th February:

In the last few months Friends in Pyrmont have been doing a great deal of sewing; making warm slippers, mittens, caps and waistcoats for the Jews who face special hardship this winter. About 25 people attend our Meeting for Worship regularly. Instead of our usual Wednesday evening study group, we are now meeting at Helene Glauner's house for a sewing bee.

At the January Quarterly Meeting, 12 Friends were able to attend from further afield. Those of us who live in Pyrmont contribute to travel costs of others, through a fares pooling scheme we have started. We provided meals as usual at the Quakerhouse, without asking our visitors to bring rations. This time we had soup on two evenings, and served cabbage cooked with apples and caraway seeds, and potatoes, for lunch. We discovered some canned plums in our stores, which had been picked from the tree in our garden and preserved five years ago, also hot drinks.

All the Friends in our district seem well, but a number of them who have sons in 'far-away places' yearn for their safe return. Theodor, the son of Magda Bauman in Fuerth, has sadly died of wounds. August Fricke's two sons are well.

Mitzi Jordan has been having health problems, and has been away for three weeks. [Her daughter Hannah told me in 1992, that 'Mitzi was arrested while attending the Berlin Quaker Meeting together with Emil Fuchs and others. After three weeks, the others were released and my father who was an Aryan eventually also secured Mitzi's release'.] Lydia W... is still in the Sanatorium, and has been away for three months, we are anxious about her. Leonora Burnitz is fairly well now but is overstrained with a good deal of hospital work.

The Quaker publishing business is doing surprisingly well and we are selling more Quaker books. The *Erbgut*/Heritage leaflets are extremely popular, but the stocks are running low and there is no paper for reprinting.

Erbgut/Heritage Leaflets

The *Erbgut*/Heritage leaflets outlining the beliefs of outstanding world figures, were the inspiration of Pastor Mensching of the Fellowship of Reconciliation in Bueckeberg. The beliefs of great thinkers, such as Gandhi, Nansen and Schweitzer, were condensed into a small leaflet format, easily fitting into an envelope. They were widely circulated in Nazi Germany where freedom of thought hardly existed. They sold in great numbers and Leonhard published 54 different titles. When Friends were despatching parcels to the Jews or POWs, or wrote to the soldiers at the Front, they frequently enclosed a few *Erbgut* leaflets. The recipients who had little to read during their disrupted wartime life, appreciated the brief respite from hate and the timeless ethical values which these leaflets offered.

Der Quaker – a Monthly Journal

On 9th March, Leonhard received a three line notification from *Reichspresse Kammer* (National Press Council) ordering the cessation of publication of *Der Quaker*. Although Leonhard and August Fricke, the editor, had been expecting this, they were extremely upset. Many other church-related journals were also closed down. Since the March issue was already with the printers, Leonhard took the risk of publishing it. Publication was not to resume until 1946.[2]

Both Mary and Leonhard went through a spell of poor health. Two weeks after his return from Berlin, Leonhard was still unwell and spending time in bed. In addition to prolonged dental treatment, Mary fainted on the outdoor staircase at the Quakerhouse and had to be brought home by ambulance.

Jews Forced Out of their Homes to Poland

Most of the information which follows was gathered from Mary's diary, but is supplemented by a list produced by Walter Fink, the Pyrmont archivist. His list contains the names of 45 former Jewish residents of Bad Pyrmont, giving their date of birth, departure date and destination. Nine of the people on Fink's list were exiled to Poland. Sixteen other names on his list were people whom Mary had helped to emigrate before the war began.[3]

Early in 1942 the remaining Jews were told that they would be taken from their homes to collecting centres for transportation to labour camps in the East. The Lichtenstein family were among the first to leave and were told to be ready on a certain evening in March. The family included Hedwig, Fritz and Berta, all middle-aged and their old mother Laura, who was 80 years old. Leonhard and Mary joined them during the early evening of their departure, to sit and wait with them. Eventually at 2 am, when the streets were empty, the Gestapo collected them, leaving Leonhard and Mary to walk home through the quiet, snow-covered streets. On hearing about this episode years later, I think how easily the Gestapo could also have taken Leonhard and Mary that night.

According to Walter Fink's list, Laura Lichtenstein was taken to a hospital in Hanover, but was then sent on to the Jewish hospital in Warsaw on 27th March. Her daughters left Pyrmont for Warsaw on 4th April, but her son Fritz was sent to Auschwitz. Leonhard and Mary had no doubt hoped that their presence would be of comfort and might have some effect on the behaviour of the men making the arrest.

The collection centre for the Jews from Bad Pyrmont and the surrounding area was at 51 Bahnhofstrasse, near the railway station. It has since been demolished. On 16th March Mary wrote in her diary:

The old, the sick and the children have been crowded together for a couple of weeks, with new arrivals being brought in all the time. We have been going every day to do whatever we can to help with packing, taking messages and shopping. It was all so difficult. Most people were so very tense and strained, and many found it almost impossible to think straight or make decisions about anything. I took pans of cooked food for them.

I was particularly sad for Jenny Emanuel and Anna Salomon, who just before war broke out had completed all arrangements to go to relatives in Paraguay; they had visas, tickets booked etc, but could not leave, because overseas travel became impossible. They then made similar arrangements to join relatives in Sweden, but once again were refused permission to leave. It was a great trial to them, and to us also.

Alma Speyer, aged 61, and her sister Berta of Steinheim [daughters of the horse dealer] were among the group at the Bahnhofstrasse, but Selma, aged 66, was left at home. Berta had expected to go with her aged mother to the hospital in Hanover, but at the last moment the police stopped her. She took this very hard, however Berta Maas, a Pyrmont Quaker, went with the old lady to the hospital.

Leonhard and I stayed with the Jews, helping them to prepare sandwiches and talking with them until 2.30 am. One group left for Poland at 8 am the next morning on 28th March and a second group left on 8th April.

The three or four Friends from Pyrmont Meeting who had supported the Jews before their departure were exhausted and devastated.

On 30th April Mary heard that Martha Ursell and her sister, daughters of one of the non-Aryan Quakers, had also been taken to Poland. Mary had helped her brother, Erich, and sisters, Lisa and Margarethe, go to England just before the war broke out in 1939. Mary wrote to Laura Lichtenstein and sent her a wool jacket and a cake, hoping it would reach her at the Hanover hospital.

During April Mary devoted all her energy to planting vegetables in the Quakerhouse garden and in the distant Pum-Birn garden. A few weeks after the Jews had left for Poland, Mary received a letter from Israel and Anna Heyman, saying that they had arrived in Warsaw on 10th April and would greatly appreciate a food parcel. On 16th May Leonhard and Mary visited Selma Speyer, who had been allowed to remain in Steinheim. She told them about the brutalities which had occurred there during the departure of her family. Selma gave them some clothing which they sent to Poland, since it was only Aryans who could use the post office.

The Pyrmont Jews took small items of jewellery with them when they left, hoping to barter them for necessities. But they sometimes gave larger items of household silver and porcelain to Mary or other friends to look after. No-one survived to claim them, though after the war Mary took great pleasure in being able to restore some of these treasures to other family members who had managed to emigrate. This was not possible in all cases and there were a few things which she kept as reminders of their former owners.

On 2nd May there was another Quarterly Meeting in Pyrmont. Mary said everyone was feeling depressed about the fate of the Jews, she was scarcely sleeping at night. She said that many of the Friends spent a great deal of effort and money on sending parcels to Poland. She felt very exhausted, which was not helped when the dentist decided to remove her last teeth in preparation for a new denture.

The departure of the Jews marked another turning point in Mary's life. Just as the outbreak of war had put an end to her emigration work, so their departure now brought to an end her caring efforts. If the Quakers' warmth and humanity had the effect of helping the Jews to accept their fate calmly, did this make the process of their transportation easier for the Nazis? If the Jews had refused to go, or had been hysterical or tried to escape, the Gestapo would have used more brutality to get them moving. Only the nimble young might have had thoughts of escape, but no one could have risked helping them.

Events of the War

On the 27th February there was a surprise British parachute drop over Dieppe and Le Havre, making use of the newly-developed radar monitoring system by which British forces could follow troop movements on the ground, at sea or in the air.

On 15th May new anti-Jewish regulations were issued by Heydrich:

- all Jews living in Germany are forbidden to keep pets of any kind.
- all Jews are forbidden to go to any Aryan barber or hair-dressing salon.
- all Jews are compelled to identify themselves by wearing the yellow Star of David on their clothing.
- no Jews are to be permitted to draw a tobacco ration.

On the night of 30-31 May the RAF staged their largest night-time bombing raid, using a thousand planes to cause the destruction of Cologne and Berlin. The centre of Cologne was reduced to a rubble of smouldering ash, though the shell of the ancient cathedral spire remained erect. The suburbs also sustained severe damage and more than 2,000 families were made homeless. The British said this massive attack proved more effective than many smaller raids would have been.[4] Though Britain was short of aircraft, massive raids followed against Bremen, Frankfurt and Essen. The railways and motorway communication lines were targeted. During 1942 industrial production in Germany increased, largely because the concentration camps, such as Buchenwald, were providing slave labour for industry.

By midsummer the German forces renewed activity on the Russian Front. As they advanced towards Stalingrad they took a large number of prisoners. Jews and Communist functionaries were shot, and no provision was made for feeding the civilian population. The German army was told it did not matter how many people died. The weaknesses of Hitler's military strategies were becoming increasingly recognised. Generals offering advice were summarily dismissed. Hitler's overriding ambition and political fanaticism determined all decisions. He lived a solitary life, spending most of his days in the isolation of his *bunker*.

CHAPTER XIV

Leonhard's Arrest 29th May 1942

LEONHARD'S ACCOUNT OF HIS PERIOD in Buchenwald comes from a talk he gave to a Quaker gathering in Pyrmont on 6th October 1947. This formed the basis of an article 'Als Gast bei Adolf Hitler in Buchenwald' ('Guest of Adolf Hitler in Buchenwald') published in *Der Quaker* in 1975, and in English in the *Quaker Monthly* November 1979. Leonhard and I re-edited the text several times together in the course of translating it into English. Mary's diary entries add more details of Leonhard's interrogation in Hanover and the many house searches and questioning she endured in Pyrmont. The letters Mary exchanged with Hans Albrecht are still among our family papers. Hans, as Clerk of the Yearly Meeting was Leonhard's employer as warden of the Quakerhouse. Mary therefore sought his advice about how she should plead for Leonhard's release and in coping with problems relating to the Quakerhouse during Leonhard's absence. The memoirs of other Buchenwald prisoners have helped me to understand the system through which Leonhard suffered.

Arrest at Stuttgart, 29th May 1942

Although Leonhard understood how anxious Mary felt after the Jews had left, he had been preoccupied with preparing for the Quaker finance committee meeting in Stuttgart. Among his papers I found a card written by his hosts there saying: 'We will meet you on May 29th at the station. What a pity Mary will not be coming with you'.

In his article Leonhard wrote:

In the six months after the United States entered the war the Gestapo felt under no restraints and took relentless action against any groups from whom they could expect the slightest resistance. I was fairly certain that I would not be left at liberty for much longer, but I could see no precautions to take.

I left on the afternoon train for Stuttgart and the train arrived rather late in the evening. I was greeted on the platform by two or three Quakers and one of them told me there were two strangers who wished to speak to me. I soon became aware that they were from the Gestapo, as they asked me to go with them because they had enquiries to make. One of the officials took me to a prison and announced, 'You are under arrest'. When I asked what the charge was, he said nothing beyond the fact that the Gestapo in Hanover had sent a telegram telling them to arrest me. My attempts to travel straight back to Hanover at my own expense were useless. I was held in criminal detention. I had at that time no conception about the procedures of committal to prison and I had an extremely difficult and harsh experience in conforming to all the requests that were made of me. After I had been thoroughly searched and had my personal belongings taken, I was placed in a cell which was already crowded to overflowing with people. Here I made my first acquaintance with bedbugs. The other prisoners were decent and helpful.[1]

Eugen Kogon in his book about Buchenwald, *The Theory and Practice of Hell*, describes the initial arrest procedures as follows:

Prisoners were usually arrested at home, preferably at night, and placed in police jail. They might be kept for days or weeks in an isolation cell, or with as many as 20 or 30 others. Treatment at the hands of the police varied, depending on the whim of the officers . . . After a certain time, at any hour of the day or night, the prisoner was brought up for interrogation. Those who were lucky were not beaten, but at the very least there was mental torment.[2]

Leonhard explained what happened to him:

After five days, on 6th June I was taken with the 'prisoner transport' group to Bruchsaal where I spent 10 days with all kinds of people under arrest, including convicts and habitual criminals. On arrival in the town we were marched through the streets to the prison, controlled by dogs and wearing handcuffs, for everyone to stare at. We were relatively well cared for here and were given light work to do, glueing paper bags. On the 16th June our 'prisoner transport' group was moved on again to Frankfurt-on-Main, where we were held in a building which had once served as a Jewish concert hall. Here we had to learn to manage without any food at all for several days. The next staging post was the prison in Kassel where we were fed and were reasonably well treated. After a few days my group of 300 prisoners travelled on to Hanover.

We arrived there on 25th June, the journey having taken 26 days. I would never have believed that distances in Germany could be so great! In Hanover I was given cell number 163, where I was to spend 69 days in solitary confinement. As I paced the cell I measured it as

4½ shoe lengths wide and 12½ shoe lengths long, i.e. about one metre wide and three metres long. It was furnished with an iron bedstead, a mattress and pillow. Later on I was also given some sheets and a towel. There was also a stool and a folding table, a bowl and water jug, a beaker and slop bucket. Food was in very short supply, though I was later treated somewhat better, when I found kind-hearted warders.

A couple of hours after arrival in Hanover I was taken in a small Honomag car to the Gestapo headquarters, where I was put in one of the notorious cellars, until a particular officer saw fit to interrogate me. This Herr Nonne showed his friendliest face and pretended to be indignant about the treatment meeted out to me since my arrest in Stuttgart. He allowed me to phone my wife, Mary, and also permitted her to visit me the next morning.[1]

When some weeks later Mary visited the Gestapo HQ in Berlin to plead for Leonhard's release, she learned that it was during this first night of interrogation that he had signed a statement which formed the basis of the charges made against him, saying he was a 'convinced pacifist'. They both later denied using these words on the grounds that to be a pacifist during the Nazi period was a capital offence which had political implications and that Quakers believe refusal to bear arms is only one aspect of a lifelong commitment to peace.

Mary's Troubles in Pyrmont

When Leonhard had left for Stuttgart on Friday 29th May, he knew how anxious Mary had been feeling about their safety. She was exhausted by having to care for Alfred Woore. She was waiting for new dentures, was in poor health and almost 60 years old. Leonhard was seven years younger, and reasonably healthy. During the weekend of 30-31 May, Mary wrote in her diary:

The Gestapo came and made a thorough house search for many hours both at the Quakerhouse and in our home. They took away many files and papers and any money they could find. When they left they took my keys and sealed up the Quakerhouse, saying Friends could no longer have access. I asked for a receipt listing items they had taken away. The Gestapo official, Wenger, said he was under no obligation to give a receipt, but I persisted and wrote the following list while he looked on:

Men from the Hanover District Secret National Police [Gestapo], today removed the following property from the home and office of the Leonhard Friedrich Verlag:

1. Two bank books showing a balance of R.M.11,624.20.

2. Three sealed packets of coins taken from the safe.

3. One unsealed package of coins, and a medal belonging to Emma Cadbury. [Given to her by the Austrian Government, in recognition of welfare services rendered by the American Friends Service Committee in the years 1924-38 in Vienna.]

The accuracy of this statement is vouched for by A. Mary Friedrich, dated 30th May 1942.

Leonhard later wrote about this incident in *Der Quaker,* July 1975:

The official [Wenger] hoped thereby finally to wind up the work of the Society of Friends in Germany. They certainly prevented any activity from taking place at the Quakerhouse, but the life and spirit of the work continued from next door. What Mary endured at the hands of the Gestapo, and how she defended the interests of the Quakerhouse, is now almost impossible to describe.[1]

Mary reported the house search to Hans Albrecht, emphasising that the Gestapo had particularly searched for the deeds of the house at Uelzenerstrasse in Lueneburg, which had been left to the Quakers by Marie Willfuer. Her will had been proved and the deeds of the property and some boxes of books and personal things had been handed over by the Court to Leonhard, as the treasurer of the Society of Friends, on 23rd April 1942. For safekeeping, Leonhard decided quite deliberately to misfile the deeds among a large number of his files. Mary had no idea where they could be. However, on 12th August 1942, while Leonhard was held in Hanover, Mary opened a letter addressed to Leonhard saying that the inheritance certificate (*Erbschein*) had now been withdrawn from the Society of Friends and given to Marie's brother OberRegierungsrat Gustav Willfuer. This dispute could well have been the trigger for Leonhard's arrest.

Mary had no way of getting in touch with Leonhard after the house search. She was still expecting him home on Wednesday 3rd June, and waited up for him until past midnight. Eventually, on the Thursday morning, a letter came from the Stuttgart Friends giving her the disturbing news of his arrest. She immediately consulted the Pyrmont solicitor, Dr Heinrich Drinkuth, who had long been legal adviser to the Quakers.

On the night of Friday 5th June she was woken by a policeman knocking on her door to say that black-out regulations were being infringed at the Quakerhouse. The Gestapo had left a light burning there after the house search, but as Mary had no key, there was nothing she could do.

Over the next few days Mary sought advice about how to help Leonhard from local Quakers. On 12th June she went to the Gestapo office in Hanover in a futile attempt to discover Leonhard's whereabouts.

She shared her worries with her friends the Wiedings, who had themselves experienced arrest and imprisonment. She had to turn in Leonhard's ration books and enquired if his health insurance would cover the costs of the expensive dental treatment she had just begun. She was distressed to discover that the Berlin Quaker office had inadvertently let the payments lapse, but soon managed to resolve the problem satisfactorily.

Mary's diary, 21-26 June:

> This is the second Sunday since the Quakerhouse was sealed up. We have held our Meeting for Worship at Helene Glauner's house. Trudy Mergel and Alice Marx came home to lunch with me. Trudy kindly spent two days the following week helping me to write letters and tidying up the chaos the Gestapo had left.
>
> On Thursday 25th June, I received a phone call from Herr Nonne of the Gestapo in Hanover to say they were holding Leonhard. He also let me speak a few words with him. Leonhard had arrived and I was told I could visit him the next day.
>
> On 26th June I was glad that Kati Lotz came with me to the Gestapo building at Schlaeger strasse. We could only see Leonhard for five minutes in the presence of a policeman. But I was told I could have a longer visit if I returned the next day between 3-5 pm, which I did. Leonhard looked so thin and shaken. He was unshaven, without a shirt collar or braces and had diarrhoea and a bad cold. He had been unable to change his clothes since he left home a month ago. I was allowed to take some of them home to wash, and found them infested with fleas. Next day I brought him some underwear and collars. I also visited the solicitor again. I then went to the Pyrmont police station, to make some enquiries about the possibility of Alfred Woore returning to the guest-house at Ruhpolding.

In order to assist Leonhard with his statements during interrogation, Mary was asked to provide documentary evidence about the Quaker attitudes on various issues. This took time and careful thought. For her next visit Mary decided to take a leaflet Friends had published about the Versailles Peace Treaty in 1919 and a copy of a statement Hans Albrecht had written for official purposes on 14th February 1936, stating that the *'Gesellschaft Der Freunde'* was a religious organisation without political aims.[3]

Hans Albrecht wrote to Leonhard on 3rd June in response to Mary's letter about the house search and closing of the Quakerhouse. He obviously did not appreciate the severity of Leonhard's situation:

> I assume that you are at home again. I had heard that the Gestapo had been searching your home and had removed money and bank

books and sealed off the Quakerhouse. I cannot imagine what reasons there could be for this: we have always been so careful, especially in money matters. So I presume that someone has denounced us. I therefore ask you to consult a solicitor immediately. I shall be going on holiday shortly, but can be contacted at the Hotel Krone in Wasserberg. Greetings to you and Mary . . . . Hans.[4]

Frau Mundhenk, a former cleaning lady, hearing of Mary's troubles, came bearing very welcome gifts of sausages and eggs. Toot van Oordt, the Dutch Quaker who worked in the Paris Centre and later in the South of France, came to lunch. Mary consulted Martha Seebohm about the problems she had with Alfred Woore. A Pyrmont policeman had warned Mary that Alfred's presence in their home had caused problems for Leonhard during his interrogation, as it appeared that they were unpatriotically sheltering an Englishman. Mary went to the bank to see what could be done about the frozen Quaker bank accounts and had a very welcome dinner at the Buchingers, which was to become a weekly event.

Mary's diary, 5th July:

I had a two hour visit with Leonhard in Hanover today, this time. I was surprised to hear that a statement from Leonhard's interrogation had already been sent to Gestapo Headquarters in Berlin. Afterwards, I had an appointment with Herr Bock at the Jewish Old People's Home at 16 Ellern strasse in Hanover, where the Gestapo sent elderly Jews. I visited the Wiedings again. On Monday I at last got my new denture and had a number of visitors. I sent a 25 word Red Cross message to Brenda in London, to tell her about Leonhard's arrest. [This was how I first heard the news some weeks later. I well remember the pain and sorrow I felt in reading it, as I walked from the Whitechapel Friends Ambulance Unit hostel to the Hackney hospital where I was a trainee dresser in the out-patients department.]

On Friday I again took the early train to Hanover, had lunch with the Wiedings and visited Leonhard. We had a short time together today as they kept me waiting for Leonhard, until the guard had returned from his lunch. Leonhard looks so thin and weak. He has only been outdoors for 20 minutes since coming here. He had his first bath today.

Hans Albrecht wrote on 9th July expressed great understanding and sympathy now that he had grasped what had happened. He stressed the importance of being truthful during interrogation. He was going to supply Mary's solicitor with information about the 'Quaker position' and would follow up with an official he knew in Berlin.[4]

Mary's diary, 17th July:

Went to Hanover expecting to see Leonhard, but I had a wasted journey because Herr Nonne, the *Oberkriminal Sekretair*, had not left written permission for a visit, so Herr Mueller would not let me see him.

On Saturday 18th July Mary visited young Dr Ott Buchinger who was home on sick leave from the North Africa front suffering from dysentery. He was serving as medical officer in Rommel's army. He wanted Mary to meet Marlies Drinkuth, the stepdaughter of Mary's solicitor, to whom he had just become engaged.

Mary's diary, 18th July:

Marlies was 18 years old, I talked with them as a Quaker Elder about their engagement. I was glad to have the company of Almuth Niemann from Bremen and Edith Alexander from Hamelin for the weekend. (Illustrations 27 and 28)

Mary's diary, 20th July:

We were shocked to learn that poor Trudy Mergel had taken her own life by throwing herself under a train. I went to the funeral service for her at the town cemetery chapel.

27 and 28. *Dr Otto Buchinger Snr, who opened a fasting Klinik in Pyrmont in 1934. His son Dr Ott Buchinger, on leave from North African Front in 1942.*

My visit to Leonhard was most difficult, we were under close observation all the time. On the return journey I felt very anxious and exhausted. When I reached home I found Alfred had made a dreadful mess in our flat and had helped himself to what little food he found in our larder.

August Fricke, the editor of *Der Quaker* the monthly journal, came to stay for the weekend, and while we talked, we spent most of the time podding peas for preserving. On Monday I had another dental appointment, and visited the Tax Office. Seutemanns were just back from Hagen where they had been visiting the few remaining members of the Jewish community.

Hans Albrecht wrote again on 21st July, apologising that he was unable to come to Hanover for the next prison visiting day:

> Everything you say about the interrogation indicates that none of them know what they are looking for. This is the usual Gestapo method, whereby they hope to uncover the unexpected. They just cannot believe that there are no circumstances in which Quakers will tell lies. I told the Regierungsrat in Berlin that he does not have to arrest us to discover we have nothing to hide. Your courage will make Leonhard's burden easier.[4]

Mary's diary, 31st July:

> The Gestapo interrogator, Mueller, said I could now only visit Leonhard once a fortnight. I found Leonhard in very low spirits again. On the return journey I decided that I must speak to someone at the Gestapo headquarters in Berlin, to see if I could do anything for him there.

Mary Visits the Gestapo HQ in Berlin

Mary must have felt that the interrogation was grinding Leonhard into the ground, though they could pin no criminal charge on him and decisions about his sentencing had shifted to Berlin. She asked for the help of Franz Hoffman, a Danish member of the Berlin Quaker office, whom she knew as the co-ordinator of the scheme to send parcels to POWs. Franz and his wife Lotte invited her to stay, saying that Hans Albrecht was also expected. Mary was glad to attend the Berlin Meeting for Worship on Sunday. The next day Franz Hoffman accompanied her for the interview with Regierungsrat Hagenbruch at the Gestapo headquarters at 7 Prinz Albrecht Strasse, a huge gloomy building in the centre of Berlin. When I saw it in 1989, decades after it had been bombed, only the notorious torture dungeons were visible.

Christabel Bielenberg, an Irish woman who went on a similar mission to the Gestapo headquarters to plead for her German husband in 1944, wrote:

> My knees were knocking together in fear as I walked up the huge cold staircase to the 5th floor. At each landing I passed the padlocked door of the empty lift shaft . . . I was waiting for my turn to be interviewed and sat on a chair against the wall and watched four typists taking down statements from four prisoners. I noticed the prisoners were sitting awkwardly and realised that this was because they were chained hand to foot. When they got up their movements were impeded because they had no shoelaces or braces and had to hold their trousers. One of the typists became impatient about the length of the statement. The prisoner said: 'You must excuse me for taking so much of your time, but this statement is extremely important for me'. The woman then suddenly slapped his face, but continued typing. This experience threw me into an intense and silent fury . . . but I was no longer afraid.[5]

In Mary's notes on her interview with Regierungsrat Hagenbruch at Gestapo headquarters, 3rd August 1942, she recorded that it had been a very tough interview. The next day she left some notes for Hans Albrecht, who would be returning to Berlin a few days later:

> Hagenbruch read the statement to me which Leonhard had signed during interrogation. I immediately noticed the phrase 'I am a convinced pacifist'. I just could not believe he would have said that. For years we have been using the phrase '*Friedensfreund*', or 'Friends of Peace', to differentiate ourselves from some pacifists in Germany who held political views with which we could not identify. I said we were too busy with welfare work to have time to make peace propaganda, and had never proselytised. Hagenbruch then referred to the two *Erbgut*/Heritage leaflets about Peter Rossiger and Christof Blumhart, which Nazis regarded as seditious pacifist propaganda.

The leaflet about Peter Rossiger, the son of a poor farmer born in 1843, dealt with his views on the upbringing of children. He wrote about the need to surround children with love and stressed the emptiness of formal religious dogma, which many recognise but few dare to speak about. He wrote about the false roots of patriotism and the killing of innocent people out of a sense of mistaken idealism.

The second leaflet to which the Nazis objected to was about Christof Blumhart, also born in 1843, into a clergyman's family in the Black Forest. He was concerned about poverty and believed in the power of good to overcome evil; that we live to serve God and in doing so become more whole; and that service to mankind is more important than political ideologies. Blumhart said: 'There is suffering in this world, but it will pass. Nothing is so dark as a man who is bitter about his fate. Pray for your persecutor: you need fear nothing if you adhere to that which is good.'

Hagenbruch having read these leaflets faced Mary angrily and asked: 'What have you to say about your welfare work for the Jews?'

Mary replied: 'We helped anyone who came to us in need.' She reminded him of articles which appeared in official newspapers, saying no one should prevent the Jews from emigrating. She said she had helped 33 families to emigrate, and considered this was in accordance with the published policies of the State.

Hagenbruch said: 'Leonhard met an acquaintance on the train to Stuttgart, who was travelling on to Warsaw. Why were two letters to Warsaw found in this man's briefcase?'

Mary replied: 'I don't know.'

Hagenbruch asked: 'Why was Leonhard so anxious to help the Jews?'

Mary replied: 'He was not. This was my work. Leonhard worked hard to earn a living from the Verlag, he had no spare time.'

Mary asked: 'Will Leonhard be charged in a Court of law?'

Hagenbruch replied: 'No, it will not be public. Why does Leonhard refuse to do military service?'

Mary replied: 'He has not refused, he has not been called up. He is 53 years of age and has not had to consider the question.'

Then some conversation about the Quaker peace testimony followed and Hagenbruch asked:

'Why were Marxist books found in the Quakerhouse?'

Mary replied: 'There was no Marxist literature in our Library. However some unopened boxes had arrived from the house which the Quakers had recently inherited in Lueneburg. During the Gestapo house search the boxes were opened for the first time, and this is where some Marxist books were found, along with household items and family silver.'

Hagenbruch asked: 'How do we know you are not storing these things for someone who has gone into hiding?'

Mary replied: 'The label on the boxes, clearly indicates that they were part of the inheritance from Lueneburg.'

Mary ended her report:

This is what I remember of the interview. If you should think that this was just a cold official discussion, I assure you it was extremely heated and angry at times. I was, however, surprised not to feel much personal hatred for Hagenbruch. Though I was fearful and anxious about the confusion of Quaker peace work with pacifism. Most disturbing of all, is the knowledge that Leonhard must remain in custody until he shows some change of attitude to that question. As Leonhard is to be *personally* punished for his beliefs and the Verlag is to be closed, I think no time should be wasted in asking for access to the Quakerhouse and for the restoration of bank accounts belonging to the Society of Friends.

Hans Albrecht, after an introductory paragraph then wrote the following in Leonhard's defence to Regierungsrat Hagenbruch at the Gestapo headquarters in Berlin:

7th August 1942

When I previously spoke to Regierungsrat Roth, I said Quaker peace work is intended in principle to abolish the use of war as a method to settle disputes, but this does not relate to times when the very existence of a whole people is threatened. Our concern is to reduce hatred through mutual understanding, and to put right injustices. For examples, I refer to the Quaker school-feeding programme during the 'blockade' after the First World War; our efforts against the injustice of the Versailles Peace Treaty; our help for the German minority in Memelland and Lithuania; and the school-feeding programme for hungry children in Sudetenland. I remind you of these things, to help you to understand what Quaker peace work entails. We do not associate with political pacifists or those who would betray their country in time of war.

If Leonhard Friedrich has been described as a pacifist in the protocol, the meaning of 'pacifist' should be interpreted as I have suggested. Finally I should make it clear that the German Quakers have no international links or dependency on Quakerism in England, even though the Society was established there. Our Quaker roots lie in German mysticism.[6]

Hans signed off the letter with 'Heil Hitler', which is startling to those of us who remember the tremendous efforts Friends made to avoid this official greeting. But it was on Hans Albrecht's initiative that Friends at the Frankfurt Quarterly Meeting in 1933 were advised to be selective about the time and issue on which to make a personal stand. On this occasion he was writing to one of the highest Gestapo officials, pleading for the release of a Quaker employee and could hardly have avoided this letter ending. He certainly tried his utmost to defend Leonhard, but I think other leading Quakers would have written differently.

Back in Pyrmont

Mary arrived home to find Alfred Woore had again created chaos in the flat. After cleaning up, she thought through some of her problems. She was short of money. She calculated that she needed a minimum of 70 marks a month for rent and a further 147 marks to cover food, medical and other bills. She enquired if she was eligible for welfare allowances. She also asked the Gestapo to release an allowance from Leonhard's closed bank account. Both of these requests were turned down.

She also made up her mind that she could no longer cope with Alfred Woore or afford to keep him and arranged to return him to the guesthouse at Ruhpolding. He had been living with the Friedrichs for almost two years. In her diary she wrote:

> It was hard to be firm about this. While I was washing his clothes and packing them for the journey, he was still pleading to be given another chance. But the local Quakers and Martha Seebohm in particular, helped me and took him to the station for the 8 am train on the 10th August.

Mary wondered if her intervention in Berlin was going to help Leonhard? Her lawyer, Drinkuth, did not seem to be making much progress, although he was helpful in drafting her letters in legally acceptable language.

On 15th August she went to see Leonhard again, and had to tell him that Hagenbruch had said: 'He has to stay in prison until he alters his attitudes.' In her diary she wrote:

> I found him very sad and his body was shaking. He was still being taken for frequent interrogations and never knew when they would fetch him. He said he had read the Bible constantly when he was alone. He had read John's Gospel many times, and Corinthians 13 daily.

Mary's diary, 17th August:

> I went to the town hall about the regulations concerning our garden at Loewensen. I took shoes to be repaired. The next day I worked in the garden from 7 am and did not get home until almost midnight. On Wednesday Hans Seutemann helped me with the accounts and came with me to the Tax Office to explain that since the Verlag was closed, our tax liability should also have closed.

On Saturday 4th September Mary went to Berlin for the Executive Committee, staying with Franz and Lotte Hoffmann again. She arranged another interview with Hagenbruch. She wrote in her diary:

> I could find my way around more easily this time. I met Johanna Rieber in 'Unter den Linden' to talk about Leonhard. I had dinner with

Margarethe Lachmund, Grete Sumpf and Kate Tacke. I really enjoyed just sitting around most of the day. The following day was the Executive Committee. I was so very thankful that they decided to pay Leonhard's warden's allowance over to me. Everybody was so kind and thoughtful and sent loving greetings to Leonhard. They showed great appreciation for all he had done for the Yearly Meeting, and prayed for health and strength for him, in his suffering.

Mary's diary, 7th September:

Grete Sumpf, from the Vienna Centre, came with me for a second interview with the Gestapo official, Hagenbruch. It was another very unpleasant interview, held under dazzling interrogation lights. He said Leonhard would be sent to a concentration camp. I was devastated. I caught the next train to Hanover, and spoke with Mueller, the interrogator, who merely asked if I had been successful in getting social welfare money. I spent the night with the Wiedings, who gave me some good things for Leonhard. On Wednesday I was able to visit Leonhard again, and I had to tell him they might be sending him to Dachau. We both wept. I thought he looked very nice today: he had just shaved, but he was so pale and his hands were particularly white. How shall we live through this? May the time be shortened somehow.

Mary's diary, 9th September:

Gusti Fuchs an old Friend from Cologne came to stay, but she was ill and remained in bed most of the time. She had been shattered by the RAF air attack on the city on 30th May, when more than a thousand planes had dropped bombs.

On 13th September Mary wrote again to the Regierungsrat Hagenbruch in Berlin to say:

I have discussed our conversations with my husband. He said he had never refused any service to the state, so it is wrong to assume he would refuse military service if this were required of him. Though the Society of Friends is very concerned that international disputes be settled peacefully, individual members have always made their personal decisions about military service. Up to the present time, I believe no German Quaker has refused military service. May I again ask that Leonhard be allowed to read the indictment himself and be given writing materials in order to defend himself on this important issue. I also beg you to release him.

During the next week Mary was busy on domestic chores. She had another visitor taking a brief respite from the bombing in Bremen. Mary spent most of her days moving the firewood from the Quakerhouse garden to her cellar, pulling it along in her handcart, and became very exhausted.

Mary's diary, 16th September:

Gestapo were at the Quakerhouse again.

On 29th September Mary made her final visit to Leonhard in Hanover. He had now seen the indictment, and was allowed pencil and paper to write his own defence, a copy of which I found among the family papers, dated 30th September 1942. It is addressed to Hagenbruch in Berlin, though it seems unlikely that he received it. In her diary Mary wrote:

> Leonhard appeared hopeful and courageous, and seemed generally somewhat better. For me it was a terrible day. When I got home I was touched to find Frau Mundhenk had left a cake for me.

Leonhard's indictment was written on a printed red card which he carried in his wallet for the rest of his life. The colour red indicated his category as a political prisoner. It read as follows:

Issued by, *Geheime Staatspolizei*, Prinz Albrecht Str. 8 BERLIN

Case number: 1V C2 – H nr F 9818

18th September 1942.

According to the findings of the Gestapo (*Geheime Staatspolizei*), his conduct endangers the existence and security of the people and the state. This is occasioned by his politically negative attitude to the National Socialist state, and is evidenced by his pacifist and pro-Jewish attitudes, particularly in the context of his leading role in the Society of Friends (Quakers). He exercises an undesirable influence on the neighbourhood and those around him and thereby undermines the unity of the German people, which is of special importance in time of war.

signed:

I.V. Mueller

confirmed, with a rubber stamp, and signed

Nonne, Oberkriminalrat Secretary

Concentration camps were created by the Nazis in order to eliminate every trace of actual or potential opposition to their rule. Other political prisoners were charged with the similarly vague accusations.

Leonhard in his article *Guest of Adolf Hitler*, later wrote:

> I will say nothing about the interrogation procedures, or the suffering I was subjected to. What I had to endure reduced me to an extremely low physical and spiritual condition. The endless stress of repeated interrogations affected me badly. The process dragged on for weeks. My case was later taken over by the Gestapo official Mueller, who was unpleasant in every conceivable manner. Mary was allowed to visit me, sometimes weekly, sometimes fortnightly. The Gestapo

tried by every means to discover something with which they could charge me, but all the accusations proved to be groundless. Their charge was based on my personal attitude and that of the Society of Friends. It became quite clear to me that they wanted to close the Quakerhouse in Pyrmont and so paralyse the activities and concerns of the Society of Friends. The matter was then referred to the Berlin Gestapo Headquarters at 7 Prinz Albrechtstrasse. I was greatly shocked when I was allowed to read the indictment at the end of September.

I appealed against the charges, but heard absolutely nothing further. I pointed out that the indictment was made out in the name of my brother Bernhard, who had emigrated to America in 1912, that my name was Leonhard. On 3rd October I left Hanover, and arrived at Buchenwald on the 5th, having spent two nights on the way in a prison in Halle, where there was very great overcrowding, incredibly bad food, and lots of bugs and vermin.[1]

Leonhard had endured 97 days in solitary confinement in a tiny cell in the Hanover prison from 25th June to 3rd October. He was subjected to interrogation, by night or day and was frequently held in the torture dungeons, which he never described to us. At the end of all the suffering he had endured, he discovered that the indictment was based on the statement he signed in the dungeon on the night of his arrival. This interrogation had immediately followed the gruelling 31-day journey in a 'prisoner transport'. He was under extreme pressure and was promised that if he signed the statement he could see Mary and be released shortly.

Back in Pyrmont

While Leonhard was on his way to Buchenwald, Mary was comforted by a visit from Ernst Mai and his wife. On 2nd October Mary travelled to Berlin again for the Quaker Executive Committee, staying with the Hoffmans. Hans Albrecht was there so they discussed Leonhard's problems. One evening the Quakers took her to an enjoyable Bach concert. On the 5th October she returned home on a very crowded train and enjoyed the Seutemann's invitation to supper on her way home.

The next morning she went to see Drinkuth, the solicitor, to help him prepare Leonhard's case for Hagenbruch in Berlin. Mary wrote 'Leonhard's life story' for this purpose with Hans Seutemann's help. Ott Buchinger jnr. has recently told me that in 1942 Dr Heinrich Karl Drinkuth, the solicitor, (born 1897), whilst advising Mary, was also a Captain in the army serving as legal staff officer to General Paul von Hase, later executed for taking part in the 20th July 1944 plot. Drinkuth had no official Nazi position, although he could not have practised as a lawyer and tax adviser without being a Nazi Party member. It was helpful for Leonhard to be represented by someone wearing army uniform, whom the Nazis recognised as a reliable negotiator.

Mary's diary, 9th October:

> I worked all day in the Pum-Birn garden digging up 4 cwt of potatoes. When I got back exhausted and dirty, I found the Gestapo man Mueller from Hanover had been to take away more things from the Quakerhouse. He also brought me Leonhard's keys to our flat. I have no news of where Leonhard is. I had Sunday lunch at the Buchinger's Klinik dining room again, which saves my rations and makes a pleasant change. This evening I chatted for a long time with a lady from Bremen who has come to stay with me for three weeks. I have listened to her sad life story. Having visitors means one has to make time for them, but I am very thankful for her presence and her help in the flat. I am so exhausted I cannot sleep and get cramp in the night. I have spent the last few rainy days moving potatoes. Had a lovely Red Cross message from Brenda.

Mary's diary, 17th October:

> Gestapo men called me to the Quakerhouse for the sixth time.

Mary's diary, 18th October:

> After lunch at Buchingers I went to see the Richters who live near Friedensthal. Kurt upset me when he said the Pyrmont Friends felt Leonhard was suffering because I had been too persistent in working for his release. He also suggested that if only we had contributed to the Nazi collections for *Winterhilfe*, we might have avoided our current difficulties.
>
> This conversation led me to take a long trip to Kassel to talk things over with the Frickes and Grete Sumpf. On my return I resolved to seek out every member of the Pyrmont group individually to try and make my peace with them. The weather is very wet now and I'm getting a lot of sewing done. My winter coat needs a thicker lining.

Mary's diary, 31st October:

> I went to see the Friends in Kassel again for the day, and discussed Leonhard's problems in detail with Grete Sumpf. The next morning I went to Meeting for Worship in Pyrmont and gave them news about the Kassel Friends. I must have made a tactless comparison between Rotraut and some other young person. It renewed a storm of ill feeling against me, and really shocked Helene Engel Reimers who supported me. A few days later I invited several of the Quakers who had

been upset by me to dinner, and by the end of the week I felt the 'war' against me was blowing over.

From time to time Mary was tactless, which created ill feeling in the local group, but she obviously had warm relations with others. Ten days later Mary went to Berlin for another Quaker Executive Committee, where she felt very supported by Martha and Fritz Legatis and also Sigrid Quade.

Mary's diary, 21st November:

> They were so understanding and thought very highly of Leonhard in Berlin. I also visited Olga Halle and Emil Fuchs and his son Gerhard. I was staying with Martha Roehm who works in the Quaker Centre at Prinz Louis Ferdinandstrasse 2. This visit was not so rushed, giving me the opportunity to look at famous landmarks. I found my own way to the Potsdammer Platz and back through the Wilhelm Strasse. I also went past Hitler's Chancery and saw the burnt-out shell of the Reichstag and Unter den Linden.

Back in Pyrmont

On 2nd December Mary returned home to find the Gestapo had been at the Quakerhouse and her home for the seventh time. They had disconnected the telephone and Mary complained about this to the post office.

On 3rd December Mary wrote to the Camp Commandant SS Colonel Pister at Buchenwald:

> I am enquiring about my husband, Leonhard Friedrich, a publisher who was arrested and sent to you on 1st October, according to information I received from the Hanover Gestapo. I have heard nothing from my husband although I have written a number of letters and sent him money. I would like to know if he has arrived at Buchenwald and if he is permitted to receive letters, or if he needs money? How should I address letters and how often may I write?

The letter was handwritten in German by someone else, but signed by Mary. The Commandant's reply is written on the reverse side, with the official rubber stamp and dated 14th December:

> Frau Friedrich, your husband has been instructed to write to you immediately.

This was soon followed by a brief letter from Leonhard saying Mary could write twice a month. She could send him parcels and money, and he would particularly like to receive his pipe and tobacco. He should be addressed as prisoner number 9164 residing at Block 45. Mary was very relieved to know that Leonhard was alive. Although she knew he would be suffering, there were now practical things she could do for him. Those who received some food supplements and clothing had a much better chance of survival.

Having made contact with the Commandant, Mary wrote to ask him to return her eight letters with the 10 mark enclosures, if they had not been delivered to Leonhard. She then received a reply saying the letters and contents had already been returned to the sender. It was this sort of persistence which the Pyrmont Quakers considered inadvisable.

The weather was getting frosty, so Mary wrote to the Pyrmont Gestapo, saying they should drain the water system at the Quakerhouse because the pipes were liable to freeze. This resulted in a request for her to go to the police station, where they kept her waiting all day to no purpose. Five Gestapo men then spent another day searching at the Quakerhouse. This was their eighth visit.

Parcels to Leonhard

On 14th December Mary received a second card from Leonhard, telling her his spectacles were broken and asking her to get a new pair made up for him, which she was able to do, because she had his prescription. He was extremely short-sighted and was helpless without them.

Mary sent numerous parcels to Leonhard, keeping a list of contents and dates of despatch. A new regulation had been made soon after he arrived at Buchenwald, permitting relatives to send regular parcels to German prisoners, but not to Jews. This had previously only been allowed for 'privileged' prisoners, who unlike Leonhard, were also permitted family visits. Parcels were opened and inspected by the Waffen SS guards, who removed choice items for their own use.

The contents of first parcel, sent on 10th December, were 3 lbs bread, a jar of marmalade, ½lb cottage cheese, ¼lb butter, seven apples, toothpaste and shampoo. Mary's second parcel, sent on 18th December, contained 3 pairs wool socks, boots, slippers, crepe bandages, blanket, jersey, underwear, cotton bag to carry bread, sewing kit, braces and shoe brushes.

Leonhard and Mary had sent countless welfare parcels to Jews in Poland and knew what was needed. All personal clothing was removed from prisoners when they arrived. Their shoes were exchanged for rough wooden clogs, which were worn without socks. Everyone soon had sore and ulcerated feet, despite tying old rags around them. If a man could no longer walk, he could neither work nor line up for food. The chances of his survival were then poor.

For three weeks in December, Mary had Elinore Schroeder, a Quaker, staying with her whilst waiting for a bed in the Pyrmont orthopaedic hospital. Elinore was an air-raid casualty who had recently had a leg amputated. Mary got to know her well and enjoyed her company. As Christmas was approaching Mary, who was almost a vegetarian, was asked to help Frau Mundhenk, her former cleaning lady, to cut up two pigs that were being slaughtered, so she had meat this year.

On 21st December the Gestapo came for the ninth time and took Mary with them to the Quakerhouse to look for the Lueneburg inheritance certificate yet again. Mary wrote an astonishing number of Christmas letters, prepared small presents for 20 people and exchanged many visits with Pyrmont Quakers. She had Christmas dinner with the Buchinger family and was pleased to see two of their grandchildren wearing some of my outgrown dresses. In the quiet hours when Mary was alone she wrote up my childhood story and listened to the midnight Christmas Eve service on the BBC. It was her first Christmas alone. Leonhard was enduring the hardest time, surviving in the stone quarry at Buchenwald.

CHAPTER XV

Initiation to Buchenwald 1942-3

ON A SUNNY MORNING IN May 1989, I took the bus from Weimar to Buchenwald, open to visitors as a concentration camp memorial. Leonhard had taken my mother to see it in 1957. It was an experience they needed to share, but a further 30 years had passed before I could bring myself to visit the place where he had been a prisoner for 130 weeks between 1942-5. He was one of the 21,000 survivors who were liberated by the US army.

As the bus climbed seven miles up the Ettersberg plateau from Weimar, I felt misgivings about the visit, but some reassurance in wearing Leonhard's Buchenwald tie-pin on my lapel. It was given him after the war and gave his number and the dates of his imprisonment.

The bus dropped me at the top of the thickly wooded Ettersberg hill beside the visitors centre, which is in the semicircle of substantial barracks, that once provided accommodation for the SS guards and their families. To my right were the ruins of the railway terminal through which Leonhard and countless train-loads of prisoners had arrived after many days of travel. Exhausted new arrivals were separated from their families and driven down a path named the Karacho Way, through the main entrance gate by shouting SS officers wielding sticks to beat the dazed new arrivals along.

The Gate House is a single-storey building with a clock tower over the entrance (illustrated on back cover). On its right-hand side was the office of the Camp Commandant, to which prisoners dreaded being summoned when they heard their number being called over the public address system. On the left were 10 cells used for solitary confinement and torture. I peered past the flap doors through which food had been handed, and saw how dark and small they were, about one metre wide and two metres long. Through the dim light I saw wreaths and photos of famous prisoners who had suffered agonising deaths in each cell. (Illustration 29)

The Gate House is positioned just below the hilltop and on coming through it, the entire camp fanned out on the slope below me, covering

XV INITIATION TO BUCHENWALD 1942-3 161

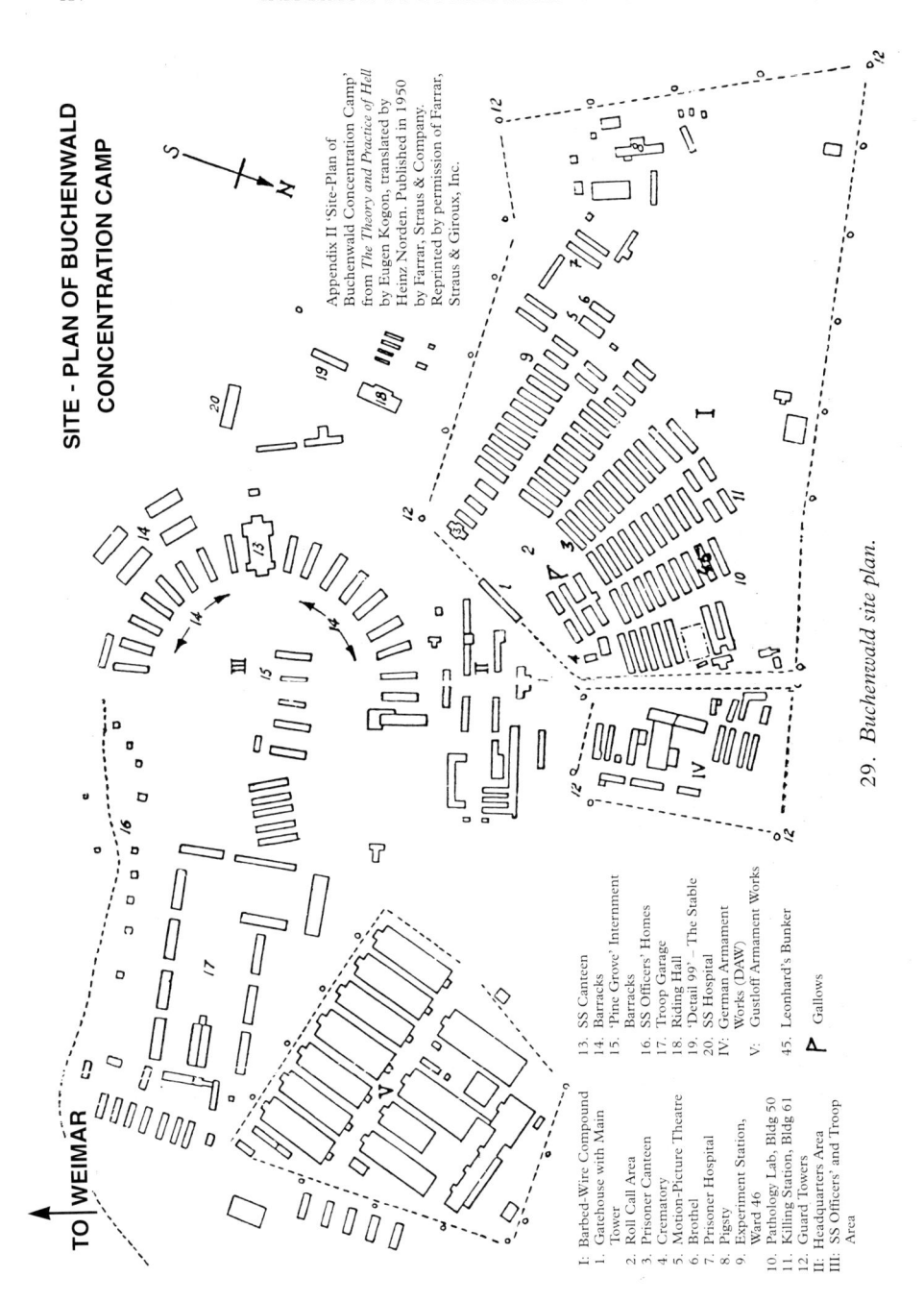

SITE - PLAN OF BUCHENWALD CONCENTRATION CAMP

Appendix II 'Site-Plan of Buchenwald Concentration Camp' from *The Theory and Practice of Hell* by Eugen Kogon, translated by Heinz Norden. Published in 1950 by Farrar, Straus & Company. Reprinted by permission of Farrar, Straus & Giroux, Inc.

I: Barbed-Wire Compound
1. Gatehouse with Main Tower
2. Roll Call Area
3. Prisoner Canteen
4. Crematory
5. Motion-Picture Theatre
6. Brothel
7. Prisoner Hospital
8. Pigsty
9. Experiment Station, Ward 46
10. Pathology Lab, Bldg 50
11. Killing Station, Bldg 61
12. Guard Towers
II: Headquarters Area
III: SS Officers' and Troop Area
13. SS Canteen
14. Barracks
15. 'Pine Grove' Internment Barracks
16. SS Officers' Homes
17. Troop Garage
18. Riding Hall
19. 'Detail 99' – The Stable
20. SS Hospital
IV: German Armament Works (DAW)
V: Gustloff Armament Works
45. Leonhard's Bunker
△ Gallows

29. *Buchenwald site plan.*

a large area. Some of the original perimeter electric fence with double barbed wire is still standing, punctuated at intervals by observation towers. I walked across the enormous roll-call area, where each day at 5 am and again at 6 pm the entire camp of 50,000 men were numbered and checked while standing to attention. Men were woken by a whistle at 4.30 am. They washed themselves, stripped to the waist at huge basins, 12 men at a time, often without soap and towels. There was no privacy in the toilet, for which there was always a queue. At the roll-call they stood arm-in-arm, 12 abreast and 12 rows deep. The sick and dying were held up by their comrades until the count had taken place. The dead could not be taken to the mortuary until after the roll-call and the sick could not report to the clinic until after they had been counted. When all went smoothly, the process would take an hour, but in the evening, after work and facing the dazzling floodlights, it could take five hours or more. During the roll-call, all kinds of degrading punishments were meted out, whilst others had to watch or were led in song to cover the screams of agony of those tied to the whipping block whilst being lashed. The singing was often accompanied by a brass band of 50 prisoner musicians who wore smart red uniforms. Many of the musicians were Gypsies or Jews. Men had to stand on the parade ground in freezing winter wind, snow and rain, and also in the baking summer sun. During my visit to the camp on a sunny day in May, I felt a persistent chilly east wind blowing. The ground where I was standing was now covered in tarmac, but for Leonhard it had been a quagmire in winter and a dustbowl in summer.

From this high vantage point, 2,400 feet above sea level, I could see for miles over the distant countryside towards the Harz mountains in the north, the Thuringer forest to the south-west and the plain of Saxony in the east. Nearby, I saw outlined on the ground, the sites of 50 densely-built prisoners' barracks, which once provided accommodation for 50,000 men.

I sought out Block 45 in which Leonhard had lived. This had been a two-storey brick structure with four rooms. I stepped over the low foundation wall which still remained and paced the length and breadth several times in thought and prayer. The metal shoe-scrapers for removing mud were still beside the entrance and some broken red floor tiles lay where the washroom and toilets had been. I picked up a fragment of a washbasin or toilet bearing the blue marking of *Victoria Waffen SS* along with the double lightning Gestapo insignia. Most of the block houses were single-storey barn-like wooden structures, with windows set high up in the walls. By the entrance there was also a small room for the Kapo, or Block Leader, and his prisoner assistants. The Block Leader was generally a low grade SS man, who slept in the family barracks outside the fence. (Illustration 30)

30. *Block 45 where Leonhard lived. Note broken washroom floor tiles and boot scraper.*

From a reconstruction in the museum I saw that prisoners dormitories were filled with closely-fitted rows of double or treble wooden bunks placed only 30 cm apart. The men slept on bare boards, head-to-toe with three or more men to a bunk. Larger bunks used when the camp population increased sometimes held 13 men. There may at times have been 1,000 men squeezed into a four-dormitory block. In a clearing in the centre of the rooms, there was an iron brazier to provide heat in the winter and a few tables and benches. Meals had to be eaten quickly, and prisoners took turns to sit down to eat. For breakfast there was a mug of coffee substitute, made of roasted boiled bran, and a slice of bread. No food was provided at midday. Supper consisted of a greasy soup with root vegetables and bits of gristle floating in it, with a slice of bread.

I then visited the crematorium, which was hidden behind a wall. Buchenwald's primary role became that of a production centre to exploit labour, rather than to exterminate the inmates, as in Auschwitz. Although many Jews passed through Buchenwald, relatively few were kept there, unless they had some special skill as doctors or scientists. The Jews who came were isolated in Little Camp, where they endured the worst living conditions. In later years many were in transit, staying only for short periods on their way to the extermination camps. I felt moved to see the six ovens in which piles of wasted bodies were cremated. There was also a pathology laboratory where the bodies of prisoners who had been subjected to medical experiments were cut up for examination. On display was a lamp shade made from human skin. Altogether 65,000 prisoners died in the camp or on extermination marches.

I later walked for a mile or so through the beech forest to the stone quarry where, in the winter of 1942, Leonhard had endured his harshest 12 weeks as part of a 'punishment work squad'. The prisoners had worked with pick and shovel, carrying the rocks up a steep bank on their shoulders or in wooden boxes, for building the crematorium. I picked up a sharp limestone rock to see how it felt in my hands. Mercifully all evidence of past human brutality has disappeared under a covering of grass. In the midday sun I watched a shepherd and his dogs lying in the shade of a tree, looking after a grazing flock of sheep.

I then walked to the other side of the camp to the site of the Gustloff II factory, where Leonhard worked for much of his time. Many prisoners were rented out as labourers to factories, making huge profits for companies in which the Camp Commandant held shares. For example Colonel SS Pister, to whom Mary had written about contact with Leonhard, was not merely Commandant of Buchenwald. He was also General Manager of the German Armament Works, with a salary and profit sharing interest in the Gustloff works, and others. The prisoners earnings eventually covered the costs of running the camp and paid the Gestapo guards, who then ceased to be a charge on the state. Any economies that could be made in running the camp lined the pockets of the Gestapo. After the winter of 1942 there was an increase in the numbers of Buchenwald prisoners who were sent to work in more than a hundred factories all over Germany. They endured appalling conditions, frequently living and working underground. The Gestapo at Buchenwald received 6 Marks a day for each factory worker supplied.[1, 2]

Finally I visited the museum where the history of the camp was traced from its origins in 1937. The exhibits were set up in consultation with former prisoners during the 1960s. The majority of Buchenwald's visitors had always been East Germans and groups from the Soviet Union and Poland, so of course the legends of prisoner resistance, were depicted as entirely organised by the Communists. The Communists were certainly among the first groups who showed the discipline to organise some protection for themselves from the Gestapo and the criminals among the prisoners. But from 1943 onwards prisoners of war were also brought into Buchenwald and were housed in national groups, which eventually facilitated their leading role in organising the prisoner resistance.

At the end of my visit to the museum, which was in the former storehouse, I met Dr Giesela Seitel, the archivist, who verified the details of Leonhard's imprisonment on the computer records.

Leonhard Tells of his First Months in Buchenwald

In the article *Guest of Adolf Hitler*, Leonhard writes:

Our reception in Buchenwald was in no way welcoming. When we arrived on the 5th October 1942, our first contacts with the SS guards were most unpleasant. Our personal details were noted and we had to give up all the remaining belongings we had brought in our small suitcases. Then we were taken to the so-called bath house, where we undressed and left our clothes in a heap. We were then pushed into a bath of disinfectant. After this we were lined-up to be at the mercy of the barbers, who were instructed to shave off every hair from our heads and other parts of our body. After a so-called medical examination and whilst we were still in a naked line, we walked through the clothing department to be issued with the Buchenwald regulation vests, pants, trousers and jackets which were thrown at us regardless of size. There were no socks or shoes: we were instead given wooden clogs, which soon rubbed raw patches on our feet. When we finally stood up clothed in our striped pyjama suits and caps, we looked ridiculous and could hardly recognise our mates, or even ourselves.

We were then given our personal identification number. Mine was 9164, a fairly low number which may have belonged to someone who had died. I discovered that low numbers were prized, because there was an assumption that one must have been in the camp long enough to know one's way around. We were also allocated an insignia and a colour for the striped pyjama-style uniforms we wore. Mine was a red triangle, the absence of a letter before it denoting I was a German. I should explain what the various colours meant. I was given red as a political prisoner, green was for habitual criminals, black for those regarded as anti-social, pink for homosexuals, violet for Jehovah's Witnesses, and brown for Gypsies. The Jews of course, were given the yellow Star of David. When I was put to work in the quarry I also had a black circle marked around my insignia, indicating I was a political prisoner in disgrace and in the penal work gang.

We were then taken to one of the barracks, where we were to live, isolated from contact with other camp inmates. I was surprised to find myself in a group, not only of political prisoners, but with all types of criminals and thieves. At the time when I was committed, there were about 8,000 to 10,000 inmates, whereas the population later grew to 47,000.

During the first few days we were allocated to various kinds of unskilled work. Then I was allocated to a work team digging drainage ditches and levelling the ground in Weimar, where new factories were being built. We had picks and shovels for this heavy work which caused terrible pain in my hands. I also suffered dreadfully from sores which developed on my bare feet, through wearing the rough wooden clogs. I was 53 years old at this time and had been a sedentary office worker all of my adult life. We were woken at 4.30 am and had a quick mug of 'coffee' and a slice of bread for breakfast. This was followed by the roll-call. We started work at 7 am, and took another slice of bread with us, if we had managed to save one. This had to last until we finished work and the roll-call at 6 pm or later. In cold, wet weather we had no chance of drying our clothes.

For some reason which I still do not understand I was then transferred to the punishment work squad. Perhaps someone in the Labour Allocation Office felt I was a stubborn character who would never serve their purposes, so the sooner I was broken down in health and spirit, the better. The punishment squad was housed in a special block, separate from the rest of the camp. The treatment I endured there defies all description, the worst of it came from the hands of fellow prisoners of the criminal categories, who had the upper hand. I gradually discovered the types of crime they had committed and realised I was among the dregs of society, from whom we need protection.

After some weeks, in midwinter, I was transferred to the stone quarry commando, where people were literally worked to death, often in quite a short time. Whilst there, I sometimes thought about the book *Ben Hur* and the stories told in the Old Testament about slavery in Egypt. I was part of a human chain, one man behind another carrying rocks. We could not walk in line, we were forced into a trotting pace. I spent 12 weeks excavating stone to build one of the camp crematoria. My health was deteriorating rapidly. I had no particular complaint, I just became weaker, due to lack of food. But even in this awful place I occasionally found good individuals.[3]

To reach the quarry the prisoners had to march miles along a path through the forest of pine and birch trees. Many prisoners were hanged in these woods. Their cries, as they suffered gruesome slow deaths, disturbed the birds and wildlife, who vanished from the area. This is vividly described by Stan Sattler, one of the prisoners:

> The open-cut mine looked like a big hole nearly 40 metres deep and 80 or more metres wide. Hundreds of prisoners had worked here with pick and shovel, with hammer or iron bars. The way down was by a narrow serpentine path, wide enough for one man. On a rainy day it

was slippery and dangerous. We had to pick up rocks and carry them to the top of the quarry, non-stop all day. To avoid dizziness on the high narrow ledge, I kept my eyes on the ground. After 10 hours, we returned to camp, carrying a rock all the way back. Every evening my shoulders ached, and the skin which was only covered by a thin pyjama top was badly chafed.[4]

Leonhard's account continued:

I had no news from home, and was not allowed to write. One evening in November 1942, after the roll-call, I was summoned to the Camp Commandant's office over the public address system. This kind of summons was greatly feared, because it could lead to further trouble or the isolation cells. When I arrived at the office, the Commandant was very angry and accused me of not having written home. When I explained I had not been allowed to do so, I was ordered, to my great joy, to send off a letter that very night. I later discovered this had come about because Mary had addressed an enquiry to the Commandant. I found that a new directive had been issued, to the effect that all German political prisoners were permitted to receive parcels of food and essential clothing from their homes. I was able to write to Mary and tell her I could do with some boots and other things. From this time onwards my health improved, largely because I was receiving regular parcels from home. Other friends also contributed items to the parcels Mary sent. I could hardly have survived the brutal treatment had it not been for this material support, and the awareness of the thoughts and prayers of so many friends was a real encouragement to me.

After some weeks in the stone quarry I was transferred to the sewerage and drainage squad. Our team was to dig service ditches in the camp for the new barracks that were being constructed, for the steadily increasing number of prisoners. We had to carry out all the tasks of digging ditches, carrying and laying heavy drain-pipes, and then covering them over using only hand tools and frequently standing in water-logged trenches. I generally worked with bandaged hands. I was extremely exhausted and weak, but somehow I managed. While working out of doors in the camp we were particularly vulnerable to all kinds of harassment by the SS men passing by. They prowled around taking every opportunity to intimidate and to kick us, or make complaints about our work. Complaints could lead to a beating, or even hanging in the forest.

During the first winter in 1942-3 we were supplied with very thin coats which afforded little protection against the snow and icy winds. As soon as the sky was a little brighter we were ordered to take our coats off and continued to work shivering with cold. The next winter we were given good heavy army surplus coats, but the SS meanly spoilt the benefit we might have felt, by cutting out an eight-inch circle of the material at the centre of the back, so that the cold wind blew down our spines.

While on this job I got into trouble for wearing a pair of gloves which Mary had knitted for me. My hands were sore and blistered. The SS man in charge ordered me to take off the gloves, and reprimanded me for being slow and disobedient. When his back was turned, I put them on again, but he unfortunately noticed. He took his whip and gave me a severe lashing. One of the blows caught my face, and I fell in the mud and lost consciousness. Fortunately I recovered and managed to stand up before they could take me to the sick bay. The Gestapo administration required that any beating be reported again the next day and written in a punishment log book, which was periodically inspected by the Berlin HQ. I dreaded having to report the next morning, because the beating would frequently then be repeated. The SS officer to whom I reported asked why I was in Buchenwald, since I was not a Jew. I said I really did not know, but the charge against me was that as a Quaker, I was said 'to exercise an unsuitable influence on the neighbourhood'. He then asked me some questions about the Quakers. He became thoughtful and said that his mother, who was now dead, had told him his life had been saved by the school-feeding programme provided by American Quakers after the First World War. In view of this he would help me, by taking me on his personal staff, if I would sign a statement of allegiance to the National Socialist state. But to sign such a statement, or to be on the personal staff of a Gestapo official, was the last thing I wanted to do.

He was surprised I did not seem keen, but ordered me to think about it and to report to him the next day. I spent a sleepless anxious night worrying about what would happen. Once again, he did not whip me, but offered a job in the munitions factory, where I would also earn some money and be moved out of the 'punishment block'. This was quite a dilemma for a Quaker! I replied I could not make bombs to drop on London, because my daughter was living there. The SS man was again surprised, but said that as the father of five children he could understand my feelings. He really did want to help me and eventually found me a job in a factory tool-store. This was good work for me: it began in June 1943 and continued until my release. I simply handed over tools and supplies for use in the factory and kept records of their return. I now had the opportunity of a certain personal independence, at least during the working hours of the day, though I still encountered a lot of unpleasantness now and then, which I managed to cope with.

About the torture and ill-treatment meted out to me and others, I will tell very little because it is now well-known. I can only say that I experienced my full share. But in the end, by divine providence, I was spared the worst.[3]

Many others have written of their experiences in Buchenwald, I have been particularly helped by reading *The Theory and Practice of Hell* by Eugen Kogon, a German Catholic who was there from 1937 until the end of the war. He recorded his experiences with objectivity, describing how concentration camps functioned. He later became Professor of Political Science at Munich University. He described what a prisoner was likely to experience after he had survived the early weeks in Buchenwald.

Within the first three months fellow inmates could see how a new prisoner would cope. If he survived the initial period without becoming a physical wreck, without having lost his will to live and without having become the subject of someone's extreme bullying, then the prisoner might find he could gradually adapt to this horrific life. Some survived by joining the criminal camp underworld. Others found ways of maintaining their former values. But men who carried only their social or middle-class standards, without any deep conviction, were lost on the first day.

Admission to the concentration camp created a shock to the personality of many men who either broke and disintegrated, or broke to be re-built, sometimes their personality gained inward perspectives. But no-one remained unchanged. In the process of adapting to such a life, it was hard to retain any recognisable aspect of one's personality. The prison community seldom offered the newcomer any consideration or understanding during this period of initiation. The long-term inmates seemed to lose their emotional response to the suffering of others and had also needed to develop a protective shell to withstand their own physical suffering.

After the first shock of life in Buchenwald, many prisoners contemplated suicide, while others fixed their hope on a belief that they would be among those selected for work, and not death. Many found they could become accustomed to suffering from cold, hunger and sores. They even learned to sleep under unspeakable conditions, and determined to try and look as smart and healthy as they could.[5]

When, after the war, friends asked Leonhard how he survived these experiences, he sometimes said: 'I simply put my head down and clung like a limpet to the rock, letting the waves wash over me'. Other writers have echoed this, saying that such attitudes were necessary for survival.

Camp Organisation

The Buchenwald concentration camp had been opened in 1937 under the aegis of the Gestapo headquarters at Prinz Albrecht Strasse in Berlin. The management of Buchenwald was in the hands of the black uniformed SS Corps bearing the skull Death Head and their double-lightning insignia. After basic military and obedience training, this elite corps was drilled to suppress their own feelings of humanity, to the Nazi cause and to exert brutality on 'inferior races'. If they failed, or showed any human sympathy, their heads were shaved and they themselves became prisoners. These demoted former Gestapo men who had failed to measure up to the discipline expected of them were particularly dangerous, because they would tell tales on the others in the hope of regaining privileges for themselves.

The Buchenwald Camp Commandant and the Gestapo officers assisting him depended heavily on selected prisoners for organising the daily routine and work teams. The Berlin Gestapo Headquarters and their inspectorate governed all aspects of management. But despite their many regulations and administrative procedures, there was immense opportunity for graft, so that some members of the SS Corps could live in luxury while doing their regular duties.

The criminals, and to some extent the Communists of German nationality, were favoured for leadership positions in Buchenwald's camp organisation. Some were appointed Block Kapos serving under the low-grade SS officers or put in charge of labour squads. Prisoners who held such positions made themselves more comfortable, benefiting from the power they held over others. However, when the labour of prisoners became strategic to the war effort, it became apparent that work group leaders lacked the administrative skills necessary to operate the complex allocation of labour. Extra help was drafted in from the political prisoners. This enabled a few more well motivated people to rise into positions of leadership. The 'politicals' in the Labour Allocation Office were sometimes able to protect some outstanding people, when the Gestapo were pursuing them. But protection for Jews was almost unheard of.

CHAPTER XVI

Mary on her Own 1943

MARY STAYED AT HOME AS much as she could during the January winter blizzards, often risking tuning the radio to the BBC. One evening she heard the evensong service from her sister Florrie's church in Southgate and felt close to life in England. It was the fourth year of the war, which would soon have lasted as long as the First World War. Mary, along with many others, began to feel the war must be drawing to an end in 1943 because the German army was doing badly on the Eastern Front.

Mary's diary, 6th January:

> I was exhausted and tired, and promised myself a much needed restful day. But four Gestapo men accompanied by Wenger, the Chief of Police, fetched me to the Quakerhouse to answer more questions while they made further searches and removed the telephone. They let me bring home Brenda's toboggan and doll's house, which had been stored in the Quakerhouse attic. I also found three of Brenda's dolls in her pram which I was able to give to Ingrid Buchinger's daughters.

Mary's diary, 15th January:

> Albert Graf is very ill in the Hanover hospital. I was very pleased to hear from Buchenwald that I could send parcels of food and tobacco to Leonhard. I had just received some food for him from Margarethe Lachmund and his cousin in Marktbreit and was able to bake him a late Christmas *stollen*. I took some cottage cheese to a friend who gave me some coupons toward the next parcel.

Mary's diary, 30th January:

> Today is the 10th anniversary of Hitler as *Reichskanzler*. I had really hoped that there might have been an amnesty for Leonhard on this occasion. I have been thinking so much about my family. I believe God will bring Leonhard back from Buchenwald when he has completed his service there. I have had a wonderful day of quiet communion and peace. The 91st Psalm has been a great comfort to me.

In February Mary heard from Leonhard, saying he had received her parcels and had great pleasure in knowing that several other Friends had contributed to them. Leonhard could only write a few lines to Mary every few months and Gestapo censorship limited what he could say. Her relief in hearing from Leonhard was tempered by three visits which the Gestapo made to the Quakerhouse on 16th, 19th and 24th February.

Mary's diary, 25th February:

> I was required to go to the Finance Department at the Town Hall about our Pum-Birn garden. I was asked what rent I was paying? I was of course not paying any, since the Sturmthals had given it to us. The official was extremely unpleasant and said I was a law-breaker in accepting the garden from a Jew. I was very worried and could not sleep. The next day I visited Drinkuth, our solicitor, who was unable to find any legal document transferring the garden to us.

German Resistance Groups Against Hitler

After Montgomery's success against Rommel in North Africa in November 1942, Hitler experienced further military humiliation on the Eastern Front. During the winter many thousands of young men had died. Finally, on 30th January 1943 General Paulus surrendered to the Soviet forces at Stalingrad, in defiance of Hitler's orders. The German 6th Army had been reduced from 300,000 men to 91,000. By the end of the summer the Soviet army had finally driven the Wehrmacht out of Kharkov and the Donetz basin. On 6th November the Russians regained Kiev and ousted the Germans from the Crimea; they never again lost the initiative.[1]

Helmut von Moltke

German military strategists were outraged by Hitler's disregard of his generals' advice. This restiveness led to the formation of several opposition groups, in which influential people from the army, the law, and the church, gathered secretly to plan for Hitler's downfall and Germany's future. One of these was Count Helmut James von Moltke, who owned country estates in Kreisau, where he could invite people to meet, without arousing suspicion. Von Moltke had studied international law and was at this time serving as legal adviser in the military intelligence service, the *Abwehr*. While on a visit to Sweden, he was able to get a letter dated 25th March 1943, transmitted to his friend Lionel Curtis, an influential Oxford don. Von Moltke wanted the British to know that an underground opposition to Hitler was developing. In his letter to Curtis he wrote:

> Another Fact: German people are very anxious about their men who have been reported missing in Russia. The Russians have allowed our men to write home, which was a very wise thing of the Russians to do. Well these letters are, on their arrival in Germany locked up or

destroyed but not allowed to reach the relatives. About 1,000 of these cards had passed the censor through some technical error. The recipients who then tried to answer in the normal way through ordinary channels were there upon arrested, questioned and kept in confinement until they realised what it would mean for them if they ever talked about the fact that they had received news from their men.[2]

Once the crematoria at the Treblinka concentration camp in Poland had been equipped with more gas ovens to cremate the Jews, it was decided to close down the Warsaw ghetto. Of the 400,000 Jews who had lived in this small walled area, now only 60,000 remained. On 19th April when the SS came to remove the ghetto Jews to Treblinka, they met with fierce opposition. It took the SS until 16th May to overcome the uprising. This heroic resistance was unique among Jewish communities during the Nazi period.[3]

Soon after the withdrawal from Stalingrad, Hitler became anxious about the attitude of his ally Mussolini, who pleaded for a peace agreement on the Eastern Front. There were further set-backs for the German and Italian troops when the Allied Forces took Tunis and Bizerta in North Africa, along with 250,000 German POWs. Soon after the Allied invasion of Sicily on 10th July, the Italian King dismissed Mussolini from office and imprisoned him in a high isolated Alpine hotel.

Marshal Badoglio was appointed to lead the Italian Government and renounced the Alliance with Germany. On 8th September he requested an armistice agreement. Meanwhile, Hitler had re-organised his forces to take Rome and other key points in Italy, forcing the King and Badoglio into hiding. Hitler managed to hold Rome until June 1944. On the 13th September 1943 Hitler had Mussolini rescued in a spectacular airborne mountain operation, bringing him for a meeting at Hitler's Rastenfeld headquarters. Whilst Mussolini was at first delighted, he would not play a puppet role and refused to resume the dictatorial position he had previously held. He returned instead to northern Italy where he lived quietly.[4]

The Pyrmont Quakerhouse

Mary's diary, 2nd March:

The Gestapo came to the Quakerhouse for their twelfth visit, after which I was ordered to the police station, to be told that the Quakerhouse was to be commandeered for the Hitler Youth.

Mary informed Willy Tangerman, a Quaker who worked for the town council and asked Martha Seebohm if her brother, the Burgermeister Seebohm, would intercede for the Quakers. The following day Mary was again due to meet Wenger at the Quakerhouse. After waiting for two hours outside the building, to which she had no key, she went to the police station, where she also found the Burgermeister, who was most helpful. The next day Wenger missed another appointment with Mary, but came on the 16th March with several policemen to clear out Leonhard's office. Mary cleaned the mould off the old leatherbound books from an earlier generation of German Quakers and stored them in her flat.

Mary's diary, 25th March:

> I was again called to see Wenger at the police station. This time he asked me if I told tales to Hans Albrecht about what had happened at the Quakerhouse? When I said 'Of course it is my duty to keep him informed', a most unpleasant 45-minute conversation took place. I related this to Kati Lotz, and then received a telegram from Hans Albrecht asking me to meet him in Berlin. I decided not to go, because I considered it unwise to be away from the Quakerhouse at this time of transition. However Kati Lotz and I went to Drinkuth the solicitor and felt somewhat relieved when he managed to get an official agreement with the Hitler Youth to regularise their use of our Quaker premises.

Since the Quakerhouse was being taken over, the Quaker Frieda Luedecke, had to remove the furniture she had stored there since 1938. She stayed with Mary for a few days while making the necessary arrangements. On 4th April Mary recorded what she had said in her diary:

> 'I have noticed that you are not much loved by the Quaker group here?' I had to agree with her. She felt she had to tell me what others were saying behind my back. Some said I see myself as a martyr. Another said she was always seeing me at street corners in town talking to different people. Yet another said I was possessive about the Quakerhouse. This gave me some miserable, sleepless nights, I felt I was being blamed for the requisitioning of the Quakerhouse.

It is easy enough for a small group of frustrated people to start blaming one person for everything that goes wrong. Mary seemed to recognise she was being scape-goated. She wrote:

> On Sunday I had a comforting lunch with Otto Buchinger snr. at his klinik. He said he had also noticed an unfriendly feeling in the Quaker group towards himself and knew they disliked him too. So perhaps we should stand together.

> On Monday morning I was ordered to the Quakerhouse to sign a paper declaring the items that Frieda Luedecke was taking away had never been the property of the Friends. When she eventually left with her furniture she begged me for some furniture and floor polish. In the end I gave her some food coupons too.

On 8th April I was summoned to visit the Chief of Police, Wenger, for the 15th time. Today he tried being pleasant. He showed me a letter asking him to question me about where the inheritance certificate for Marie Willfeur's property in Lueneburg could be. I told him I thought I had once seen it, though it was possible that I was mistaken. I have a bad memory for things that don't concern me, and had no idea where it was.

On 14th April Hans Albrecht came to Pyrmont, and spent the whole day with Kati Lotz. Two days later he went to the Burgermeister on his own and came again briefly to look at the burial ground. He did not have time to ask about Leonhard. It appears that the Pyrmont Friends considered it a mistake to ask the solicitor to draw up a legal document with the Hitler Youth. I felt I was being ignored as a Quakerhouse caretaker, instead of being treated as a responsible Friend.

This was an awkward situation for Hans Albrecht to deal with. Mary had worked lovingly for years, looking after the Quakerhouse and garden. She had planted trees and rose bushes, and grown flowers on the old stone walls. She had polished and repaired the furniture, and had sea-grass hassocks made in a women's prison for the Meeting Room, had filled the window-sills with pot plants. Others had of course also done a great deal. It is understandable that Mary was protective about the Quakerhouse. Since it had been agreed that Quakers would continue to look after the garden, Mary and Kati Lotz went to the police to negotiate the building of a fence and a garden tool shed underneath the outdoor staircase.

Bombing Creates Public Restiveness

On the Western Front, the Allies were winning the Battle of the Atlantic. Hitler's submarines were unable to stop Allied shipping convoys from reaching the Soviet Union, because radar was proving increasingly successful in detecting their underwater positions. In March the RAF, now also supported by the US Air Force, began a series of heavy air raids against German cities. It started with the Dambuster raids to destroy reservoirs producing hydro-electric power for the Ruhr factories and continued with attacks on the industrial plant at Penemuende, where the first pilotless jet-propelled rockets were produced. There were massive air raids on the cities, 16th May Kiel; 25th May Dortmund; 26th and 29th July on Hamburg. Acute shortages of manpower, raw materials and transport were affecting the morale and capacity of Germany's industries.

Hitler himself was suffering from the increasing dosages of drugs which he took to control stress. He lived in austere seclusion, spending his time in an underground bunker, seldom seeing even his most trusted colleagues. As he lost contact with ordinary people, his commands became more unrealistic.

The German generals and senior military staff became restive as Hitler repeatedly countermanded their decisions. This resulted in the growth of small opposition groups, who rather ineptly plotted against Hitler's life. However, Hitler had an uncanny feel for his own security, managing to foil assassination attempts by frequent changes of his schedule. One of the opposition groups was headed by General Beck, who had contacts with Wallenberg, an international banker in Sweden. The conspirators tried to get assurance from Britain that an assassination of Hitler would be followed by a peace agreement with the Allies. Opposition was also developing in Lutheran church circles. Pastor Dietrich Bonhoeffer managed to contact Bishop Bell of Chichester during a visit they both made to Sweden. Bonhoeffer was subsequently arrested in April 1943, which prompted Bishop Bell to speak in the House of Lords about opposition groups in Germany.[5] Bonhoeffer was held in the Buchenwald torture cells.

On 2nd July 1943 *The Friend* reported that a leaflet had been circulated among medical students in Munich and elsewhere saying:

> We have grown up in a state of brutal oppression with no freedom to express our beliefs . . . the Nazis have brought a terrible blood bath upon Germany.

As a consequence six young medical students at Munich, were hanged. An example of isolated resistance groups.

Mary's diary, 21st May:

> I went to Berlin with Kati Lotz for the Executive Committee. I met our dear friend Ernst Rummel, who had been bombed-out in Nuremberg; I spent a long time talking about Leonhard with Margarethe Lachmund, who was very understanding. I stayed with Olga Halle. An air raid restricted us to her cellar most of the night. I was thankful to be home in peaceful Pyrmont, three days later.

On her return to Pyrmont Mary discovered that the Hitler Youth were mainly young girls who were preparing the Quakerhouse as a reception centre for people whose homes had been destroyed in air raids. Two hundred chairs had been taken from the large Meeting Room, along with other Quaker furnishings, to be stored at a depository. Mary spent a long day working with the young members of the League of German Girls while they were putting up beds etc. They invited her to share their evening meal. Mary also rather enjoyed having two young soldiers allocated to work with her for several days in clearing up the Quakerhouse garden.

Caring for Bombed-out City Dwellers

Before describing how Mary shared her home with so many guests, I need to say more about her flat on the first floor of a detached villa, next door to the Quakerhouse. It was surrounded by park, farmland and forested hillsides, which she could enjoy from all the windows. The Friedrichs' flat consisted of two bedrooms and two reception rooms, separated by a sliding glass door and opening onto a sheltered south-facing balcony. Each room had a coal/wood burning stove. The kitchen and bathroom only had cold water taps. Mary also had the use of a narrow attic space under the roof tiles, as well as a small attic bedroom with a sloping ceiling. Another tenant, Frau Kuhl, also occupied two rooms at the top of the house. Knierim, the landlord, lived on the ground floor with his two unmarried sisters, one of whom Mary always referred to as the Lemon, because she was rather sour, and the other as Sister, because she was a nurse; and also their aged mother.

Throughout the summer, Mary was glad to be able to offer respite to Friends or their relatives who needed a break from the massive air raids taking place in the cities. The first visitor was Gusti Fuchs, one of the Quakers on the 'Trusted List' who came from Cologne. Then there were the Hennikers' relatives, who were bombed-out in Wuppertal. These were quickly followed by Eugen and Agnes Richter, who had lost their home and business in Barmen and later in Elberfeld. Agnes had heart trouble and a broken leg which was in plaster; her nerves were totally shattered. Mary moved out of her bedroom for them. A few days later Hannah Jordan arrived, bringing Karl Doerr, a journalist, with his blind wife and 12-year-old son. They all slept on the dining-room floor until they found a room at the Schoendorfs. Mary was able to give them some household items from her attic store, where she tidily kept all sorts of things that 'somebody might need one day'. After some rearrangements Mary found she could accommodate eight people and offer hot baths heated by a wood fire, but it was at the cost of her own privacy. At the end of July she wrote in her diary:

> My kitchen is always full of people doing their cooking. They have lost all their possessions and have suffered severe shock. They are highly strung and insecure about the future. I sometimes feel I don't know where I belong; there is nowhere to relax, so I go out gardening, but I know how fortunate I am to have my own home. I can sleep on a sofa in my own kitchen and have never felt more certain about the caring love of God.

Years later, after the war, Georg Schnetzer wrote an article for the *Friends Quarterly* in which he paid tribute to Mary's hospitality:

Leonhard and Mary Friedrich impressed me greatly by the way they lived. Their combination of simple manners and inner resolve and their practical approach, seems to epitomise the essence of Quakerism. I marvelled how Mary managed, despite her physical handicaps, to keep open house in that wonderful way; no one ever went away with empty hands or empty hearts.[6]

During July and August Mary looked after many more Quaker visitors who were exhausted or bombed-out by the heavy air raids in the cities. She was sad to hear of the arrest of Eva and Carl Hermann, the courageous Friends in Mannheim who were given long sentences of imprisonment for listening to the BBC. These were the Friends who a year earlier had supported the Mannheim Jewish community at the time of their removal to Gurs concentration camp in southern France. After the war Eva Hermann wrote a remarkable booklet about her experiences: *In Prison Yet Free* in which she recounted:

> In Mannheim, the prison was in the Castle which was hit in almost every heavy raid. Once when I expressed to the chief wardress my astonishment that there had been no casualties in the prison, she said quietly and naturally: 'In this house there is much prayer.' There is indeed much more prayer within prison walls than I had surmised and the prayers are not only for safety and protection from punishment.

Years later in 1990, I was fortunate to meet Eva, a lively 90 year old, in Pyrmont and have subsequently corresponded with her about her Nazi experiences. In a letter dated 23rd March 1992 she explained how she came to write about her prison experience:

> The moment I came to the Rest Home in 1946, Kati Lotz asked me to talk about my Nazi experiences to the group, but I resisted, 'not yet, I need more time'. This happened several times. One afternoon near the end of my stay, I found myself sitting at the table with pen and paper in front of me, writing as though it was being dictated. There seemed to be someone who knew what was needed, and that it was needed now. Every time since then, when I read a portion of it somewhere, like in *Der Quaker* December 1991, it gives me the same feeling of 'Oh yes that was my experience, but I was just the pen that wrote it down. I am grateful for Kati Lotz's insistence.[7]

On 6th August Mary invited a number of Quakers to tea, without telling them it was her 61st birthday. She was much cheered by a postcard from Leonhard, but he was not able to tell her that since June he had been in a slightly easier situation, working in the Gustloff II factory.

Mary's diary, 12th August:

> Trudy Marx, a non-Aryan attender of the Meeting, who lived in a bed-sitter, asked if she might cook her supper in my kitchen several

evenings a week. Of course I agreed. [This was the beginning of an arrangement Mary later made for a number of people, merely asking them to contribute towards the cost of fuel.]

Agnes and Eugan Richter had been living with me since June, though Eugan was frequently away in Wuppertal. One day Agnes became quite hysterical when she received a request to visit the police. She insisted that Eugan should return from Wuppertal to accompany her and later they discovered the police merely wished her to register her change of residence for ration book purposes. One day Eugan came with me to the Pum-Birn garden to dig up my potato crop. It had been a very dry summer, and the potatoes were very small. He kept grumbling that it was not worth lifting them. A few days later he travelled to Amsterdam and returned late at night with four small pullets which he insisted on keeping in my cellar. So we fed them on the smallest potatoes, but they created the most awful smell, noise and dirt, to which our landlord objected. Eventually I persuaded Eugan this project would have to stop. So he took them in the garden and chopped off their heads, and plucked them outdoors. We were about to eat our dinner at three o'clock when Trudy Marx and her two friends phoned up to say they had been unable to find anywhere to eat in town, so could they come to eat with us? Agnes quickly turned off the oven and instead of sharing our chicken, we just had beetroot and potatoes.

Mary's diary, 31st August:

We had our first air raid warning in Pyrmont, during an RAF overflight on their way to Berlin. The Richters who were with me, sheltered in our cellar.

At this time Edith Alexander, the English woman living in Hamelin, came quite often for a day or two. Although Edith was considerably younger, it must have been a pleasant relaxation for them both to speak English and be able to exchange confidences. On 31st August they listened to Winston Churchill together on the BBC. The fifth year of war was now beginning and Goebbels was challenging the people to make 'a supreme effort'.

The Quaker Apple Trees

Along the Bismarckstrasse, in the 30 yards between our house and the Quakerhouse, there were five old apple trees which belonged to the Quakerhouse. Mary was angry to discover that on 16th September the municipal authority had, without asking, picked the apples off the trees. The apples had always been shared among the members of the Meeting and a quantity of apple sauce was tinned for use at residential Quaker gatherings. While Mary was visiting the solicitor on other business, she mentioned that the town had simply taken the apples. Drinkuth must have complained to the right person, because on 5th October a truck-load of apples was returned. Of course many were bruised and had to be thrown away, but local Friends came and fetched them and the best of them were packed up and posted to Meetings in the cities. A few also went to Buchenwald.

Mary's diary, 8th September:

> Hans Albrecht came to supper and the next day took me with him to see the Burgermeister. We were told that the Quakerhouse was to be used as emergency accommodation in case Hanover were to be targeted for heavy air raids. Hans also succeeded in negotiating the release of the Quaker bank accounts which had been frozen a year ago when Leonhard was taken away.
>
> Hans came again a few weeks later and the Quaker group discussed what use they would like to see made of the Quakerhouse after the war. Hans favoured building a coffee shop in the front garden and I suggested taking up the offer of the Jewish cemetery land, which the town had earlier made to us, for landscaping as a quiet restful park equipped with deckchairs and a refreshment pavilion. At this time we had a wedding in our group, Maria, daughter of Dr Otto Buchinger Senior was marrying Helmut Wilhelmi. The wedding was held at St Joseph's House, because we had no access to our Meeting House, and both Hans Albrecht and her father ministered, making it a deeply moving occasion.

Mary's diary, 8th October:

> I had a very 'churned-up' feeling, whilst waiting all day for the Gestapo to come to the Quakerhouse. The next day there was a heavy raid on Berlin, creating chaos on the railways. My visitors from Bremen did not manage to get through to Pyrmont.

Mary's diary, 10th October:

> At 1 am I was got out of bed by two young girls from the Hitler Youth at the Quakerhouse. They had brought a lady who had suffered in an air raid on Hanover. I found dear Marie Edert on my doorstep, a Quaker friend who often came from Hanover to help me with my sewing jobs. The girls said she was in shock paralysis, she was covered in dust from head to foot and her head and eyes were bandaged. I washed her and put her to bed, and she slept most of the next day. Our friends the Wiedings also had a bad time that night. There was another heavy raid on Hanover on 18th October and the Pyrmont air raid sirens sounded off on the 20th and 31st. Marie Edert was

understandably very frightened. On the 21st Kassel was bombed and watching the sky from our balcony I saw several planes shot down. My house guests were scared to death in the cellar.

Mary had heard that there was a possibility of release for concentration camp prisoners, providing the relatives obtained an appeal form endorsed by the Burgermeister. The opportunity occurred because Leonhard's age group for military service had been called-up this year. They were conscripting men between the ages of 50-54 and boys between 15-18 years. Some of the German non-Jewish men at Buchenwald were released for military service. Most ex-concentration camp volunteers were sent ahead of the front lines on the Eastern Front, without any training and few survived.[8] Mary did not of course know this and submitted the request for Leonhard, signed by Burgermeister Seebohm, and received an acknowledgement on 12th November, but fortunately nothing happened.

Reading of this incident half a century later has been difficult for me. How could Mary, a committed Quaker who was so determined about 'doing what is right', have requested Leonhard's release for military service? Had Drinkuth advised her to do so? Had she felt under pressure from someone? Mary may have felt she had to risk making this compromising attempt for Leonhard's sake. They had by now endured 11 years of Nazi rule.

Mary's diary, 16th November:

I complained to the police about three more broken windows at the Quakerhouse and handed in a school satchel which had been found among the bushes. In the evening there was another air raid warning, they now seem to be happening every day. I sorted out the seeds I had saved for planting next year and wondered what will happen before the spring? I am thankful for a few days without visitors to enjoy my home comforts, but I wish my Leonhard could be sharing them too. I have re-roasted some coffee beans his brother Bernhard sent us from America in 1939, and shall send it to Leonhard for Christmas.

On 28th November Emil Fuchs came to speak to the Pyrmont Quaker group and spent the next morning with Mary. This must have been a farewell visit just before he went into hiding with his grandson Klaus. Mary heard of the problems at the Ommen Quaker School in the Netherlands, which the Nazis closed a few days later.

Mary's diary, 11th December:

I had been unwell, but had to go out shopping and to see the solicitor. The roads were icy and I slipped and fell three times. I sat on a step and fainted. After I had recovered I went to the dairy to buy my rations. There I met Therese Herzog, who quite impulsively offered her week's cheese ration for Leonhard. This unexpected act of kindness brought tears to my eyes.

Many of us have experienced the sudden uncontrollable welling up of tears when someone unexpectedly shows understanding of a problem we have kept to ourselves. But Mary was bruised and ill for three days and no one realised. Eventually Dr Otto Buchinger Senior came to check up on her and sent one of his nurses to help her. She rested a few more days at home, until there was only stale bread and cabbage left to eat before she went shopping again.

For Christmas Day Mary had invited a friend and decided to cook all the trimmings she would have made had she been cooking a goose. There was sage-and-onion stuffing, roast potato, lentil patties, apple sauce, etc, but the principal dish was missing. Kati Lotz had invited her to Sunday lunch and when she got home she found Marie Edert from Hanover on the doorstep again. Kurt Richter came to spend New Year's Eve with her, bringing his own supper in a thermos. It was goose soup, which he did not share, but Mary said it smelled marvellous.

Mary's Health and Spirit

During 1943 Mary had experienced over 20 house searches and interviews with the Gestapo or with the Chief of Police on matters relating to the Quakerhouse and Leonhard. Like many people, Mary and Leonhard usually spent New Year's Eve reviewing the year which had passed and looking towards the future. This year, after Kurt Richter had left, Mary shared her thoughts with her diary and God. Although she was low in health and spirit, she was trying to pick herself up. She must have been very undernourished and anxious about her dealings with the Gestapo. Also under stress having so many visitors in her home, yearning for her child and very worried about Leonhard.

Her diary showed an itemised list of 64 parcels sent to Leonhard during the year. Mary, who had obviously been eating very little herself, wrote:

The Pyrmont Friends seldom contribute to Leonhard's parcels, except for Therese Herzog's cheese ration last week. I don't know how I would manage without the bread and the Sunday lunch I regularly get from the Buchingers. I send Leonhard all my meat ration, three-quarters of the fat ration, as well as occasional cheese and quark. The Quakers here say they cannot spare anything, but fortunately others do help us. Occasionally the tobacconist provides some tobacco for Leonhard's pipe. After the New Year I felt rested and enjoyed reading. I felt drawn into God's care, and hope I can share His love for me with our Quaker group more consistently next year. I seem to be recovering from the depression and feel strength from what I hear from Brenda. I know I used to be successful in my work in England and in Nuremberg, but I have failed miserably in Pyrmont, even with dear Cilli. Have I been too simple and direct among these dry intellectual people, who appear to have such small hearts?

I am thankful that many of my needs and hopes in life have been met, but I do need a little tenderness. I have to struggle against depression and the absurdities of my temperament, manner or words. I need to be more clear-sighted and to recognise that I fill my time with exhausting work as an escape from my anxieties. The love I am passionately eager to give, I am also eager to receive. When I pour out sympathy for the needs of others, I long also to have it offered to me. I give, because I understand the hunger of others, but I am often left to starve, entirely alone. I need a lover's tender touch, and to feel my grief is understood, and my inconsistencies forgiven. They do not accept me. Please help me God.

Then Mary read Mathew Chapter 11 verses 25-30, and felt that if she shared her yoke with Jesus, who was after all a carpenter and knew how to make a well-fitting yoke, her burdens would be lighter and there could be room for happiness. Mary was desperately trying to live up to the image she had of herself. Were her high expectations of a Christian and Quaker life creating unattainable goals for herself? She was missing Leonhard and his sense of humour which at other times helped her to achieve a better sense of proportion.

CHAPTER XVII

The Allied Invasion of Europe 1944

THERE WERE NOW MANY BOMBED-OUT city dwellers looking for accommodation in Pyrmont, and the housing department surveyed all residential property to find out who could provide a room for the homeless. Mary's flat was inspected in January 1944 and her two bedrooms were requisitioned. She decided to move Leonhard's bed into the sitting room along with her own in case he should come back. It felt very crowded, but she was grateful to be in her own home. On 11th January Mary wrote in her diary:

> Every day people come to view the accommodation. There was the choirmaster and his wife; the wife of the newspaper editor who would bring her own servant and would keep the whole flat clean; the policeman who demanded a room for his cleaning lady and her five-year-old child. I said I could not take a small child, out of consideration for 95-year-old Frau Knierim downstairs. In the end I shall have Herr Rohrman, aged 64 and his housekeeper, Frl. Weiss, aged 45, from Hanover. They will move in next month and will pay me 30 marks a month.

Mary received a 25 word Red Cross message from me in London, saying I had decided to complete my two-year Social Studies Diploma at Birmingham University that summer, rather than stay on for another year to get a degree, because it seemed difficult to justify studying in wartime. This message had reached Mary within six weeks, whereas others had taken six months or a year to arrive.

Mary's diary, 17th January:

> Drinkuth called me to his office after his return from Berlin, where he had visited the Gestapo HQ and had handed Hagenbruch my latest application for Leonhard. He said we could not hope for Leonhard's release until the end of the war. He is held for reasons of 'protective security', although he appears to have done nothing to have deserved such punishment. Hagenbruch had added that it would be folly for

the State to release any of the starving prisoners from the concentration camps, while public morale in Germany was so uncertain.

Mary's diary, 29th January:

We had to hurry home from Meeting: there were so many planes flying overhead to Frankfurt-am-Main. There were night-time raids on Braunschweig and Berlin. There has been no let up in the bombing of cities. I spend a lot of time on essential shopping. I can sometimes buy half a litre of buttermilk to make cottage cheese for Leonhard, but I have a 20 minute walk there and back, to fetch it. Today I stood in line for one-and-a-half hours to buy a pound of brussels sprouts. My feet are painful, especially at night. I keep a cold water compress beside my bed, ready to put on my feet or hands, whichever hurts most. A plaster cast of my feet has been taken in order to have orthopaedic shoes made by a man who lives in the nearby village of Hagen.

The well-loved Quaker writer and poet Alfons Paquet died on 29th January, aged 63, he had suffered a heart attack during the air raid on Frankfurt. Paquet's ashes were interred in the Pyrmont Quaker burial ground. For years he had written a column in the liberal *Frankfurter Zeitung*, until the paper was closed down by the Nazis.

Mary's diary, 8th February:

Kati Lotz [age 74] is in hospital, having fallen on an icy road and broken her leg and arm. Kurt Richter [the Friend who lived near Friedensthal] seems to be very unwell. He falls asleep and appears to remember very little. Is he taking too much bromide? I took him my month's ration of porridge oats. Emma Raeydt seems to be going blind.

Mary's diary, 22nd February:

There was a massive air raid on Leipzig today. From the balcony I saw an American plane shot down 30 seconds after it had passed our house, leaving a plume of black smoke in the sky.

In the early months of 1944 conditions deteriorated throughout continental Europe. The bombing of German factories, railways and cities and the losses on the Eastern Front created great suffering. In January the Inter-Governmental Committee for Refugees and Displaced Persons (IGCR) estimated that when the war ended, there would be 30 million displaced people in Europe. Our American Friend, Patrick Malin, the Vice-Director of the IGCR, wrote about this in *The Friend* on 14th January 1944, explaining that plans for coping with the anticipated refugee problems at the end of the war were being made, through the establishment of a new organisation, called the United Nations Relief and Rehabilitation Administration (UNRRA).[1]

Mary's diary, 6th March:

> Herr Rohrman and Frl. Weiss have moved in, complete with their coal, for which I have had to find space in the cellar. They seem to be kind and pleasant.

Mary continued to put up some of her own guests, and she occasionally had two or three people sleeping in her sitting room or in her very small attic. Sometimes there were 10 people sleeping in the flat, using the kitchen and bathroom. They cooked meals in three shifts and managed quite well without getting in each others way.

Mary's diary, Easter Sunday 9th April:

> The snow is melting and I went out for the first time. The Quakerhouse garden looks dreadfully untidy. I have met a friend who has a brother in Buchenwald. He wrote to her saying that Leonhard manages to tolerate conditions, but is very homesick.

Mary's neighbour, Frau Kuhl, who lived on the top floor, said she had seen some boxes of books being taken out of the Quakerhouse. Enquiries revealed they had been taken to the papermill. Mary then told Dr Otto Buchinger, whose book stock was held with Leonhard's. Otto and Mary went to the Burgermeister, who advised them to keep quiet about it and so did Drinkuth, her solicitor. Drinkuth had met a Gestapo official in Hanover, who informed him that the Quakerhouse was going to be used as a police training centre. Mary was appalled that a Quaker Meeting House was to be used for such a purpose. Drinkuth suggested that if Hans Albrecht protested quickly, he might be able to get the use changed, which indeed happened. A young women's training group, bombed-out from Hanover, came instead.

Mary's diary, 24th April:

> Hans Albrecht came and we inspected the Quakerhouse with Wenger and Drinkuth. The place was in a dreadful condition. I was glad that Hans stayed to have supper with me afterwards.
>
> We had the most frightening night air raid. A plane was shot down over Luegde and a bomb dropped on Loewensen. Both are about three miles away in different directions, but it felt as though something was falling on our roof.

Mary's doctor prescribed a series of the renowned Pyrmont mudbaths for her arthritis. Friends who knew how difficult it was for her to queue would sometimes do her shopping or post the food parcels for Leonhard. However, after she had her new orthopaedic shoes she was more easily able to look after herself and tidy up the Quakerhouse garden.

Sister Wendolini, a nun at Georgs Villa next door, planted a vegetable garden for her at the Quakerhouse. Mary was delighted to have three rows of runner beans, two rows of tomatoes and some strawberries. She had also made friends with Daniel Drinkuth, the forester, who owned the Sennhuette restaurant and farm in the woods on the top of the Bomberg. He brought her manure for the new vegetable garden.

The long-awaited Allied landing in Normandy began on 6th June, although Mary wrote in her diary: 'It does not seem to be a very strong invasion force . . . Churchill has said it is to be known as 'D' Day'.

Mary replied to a letter from Margarethe Lachmund on 8th June:

Many thanks for your letter and for the bacon fat and biscuits for Leonhard, which I have already sent on to him. I did try to save the packing materials to return as you asked, but I'm afraid they were too tattered. I also have difficulties in finding cartons for Leonhard's parcels. Sometimes I take my cart to the pharmacy and climb two ladders into their attic, where for years they have thrown their old paper. It is very dirty, but I am thankful for it. I received your last butter coupons four weeks ago. Leonhard likes me to send as much bread as I can manage, because he shares what he can spare with others.

I do not think there is anything else that Quakers can do to help Leonhard now. I don't for a moment think I could get permission to visit him. You will have read the regulations which I sent you. It would of course be wonderful if Hans could visit him. If I were allowed to visit him, I would of course go. But any visit would be so short and we would both feel frustrated by the things we could not talk about. My visits to Leonhard in Hanover were a terrible ordeal for us both, deeply upsetting and degrading.

When Leonhard heard that his library and the books he had published had been carted off for pulping, he sent me a card saying: 'My mind dwells constantly on these and other matters. Since everything has been destroyed, I have no alternative but to start all over again'.[2]

Margarethe's husband Hans, had for many years been a High Court Judge. When the Nazis first came to power in 1933, he was removed from this position because he was not a party member. However, he was quickly re-instated by a Nazi colleague who admired his ability. Hans remained in the post until he was arrested by the Russians in 1945, and held in various Soviet prisons until 1953.

London Survives Doodlebugs

Mary heard about the V1 pilotless bombs which began falling on London a few days after the Normandy landings. People around her were very excited and believed Germany would soon be victorious.

By the end of June I had completed the Social Studies course at Birmingham University, whilst living at Woodbrooke, the Quaker College. Aged 20, I was now back in East London with the Friends Ambulance Unit in the medical students hostel of the London Hospital in Philpott Street. My work was assisting people who came to the Toynbee Hall Citizens Advice Bureau. Most of our clients were the bomb-shocked stallholders from Petticoat Lane street market, who needed help in completing their applications for war-damage claims. Many of them had come to the East End from Poland after the 1901 pogrom against the Jews. The older family members had got by without ever learning to read and write in English, although they were astute market traders. Being part of Toynbee Hall, a multi-project Settlement House under J. J. Mallon's wardenship, left a marked influence on my life.

During the summer of 1944, when the V1s were first launched, some 50 rockets came over every day from northern France. Half of them were intercepted by the RAF fighter planes and anti-aircraft fire before they could reach London. A few were caught in the cables of the barrage balloons anchored above the city to discourage low-flying enemy aircraft.

Like many young people without family responsibilities I rarely interrupted my work to go into an air raid shelter when the sirens went. But, when I was in the street and heard a Doodlebug overhead I became alert, noting the position of the nearest shelter or cover. The dangerous moment came when the mechanical buzzing noise suddenly stopped above me. The silence would then be followed by an explosion. On one such occasion, while walking along Whitechapel Road from the hostel to Aldgate East, my only shelter was in a doorway. I saw the bomb drop on St Mary's Church 100 yards ahead of me. I was very shaken by the death of a costermonger and his horse who were blown to pieces beside a lamp-post in front of me. The church was never rebuilt, but is now landscaped as a small park.

Some weeks after this incident the Luftwaffe sent soundless V2 rockets to London. The stealthy approach of these high explosive weapons was very frightening. Anyone who could get out of London did so. But those who stayed displayed great stamina and neighbourliness.

Attempt on Hitler's Life, 20th July

Plots to secure Hitler's downfall gathered momentum. Klaus von Stauffenberg, a young army staff officer, joined the von Moltke opposition group. On 20th July there was an opportunity to catch Himmler and Goering in the same room with Hitler at the *Wolf-Schanze*. Stauffenberg carried a briefcase containing a time bomb into the meeting and placed it close to Hitler. He then left the room to phone a co-conspirator to activate other parts of the plan for the take-over of key installations in Berlin. But after he had gone, someone moved the briefcase underneath a heavy table, thus reducing the effects of the explosion. Stauffenberg was on his way to Berlin when the explosion occurred, killing several people, but Hitler did not appear to be seriously hurt and even kept an interview with Mussolini that afternoon. The Stauffenberg coup plans might still have had some success, had it not been a hot day when many of the activists were away from their telephones, relaxing outdoors. Attempts to take control of Berlin failed. The conspirators were easily rounded up, Stauffenberg and three others were shot in the courtyard of a building which is now the Stauffenberg Museum of Resistance. This collection also holds records of the German Quakers, including Leonhard Friedrich. This has embarrassed a few German Quakers, who feel their non-violent resistance should not be linked with the 20th July plot.

The opposition to the Nazi regime arose from very many different groups in Germany, and might have been more successful had the coup leaders not been drawn almost entirely from the upper classes in the army, the Church and universities. Their resistance would have benefitted by having a more practical input from workers and technicians.

Normandy Invasion on 6th June – D-Day

The Allied invasion of Europe forced Hitler to deploy military resources to the Western Front, whilst also trying to hold the Russians in the East and stemming the Allied advance in Italy.

Paris was liberated by the American General Patton on 26th August. With De Gaulle beside him on the viewing stand, he presided over the Allied triumphal march through the city. The Friends Ambulance Unit attached to the Hadfield Spears Mobile Hospital also took part in the procession. Four days later, the British liberated Brussels, Louvain and Antwerp. By the 17th September it was reported in *The Friend* that Roger Wilson and Edith Pye, from London, were in Paris to contact French Quakers and enquire about relief needs.

On 11th September an American patrol crossed on to German soil. The Allies had expected to reach Aachen and the Ruhr and to cross the Rhine before winter, but the Wehrmacht managed to hold their lines. On 17th September Allied forces landed by parachute in the Netherlands taking Nijmegen, Eindhoven and Arnhem after heavy losses.

In Pyrmont

Mary's diary, 2nd July:

Leo Schulze, a friend of Pastor Mensching in Bueckeberg, came to see me. His brother, wife and two children had been taken to different concentration camps. He wanted to know if I could think of any way of helping them.

On 13th July Mary discovered more vandalism at the Quakerhouse, which she reported to the Police. Minnie Tangerman's new grave had been disturbed and the manure provided by the forester for the vegetable garden, had been thrown against the cemetery wall onto the plaques bearing names of deceased Friends. There were also 10 broken window panes and water was leaking into the library.

On 3rd August Mary heard that Edith Alexander in Hamelin had been advised by the Swedish and Swiss Consulates to prepare herself for repatriation as a British civilian. Mary realised this would also apply to Alfred Woore and Dorothy Henkel, but not to her, because she had lost her British nationality in marrying a German. Mary went to Hamelin to say goodbye to Edith and gave her the gold watch which she had bought for my 18th birthday, to bring to England. Edith's departure was delayed because her leg was broken during an air raid. When she had sufficiently recovered she moved to an internment camp at Wuertenberg and was repatriated from there. I did eventually receive the lovely watch some months before the end of the war.

During the summer, Mary was preserving her harvest of fruit, runner beans and other vegetables. She hoped to have food in the house for Leonhard, whom she was convinced would soon be returning. She had at last made an arrangement with a young couple who would work the Pum-Birn garden for her and share the garden produce.

In a letter to Margarethe Lachmund on 9th August, Mary wrote:

The Quakerhouse garden is in good order again, after the spate of vandalism. For the past two weeks I have sweated over spreading sieved compost on the vegetable beds. There is more to do before the winter, because the soil needs nourishment. I should never have been able to do all this work, if I did not love the place so much. When I am in the garden, I feel I am on sanctified ground, an island fenced around with Truth and Love and things that endure. But this fence is not always secure. Most of the good crop of raspberries and strawberries were stolen and the currant bushes have been trampled down. One afternoon 10 windows in the Quakerhouse were smashed and the roofing felt was torn from our new hut. I have much unpleasantness to put up with. The Hitler Youth have now been forbidden to enter the grounds, but of course they do come in when I am not there to chase them off. However, these are passing problems, which I don't make much of.[2]

Mary's diary, 24th August:

A US airplane came down at Hagen, setting fire to a house. Another plane was brought down on the Bomberg and three American airmen landed by parachute near the Allee. One of the men hid behind the Bomberg restaurant.

Albert Graf (1888-1956)

Albert Graf, a member of the Pyrmont Meeting, was called up for military service on 12th July, although he only had the use of one lung and had been in hospital for some weeks during the previous winter. He collapsed after his first route march and was sent home. On 24th August he was arrested and taken to Buchenwald.

Albert and his wife Gertrud, who were both 56 years old at this time, had retired to Pyrmont when Albert had lost his job as a secondary school teacher in 1935. Gertrud was a loving practical person, quite tireless in catering for countless Quaker gatherings. In the post-war years she organised welfare and social activity for displaced persons from East Pommern, who were settled in Pyrmont. Albert had been a quiet and dependable person, who enjoyed stamp collecting.

Albert Graf was denounced because he had been active in the peace movement. He was taken to Buchenwald on 24th August 1944, where he suffered greatly. The top bunk which he occupied was next to a window not far from the gallows, through which he witnessed many cruel, lingering hangings. He may also have been tortured. On his return home on 17th September 1944, it was evident that he had suffered intensely. He was no longer capable of formulating coherent sentences and frequently woke up screaming in the night. Gertrud nursed him lovingly until he died. [*Lebensbilder Deutscher Quaker*][3]

It is surprising that he was released, and a blessing that Gertrud and Albert could be together again, though his suffering continued. Leonhard had not known that Albert was in Buchenwald.

Mary's diary, 26th August:

Almuth Niemann came again and left her mother Kathe, to stay with me for a month. The old lady was bombed out of her home in Bremen and was ill and shaken. I gave up my bed for her, and had endless washing to do as she was incontinent. But Kathe was extremely grateful for my care.

Mary's diary, 11th September:

The war news is very exciting. The Allies are now on all the German borders. We had six air raid alarms today. There is bedlam in our flat, as my lodgers are very tense and anxious about the war news and quarrel with each other. I worry about Leonhard. There was a raid on Buchenwald on the 7th September in which two SS men were reported killed. It is two years since I last saw Leonhard. I have just sent him the 105th parcel. I also sent one for Manfred Pollatz, who has been in Dachau for some time.

Manfred Pollatz (1886-1964)

After the German occupation of the Netherlands in 1941, the Jewish children had to go into hiding and the Pollatzs experienced many difficulties in protecting the non-Aryan children they cared for. Manfred was imprisoned in June 1943 and eventually transferred to Dachau. Although they lived in the Netherlands, Manfred's son, Karl-Heinz, was called up for the Wehrmacht because he was a German citizen. As a Quaker he tried at first to register for non-combatant service, he suffered lengthy interrogations and was threatened. Eventually he agreed to serve, with the assurance that the safety of his family and their foster children would be respected. He was allowed to complete his medical studies at Muenster University and could go home during the vacations. When qualified as a doctor, he served in a military hospital in Haarlem. He was then posted for a few weeks to the office of the notorious SS leader Heinrich Heydrich in Berlin. While there he negotiated the release of his father from Dachau on 13th September 1944. One does not know what Karl-Heinz went through in order to obtain this. Sadly Karl-Heinz was then posted to the Eastern Front and died before the end of the year.[4]

Mary's diary, 7th October:

> An incendiary bomb was dropped on the Bomberg. We watched three planes coming down in a dog fight over Pyrmont. A train at nearby Steinheim was bombed whilst in the station. The driver was killed and many were injured. Our gas and electricity supply are frequently cut, so none of us in the flat can cook and we have to sit by candlelight in the evenings. Occasionally I am invited to eat with the nuns at Georg's Villa which is a wonderful treat.

Mary's diary, 10th October:

> The use of the Quakerhouse has been changed again. It is now to be an extension to a civilian hospital. Police Chief Wenger has been in the building and agreed to our removing all the Quaker equipment not needed for the present purposes to the attic. I have been given the key to the attic and the care of the items. Wenger seemed a bit more friendly today. At the end of his visit, he told me he had at last found the Willfuehr Lueneburg inheritance certificate in the Lohrmecken file!

We do not know what benefit Wenger expected from his lengthy and diligent search for these documents, but Marie Willfuehr's brother Gustav, eventually got possession of the property. Willfuehr was described as 'OberRegierungsrat and Obermedizinalrat', a high-ranking official in the local government and the medical services. He died in 1948, and his wife then inherited the property.

The following news item was published in *The Friend*, dated 29th September 1944:

Hans, son of Dr Otto Buchinger Senior, who is now teaching at the Quaker college of Earlham, in Richmond, Indiana, visited his brother Ott who is a POW in a wire enclosure at Alvo, Oklahoma. They were allowed five hours together. Ott had been taken prisoner in North Africa, where he had served as a doctor in Rommel's army.

Dr Ott Buchinger jnr. recently told me that conditions in the POW camp were very primitive and that the food was so bad that he decided it would be safer to fast for some weeks. He kept well and served his fellow prisoners as a doctor in the camp.

Mary's diary, 19th November:

On Sunday we held our Meeting for Worship again, with 18 Friends present. We read a very inspiring letter from Carl and Eva Hermann. Dr Otto Buchinger Snr. suggested we make use of the dark evenings without electricity for prayer and meditation and to talk with each other about our beliefs.

Drinkuths of the Sennhuette

At the end of November Mary had not been able to buy milk for a month, so she walked up the Bomberg to visit the Drinkuths and was given three glasses of milk to drink and another litre to take home. Ott Buchinger jnr. recently told me that this couple with whom Mary had made friends were Daniel and Aenne Drinkuth, cousins of Drinkuth the solicitor. It was Daniel who taught Mary about the edible fungi which could be found in the forest. Aenne was a Swiss farmer's daughter and named their inn Sennhuette, meaning Alpine pasture. A few cows and horses are still kept on the high meadows near the inn. Daniel disapproved of the Nazis and was glad to help Leonhard and Mary. Ott remembers visiting Uncle Daniel with his wife, Marlies, when he was on sick leave at home. Ott was wearing his uniform, which provoked Uncle Daniel into saying: 'If only I could get near that Adolf Hitler I would shoot him through the head!' Both of Daniel's young sons were called up just before the war ended in 1945 and died on the Eastern front.

In December Mary reported:

She was preparing Leonhard's Christmas food parcel, and re-heating the biscuits she had kept since 1941. She was sure they tasted much better than anything she could make from the ingredients that were available in 1944. The post office would not accept the parcel, because RAF bombing was creating chaos on the railways. If however, she re-packed it in five smaller containers, there was a chance of them getting through.

Mary's diary, 28th December:

I am in financial difficulties, my monthly allowance from the Berlin Quaker office has not come through. I have made one pork chop last me for four days.

For Christmas I invited Helene Engel-Reimers. We had spaghetti and tomatoes, followed by my bottled strawberries and quark. Engel stayed with me until quite late and we both enjoyed it. I slept better than I have done for weeks. We both lead isolated lives. Engel confides in no-one. I believe we live in families to share joy and sorrow. If we separate ourselves from others, we cannot fulfil our destiny. 'Love so amazing, so Divine, demands my soul, my life, my all.'

After Christmas I went shopping, but came home with nothing. I am getting very short of food. The Kuhls kindly invited me upstairs for New Year's Eve. I was not at all sorry when there was a power cut preventing us from hearing Hitler's speech on the radio.

Mary always felt Christmas should be a time of festivity. It marked another year of loneliness for her, though she seems to have been less depressed this year, because the tide of war was slowly turning. I believe she also gained strength from the understanding and encouragement she felt from a frequent correspondence with Margarethe Lachmund, in Berlin.

CHAPTER XVIII

The Final Year in Buchenwald 1944-5

Prisoners from 42 Nations

As THE WAR CONTINUED, the armaments factories manned by prisoners from the concentration camps became strategic to the German war effort. The Buchenwald industrial site now extended over six miles from the living quarters, requiring a direct rail link to Weimar. Prisoners were contracted to work in over a hundred armaments factories all over Germany. The worst conditions occurred in some of the subsidiary camps where factories and living quarters were built underground, to avoid the Allied bombing. One of these was DORA near Nordhausen, where the overcrowded living conditions led to 50 deaths a day.[1]

In Buchenwald prisoners were generally housed according to their nationality. More POWs came to the camp during 1944. There were separate Blocks for the French, Norwegian, British and Canadian airmen. POWs were exempted from labour by the Geneva Convention. But those from Eastern Europe such as the Ukraine were not protected because their countries had not ratified the Geneva POW convention.

Health

The increased industrial use of water and the escalating numbers of prisoners created water shortages at Buchenwald, which affected washing and toilet facilities. The prison doctors, many of whom were Jews or non-Aryans, organised twice-weekly medical inspections for the residential Blocks. Cleanliness was essential and there were stringent de-lousing measures for prisoners coming from Eastern Europe, where flea-born typhus was prevalent. The Buchenwald medical research teams had produced protective vaccines against typhoid and typhus for the German army, at the expense of countless prisoners who died while being used as human guinea-pigs. Eventually some prisoners valued as workers were also inoculated against typhus and dysentery, but thousands of men fell ill and died. Prisoners were chary of reporting sick at Medical Block No 16 where they risked being used in medical experiments. Some, however, were cared for in the sick bay and allowed to rest. Leonhard was thankful that he managed to avoid ever going near the place.

Eugen Kogon, author of *The Theory and Practice of Hell*, became chief orderly in the Medical Block during the final year. He was sometimes able to rescue healthy prisoners from the death list by substituting their name and number for someone who had just died. As the war was drawing to a close, he developed a special relationship with the doctor in charge, SS Major Doctor Ding-Schuler, which enabled him to ask for exceptional treatment for the camp resistance leaders. Ding-Schuler had for years needed to hide his lack of medical qualifications from the Nazis. An Allied victory was now expected and he feared for his life. This made him willing to co-operate with Kogon, hoping that Kogon would help him when the Allies took over. Ding-Schuler's personal friendship with Himmler sometimes enabled him to provide Kogon with access to useful information.[2]

Food shortages

The Buchenwald catering departments never received all the supplies to which they were entitled because the stores were pilfered by the Gestapo and then by the Kapos and others before they ever reached the kitchens. The Gestapo helped themselves to food for their horses, pets, poultry and rabbits. After the first three months in Buchenwald, most prisoners lost 50 lbs in weight. Meat was horseflesh, suspended as small fragments in a watery soup. Vegetables, which were frequently rotten, were mainly turnips, carrots and potatoes.

In the autumn of 1943 a prisoners' canteen was opened and 'money', printed on card, was introduced. Prisoners could officially receive up to 30 marks a month from their families. Mary sent Leonhard small amounts occasionally, and there were some jobs in the camp for which payments were made.

The SS personnel needed money for their luxurious life-style and devised ways of supplementing their salaries at the prisoners' expense. They demanded 'voluntary contributions' for the repair of equipment or for phoney charities. They also sold 'Viking salad' at exorbitant prices in the canteen. This salad, although filling, consisted largely of potatoes and ground fish bones. In 1944, due to Gestapo staff shortages, the canteen was turned over to the prisoners to manage and the quality of the food improved. Occasionally the prisoner canteen managers were able to obtain better supplies and served good soups, which were offered to different work teams in turn, regardless of their ability to pay.

Leonhard's survival was in part due to the food parcels Mary sent, which he generally ate in the privacy of the tool store at his work place in Gustloff II. He also had a stove there, on which he could heat water. Each parcel Mary sent contained bread, curd cheese and sausage bought from her meat ration. All the parcels were opened in front of a Gestapo official, who might pick out items such as tobacco for himself. About a third of the non-Jewish German prisoners and most of the POWs occasionally received parcels after 1941.

From 1944 onwards food was in very short supply all over Europe, particularly in the concentration camps. The POWs received monthly Red Cross parcels from Switzerland. It was not so easy for the Gestapo to help themselves to these standard packages. The POWs generously shared food with their friends. Each parcel was personally addressed and contained an acknowledgement card which the recipient had to return to the International Red Cross. This sometimes gave an opportunity to add a new name to the Red Cross lists.

Letters

German prisoners and their families were in theory permitted to exchange letters twice a month, although this was seldom achieved. In Buchenwald it was difficult to find paper and pen for writing and I still have one of Leonhard's letters written on the back of an envelope Mary sent. He received most of her letters enclosed in the food parcels.

On 4th February 1945 Leonhard wrote to Mary:

I would dearly like to write more often, but I send you a sign of life whenever possible. Our separation has been long, but I believe we shall soon be together again. Do not worry if you can no longer send parcels. I will manage, my health is not bad. It was a great comfort to hear news from you about Brenda.[3]

Mary replied on 12th February:

I was so pleased to receive your letter of 4th February, and am very glad you received some of the food packages I sent recently. I see now that the parcels take a long time to reach you and much of the food must have gone bad. I was sorry not to have been able to send anything last week. I am only getting two pounds of bread a week now, and cannot spare much. It will be lovely to have you home again, then I will never have to send another food parcel! Brenda has written to say how anxious she is about you, now I can reassure her. I have many worries about my house guests which now include a four-month-old baby. The days are too short to do all the things which need doing. With so much love, Mary.[3]

Sundays at Buchenwald

Sundays were supposed to be rest days, when the block leaders organised dormitory clean-ups and every prisoner had to tidy up his own things. Some found time for reading. Most blocks organised a bookshelf to exchange the reading material sent from home. They even had a few copies of the Nazi newspaper *Voelkischer Beobachter* available. Towards the end, a great deal of political discussion took place among some small groups of people. Some of the men who worked outside the camp in construction offices picked up foreign radio broadcasts and passed the news around. The only pleasure on Sunday was in taking a brief rest and chatting with friends and strolling around the bare and muddy enclosure. Leonhard particularly valued this respite from work. There were also a few people he enjoyed playing cards with and one of them, used a pack of cards to tell fortunes. Among the greatest hardships Leonhard felt was the utter lack of privacy, there was nowhere one could be alone. It was difficult to live among so many people, some of whom were always in a state of high tension ready to blow up, even in response to good-natured teasing. Others became very hard and insensitive. Men vied against each other to achieve privilege, by oppressing the weaker men.

In the article 'Guest of Adolf Hitler' Leonhard wrote:

> I have heard that in POW camps, a sustaining camaraderie developed among the prisoners. This could not happen in the concentration camps where we lived among stool pigeons and criminals. We could hardly trust anyone as a friend, but those with certain political affinities supported each other. If an SS guard noticed friendships developing, they separated the men. However, one or two people met with me for religious dialogue, but it was impossible to undertake any kind of religious service, which might have helped the Christians among us. I must praise the Jehovah's Witnesses who, in spite of ridicule and persecution, held firm to their beliefs in the most remarkable way. I really do believe the low morality of the life we experienced, has come about because we have individually neglected our inner life, so that our religious strength has withered. We will always find that men and women who confess their belief in God without hesitation are given strength, even in these dreadful circumstances to struggle for a better future.[3]

The people who seemed best able to survive the degradation of prison life were the selfless individuals who lightened the load for everyone around them. But these people were seldom selected by the prisoners as leaders, because they would probably have found it impossible to make the very tough decisions that the prisoners leadership group had to take.

Jews in Buchenwald

The Jews undoubtedly received the worst treatment in Buchenwald. At the time of Leonhard's arrival in October 1942 they were already being transferred from Buchenwald to the death camps in Poland. However some 200 Jews with special skills, such as doctors, lawyers and scientists, were saved from transfer by the political prisoners in the Labour Allocation Office, who listed them as bricklayers needed for the expansion of the camp. In late 1944 labour was so short that more able-bodied Jews survived as labourers. But they lived isolated in Little Camp and were abominably treated. During 1944-5 over 6,000 young Hungarian Jews came to Buchenwald, along with a similar number of Polish Jews, to work on heavy outdoor construction work.

Prisoners Resistance to the SS

During the winter of 1943-4, plots against the Nazi regime began to emerge throughout Germany, and resistance groups also developed in Buchenwald. Early in 1944 a group of Danish police officers were brought to Buchenwald as prisoners and managed to raise the standard of morale. French prisoners also retained a sense of group loyalty and some played important roles in the prisoners resistance group. Late in 1944 a group of 167 British RAF parachutists arrived, with an outstanding airman, Yeo Thomas. He later wrote about an Allied air attack on the Gustloff II factory on 24th August 1944. Incendiary bombs damaged part of the Gustloff II factory and others dropped on the adjoining accommodation Block 17. Four hundred prisoners died and many more were injured. Mary recorded her anxiety about this air raid in her diary. The Allies were also bombing other armament factories in the concentration camps of Dachau, Sachsenhausen and Auschwitz.

The Buchenwald Labour Allocation Office was increasingly staffed by political prisoners, who in 1944 were given the unenviable responsibility to select prisoners for transfer to the 136 other work sites. They knew of individuals who had special skills which might be needed by the resistance and should be saved from transfer, also of those who were in danger or showed some special leadership quality which the other prisoners valued. However, if the Gestapo suspected that one of these leaders was being protected, nothing could be done to save him. Towards the end of 1944 many more prisoners arrived at Buchenwald from concentration camps situated in the path of the advancing Allied armies, both from the Rhine valley and the Eastern Front. Food supplies became very short.

The Allied advance created great anxiety and speculation among prisoners about how their liberation would be achieved. They were worried that Himmler would make a last-minute decision to gas or bomb the camp. A few prisoners felt safer after they had stolen weapons from the factories they worked in, these were buried or bricked up in the camp. Some of the prisoners noticed that the Gestapo were becoming anxious about their own security, both in the camp and in facing the advancing Allied armies. The risks to the lives of the prisoners in the last days before liberation were very real. However, many hoped that the Gestapo would be too preoccupied with their own problems to carry out instructions from Himmler to kill them.

By the end of March 1945 the Allied advances convinced most prisoners that the end of the war was in sight. Those who knew where the hidden weapons were, debated the right moment for staging an uprising, but this was complicated because the resistance was organised in two separate groups: one under the Communists and the other under a British POW, Captain Burney.

Leonhard Described the Last Months:

> In Buchenwald conditions deteriorated markedly, as so many additional prisoners arrived during the winter of 1944-5, when the huge camps in Eastern Europe were cleared. During November, December and January they arrived by rail, travelling in open coal wagons in which people had endured journeys lasting from six to fourteen weeks. I cannot describe the suffering and misery I have seen. Food was absolutely minimal, warm clothing was non-existent and there were no sanitary facilities. In spite of the health precautions taken on arrival at Buchenwald, there was no way of isolating the sick prisoners who suffered from typhus and other diseases in the overcrowded camp, the death rate soared.

> In spite of all these torments there was no let up in the roll-call procedures. We often had to stand there for hours, sometimes five hours, until the numbers were correct. If anyone was missing, it had to be established who it was and we remained standing until he was found. These roll-calls took place in bitter winds, rain and snow, and cost many lives. I will not burden you with all the dreadful things that happened during these last weeks of roll-calls.

Most of the prisoners who had recently arrived from the Eastern camps were sent on to other camps at the end of March, but many had to walk because the railways were no longer functioning. Those who could not walk any further, or stepped aside to rest, were shot. The corpses were left in the ditches. By these means the population at Buchenwald, which had risen to 47,000 in March, had been reduced to 21,000 a few weeks later when the American army arrived on 12th April.

For several days we had heard the thunder of battle from the Erfurt direction. Himmler's orders to Brigade Commander Tirlewanger were that all the prisoners should be gassed, after which the camp was to be blown up. Fortunately we were saved by the Americans who arrived in Weimar sooner than expected. The so-called American 'enemy' arrived in time to liberate us.

Among Leonhard's papers I found a crumbling news sheet dated 16th April 1945, in which the Camp Management listed departure arrangements for Czechs, Norwegians and Russians. There was also a report of a meeting held by the former prisoners, resolving to assist the Allies to eradicate Nazism.

Eugen Kogon's account of the last days at Buchenwald provides graphic details. The Jews were summoned to the parade ground on the 4th April, to hear about a mysterious arrangement being negotiated for 'a special shipment abroad', in which Himmler was said to be doing a 'deal' in exchange for the lives of Jews. This seemed implausible to those hearing the announcement. At the time appointed for the roll-call, none of the Jews turned up. Nothing like this had ever happened before and the SS no longer dared to enforce their orders. Before the next roll-call was due, fellow prisoners spontaneously provided the Jews with opportunities to hide themselves among other groups. Prisoners names, insignia and block numbers were changed, and those men who were sufficiently agile simply disappeared into other groups. This could only happen now because the camp personnel records were getting out of hand. But the next morning 1,500 Jews remained unhidden, and were deported along with other prisoners who had arrived the previous day from Ohrdorf, a camp in Hungary.[2]

The Final Days

On 5th April news leaked out to Eugen Kogon through Dr Ding-Schuler in the Medical Block that the Weimar Gestapo had orders to shoot 46 leading men of the Prisoners' Resistance group, to coincide with the departure on foot of all the remaining prisoners. The Prisoners' Resistance group debated whether this should be the signal for the anticipated uprising, but decided that the chances of overcoming the SS were still minimal. It therefore seemed essential for one of the prisoners to escape and to communicate with the American army, now on the outskirts of Weimar. Eugen Kogon was selected for this mission, with the co-operation of Dr Ding-Schuler, who was terrified at what the Americans might do to him. Kogon, dressed in a Luftwaffe uniform, was hidden in a box being sent to Ding-Schuler's home in Weimar. As soon as the van had cleared the camp, Kogon climbed out and crossed the German lines to warn the Americans of the SS plan to destroy Buchenwald.

Two days later on 7th April, 200 SS guards armed with machine-guns came into the camp to enforce the departure of 14,000 men being sent to Dachau and Flossenburg. Forty railway goods wagons were packed with a hundred men in each wagon, which were shunted over the war-damaged railways for many days. When the group destined for Flossenburg camp reached the village of Passau, they were cared for by a church charity who found only 700 men had survived asphyxiation on this dreadful journey. On 8th April there was a long air raid alarm, during which all the remaining prisoners at Buchenwald were assembled on the parade ground for evacuation. But no further transports were organised.

On the 11th April 21,000 frightened prisoners remaining at Buchenwald were within earshot of machine-gun and artillery fire from the withdrawing Wehrmacht forces. Low-flying German aircraft could destroy the camp at any moment, especially during a roll-call. At 10.30 am, Pister the SS officer in charge, announced that the camp would be surrendered to the Americans, leaving Captain Burney, and two others of the prisoners' resistance group in charge. The prisoners did not know whether to believe him, until at midday the public address system called on all SS officers to march out of the camp in formation with their horses and to report to their duty posts outside the camp enclosure. Only the watch tower guards remained in place. By mid-afternoon, the sounds of battle drew nearer. Armed members of the Prisoners' Resistance came out of hiding, cut the wire fences and took over the high guard towers, festooning them with white sheets. The next day, 12th April, the American army arrived to find the Prisoners' Resistance group, now known as the Leadership group, had already taken charge of the camp. A few of the men with guns displayed undisciplined trigger happiness for a brief period, but all were persuaded to hand over their weapons. The prisoners voluntarily assembled in their roll-call positions, singing poignant Buchenwald songs which Leonhard often hummed in later years. There was tremendous jubilation.[5]

BUCHENWALD SONG

When daylight breaks
Before the sun wakes
The columns must march
To their backbreaking work
Into the grey of the morning.
And the trees are black
And the sky is red
And in our sack
Is a small piece of bread
In our hearts, in our hearts pain is dawning.

refrain:

Oh Buchenwald, not even kind forgetfulness
Denies that you remain my destiny,
Whoever passed through here, can only then assess
How wonderful our freedom has to be.
Oh Buchenwald, we do not moan and wail
However harsh our fate may be,
We still say firmly 'yes' to life,
For finally the day will come when we are free.

And the stones are hard
But our step is firm
And we carry our picks
And our spades,
And in my heart, in my heart there is love.
And my blood is hot
And my girl far from here
And the wind blows soft
And I hold her so dear
May she stay true to me, true to me.

refrain:

And the night is short
And the day so long
And a tune is heard
That at home was our song
We shall not let them steal our courage!
Keep in step friend of mine

March on and be brave
All that is in us is striving to live
In our hearts, in our hearts there is faith!

refrain:

This was written by a Jewish prisoner
Translation by Ruth Finch, whose father died
in Buchenwald 1938.

Arrival of the American Liberators, 12th April 1945

The liberation was described by Pierre d'Harcourt:

When the battle-worn American troops arrived in their tanks looking weary and unshaven and smoking . . . We noticed that they quailed when they saw us. We must have been a terrible sight. We were skeletally thin, dressed in ragged striped pyjama suits, with shaven heads and spoke in 30 different languages. They stared at us, and seemed fearful and suspicious . . . We may well have appeared demented, in our overwhelming joy to see them . . . It took some time before they understood about prisoners involvement in managing the camp. They made the mistake of giving the store keys to some of the criminals, who made off with the scarce supplies.[6]

The Prisoners' Leadership Group did a magnificent job in maintaining discipline during the hand-over to the Americans. They formed a management committee representing all nationalities in the camp and established relations with the 3rd US Army. At the end the camp held 5,000 Frenchmen, 3,500 Poles and Jews, 2,200 Germans, 2,000 Russians, 2,000 Czechs, 2,000 Ukrainians, 600 Yugoslavs, 400 Dutch and 3,400 others, including the British.

The Americans brought food, doctors, nurses and all kinds of help, but most important kindness. Captain Burney writes of his personal experience:

Above all I was stunned and blinded by my sudden entry into a daylight of kindness . . . I became light-headed and talkative as the protective tension which I had acquired, slowly left me. I was at ease, among men who were completely at ease with me.[7] (Illustration 31)

Freedom

How did the former prisoners react to their freedom? Some, naturally, rushed through the prison gates to escape from the place where they had suffered. But they soon encountered difficulties. The battle was still

XVIII THE FINAL YEAR IN BUCHENWALD 1944-5 205

31. *American guns drawn up outside the Buchenwald Gatehouse showing American flag after liberation.*

32. *Leonhard's friend Salomyxin, who 'read the cards', wearing Buchenwald uniform.*

raging around Weimar. They had no money and could only leave on their own two feet. Leonhard and a friend ventured a few steps through the gates to see the camp surroundings. No one shouted orders at them, and they saw the bright green leaves unfolding on the beech trees. A new feeling of goodwill and camaraderie emerged among men who had previously trusted no-one. They told bitter jokes which helped them come to terms with the life they had endured. Leonhard wrote:

> Everyone seemed to breathe again. We were no longer prisoners, and began to regain the characteristics of human beings. Sadly, many died in the early weeks of freedom. Some were sick and many were too feeble to recover. Others became ill and some died as a result of suddenly eating too much, now that food was plentiful, and the SS stores had been supplied to the camp kitchens.[4]

Leonhard and his friends were excited at the prospect of being able to go home, but had no idea when this would be possible. They had no contact with their homes, there were no functioning postal services and telephone lines everywhere were broken. Whilst Leonhard felt hopeful that Mary would still be in their flat in Bad Pyrmont, others did not know whether they still had families or homes to go back to. It must have been difficult for the men who had been incarcerated for so long, to imagine what awaited them.

Leonhard was wondering how I had fared in London and how I had survived the bombing. He realised I would now be 21 years old, though still a schoolgirl when he last saw me. His fortune-teller friend Johann Salomyxin 'read the cards' revealing that: 'She has just been married, not in a church, or registry office, but in a very large building in London.' (Illustration 32) This greatly amused Leonhard later on when he heard I had indeed been married on 26th April, to Sydney Bailey in Friends House in London. In February, when we had decided to get married, it seemed that the war could drag on for many more months.

Leonhard voluntarily spent five weeks helping the American camp administration prepare discharge papers for the departing men. The first to go, on 18th April, were the Czechs, who left on a train sent for them from Prague. The next were a group of Norwegians, who were quickly followed by the Russians, for whom the Soviet army also sent transport. The British sent a Parliamentary delegation of enquiry on 20th April, who reported:

> Although the work of cleaning up the camp had gone on busily for a week before our visit, we had the impression of intense squalor. The odour of dissolution and disease pervaded the entire area.[8]

Whilst Leonhard did not want to stay longer than was necessary, he enjoyed working alongside the Americans and talking with the men whose documentation he was preparing. He was also able to glean information about the conditions he would experience in travelling home. During these weeks, released from the anxieties he had as a prisoner, he began to recover his health and personality. He finally left on 18th May, travelling in a Buchenwald truck to Kassel and then by military train to Hanover. He may himself have prepared the travel document which I later found with his papers, written in English:

To the Commandant,

We ask your permission for the following political prisoners to leave for Kassel on their way home on 18th May 1945:

August Groel	Leonhard Friedrich
Otto Grosse	Max Mayr
Helmut Guttmann	Paul Wiesner
Otto Becker	Konrad Moebus
Helmut Lenhardt	Konstantin von Bentheim
Johann Salomyxin	

Yours faithfully,

The German Committee, Buchenwald

Leonhard arrived back in Pyrmont on Whit Sunday, 20th May, just as Mary was locking the Quakerhouse door after the Friends had left at the end of Meeting for Worship.

The Closure of Buchenwald

The Yalta Agreement arranged for Germany to be divided into four zones of occupation by the Allies. Buchenwald came into the Soviet zone, although it was liberated by the American 3rd Army. A few weeks after all the prisoners had left, the Americans handed over the camp to the Soviet occupation forces, but before doing so, they took all the Buchenwald records to the American zone as material evidence for the War Crimes Tribunal shortly to take place in Nuremberg. Some of these prisoner records are still held by the German Red Cross Society. At the end of the war, there was an intensive search for former Nazi criminals all over Germany. From 1945-51 Buchenwald was used as a detention centre where the Soviet authorities held thousands of former Nazis, who were used as forced labour in reconstruction work. Many were taken to work in the Soviet Union and few ever returned. Eventually the prisoner's living quarters were burned down and the ground was cleared. In the late 1950s a massive Soviet-style memorial was built.

At the end of my visit to Buchenwald in 1989, when I took the bus back to Weimar, I found myself sitting beside the museum attendant with whom I had spoken earlier in the day. She was about my age, and I enquired about her war-time experiences. In 1939, at the outbreak of war, she was 17, the daughter of a farmer who lived nearby. She had not understood what Buchenwald was, beyond knowing it was a place where people whom the state considered undesirable were put to work. Her father employed two Polish prisoners from the camp as labourers, whom he was expected to treat as sub-humans. One rainy day, when there was no one else around, she had given them lunch in the farm kitchen. Someone denounced her for this act of humanity, and she was imprisoned for six months. She spent the rest of the war in hiding, without a ration book or job, staying for short periods with relatives in different places. After the war she was twice married and had eight children and twenty-two grandchildren, all of whom learn why she has worked as a guide at Buchenwald for 22 years. She said how much the personal encounters with the visitors have meant to her.

CHAPTER XIX

Ending of the War 1945

Progression on the Fighting Fronts

THE GERMAN ASSAULT ON THE Ardennes was followed in early January 1945 by bitter fighting over the Saar and Upper Rhine. Both sides lost thousands of men and many more were wounded or taken prisoner. During February and March the Ruhr was heavily bombed by the RAF and American Air Force. The railways were scarcely functioning and German fighter planes were grounded for lack of fuel. Many German soldiers were surrendering to the Allies. General Eisenhower's forces were north of Duesseldorf and crossed the Rhine on 22nd March.

General Montgomery led the British army through northern Germany towards the Eastern Front. Soviet forces were approaching Danzig, having taken almost half of Prussia. Hitler moved back to the Chancellery in Berlin and on 19th March he ordered the destruction of military, industrial, transport and communication systems, so that the invaders would inherit a wasteland.

In the early days of April dramatic developments affected both Leonhard and Mary. On 5th April, the American army liberated Bad Pyrmont and on 12th April they freed Buchenwald. On the 13th April the Russians took Vienna and later that day it was announced that Franklin D. Roosevelt, the American President had suddenly died. Goebbels, with misplaced optimism, told Hitler that this was a sign that his fortunes would improve. The German Reich, which had once stretched from the Atlantic to the Caucasus now measured a mere 100 kilometres from west to east and north to south.

Hitler had intended to spend his 56th birthday, on 20th April at Berchtesgaden, with Eva Braun, his mistress, but because Berlin was being heavily bombed, she joined him in the underground bunker at the Chancellery. On 22nd April the Russians reached the outskirts of Berlin. Hitler's bunker was shaken by the bombing and he was furious at the failure of the Wehrmacht to keep the enemy at bay. Meanwhile, without Hitler's knowledge, Himmler was in the Swedish Consulate at Lubeck, attempting to negotiate Germany's surrender to the Allies through Count Bernadotte, Chairman of the Swedish Red Cross.[1]

This may have been some explanation for the extraordinary announcement, just before liberation of Buchenwald on 4th April, when the unbelieving prisoners were told that the Jews were going to Sweden. It also explains the very early departure of the Norwegian prisoners from Buchenwald on 20th April.

Although Berlin was surrounded by Soviet forces, Hitler refused to surrender. He continued to broadcast over the Berlin radio, admonishing the people to resist to the last. But for himself and his close associates, he decided that death was the only option. When he heard that Himmler had betrayed him by opening negotiations for surrender with Bernadotte, he made his last will and testament, naming Admiral Karl Doenitz as Supreme Commander and Head of State. In the small hours of the night of 29th April, Adolf Hitler married Eva Braun in the bunker and the next morning they were both found dead in their bed. The Soviet forces captured the Chancellery on 2nd May.

On 29th April the German army in Italy surrendered to the Allies, the day after Mussolini and his mistress had been killed by partisans. On 4th May north-west Germany and Denmark surrendered to General Montgomery and the following day the German naval forces showed the white flag. Three days later on 7th May General Alfred Jodl signed an 'Unconditional Surrender'. The Nazi regime and the immense human suffering it had caused over the last 12 years were ended by five-and-a-half years of war. There was great rejoicing as church bells pealed for peace all over Europe.

Final Months of the War in Pyrmont

Mary had been on her own, with her two lodgers, over Christmas and for the first two weeks of January 1945. She was very short of food and money. Her diary entries during the first week of the new year were as follows:

> Went shopping for Leonhard's parcel and got nothing, though the tobacconist provided a few cigarillos. I took my meat ration to Frau Mundhenk, who promised to come and beat my carpets.
>
> I went to Buchingers for bread, which I later gave to Katie Lotz when she said she was hungry. There was a heavy raid on Hanover, during which I sheltered in the cellar. The house shook and the windows blew open, as though Luegde, a nearby village, were being bombed, but I heard no reports of any falling in our vicinity. I have

been going up the Bomberg to the Sennhuette for milk every week, even in the snow and ice. When it is very slippery, I put old socks over my shoes.

Mary's diary, 10th January:

The Chief Police Inspector Wenger, came to tell me that the Hamelin NSV (Social Welfare Department) will be using the Quakerhouse as a nursing home for the elderly. The keys were to be handed over to Frau Baeder, the NSV representative. When she eventually arrived, Wenger was very unpleasant and gave her all the internal keys of the building, thereby putting the Quaker property stored in the attic at risk. He also said he had lost our masterkeys. Two days later I was asked to go to the police station again. He almost apologised for his behaviour and gave me various documents of Leonhard's which he had taken from our files. I was very glad to receive Leonhard's National Provincial Insurance policy, his National Employees insurance card, and a Loan Tax certificate, as well as the missing masterkeys. He said he was glad to be rid of the responsibility for the Quakerhouse, which had caused him a lot of aggravation. We shook hands and said our relationship could begin again on a new footing.

Mary's diary, 11th January:

After Meeting I found the electricity in our flat was on again and I could listen to the radio. I enjoyed hearing about the life story of the Queen of Romania, and felt sympathy for her being shunned as a foreigner. I do not wish that experience on anyone. Several more air raid warnings.

Mary's diary, 16th January:

A letter came from Leonhard which warmed my heart. He seems to understand the difficulties I have in collecting together food for his parcels and in getting them through the post office. He says he hopes to build up his strength again and provide a living for us. He is glad that we have some savings behind us, but does not seem to realise that the Gestapo took them all. There was also a sad letter from Leonore Burnitz saying that our friend, Rudolf Schlosser, had been found dead in the street after an air raid. His wife was not told until two weeks later. His passing will be a great loss to Quakers. His ashes were buried here on the 14th January, when we held a Memorial Meeting.

Mary's diary, 17th January:

The Soviet army is advancing on the Eastern Front. They have at last regained Warsaw. I had for some time thought the firewood was disappearing too rapidly from our wood pile in the cellar. Today I caught my tenant, Rohrman helping himself to it. He said he was just borrowing the wood and intended to order more from the Forestry Department. I told Drinkuth that I had found two of Leonhard's ledgers lying in the bushes at the Quakerhouse.

Difficult Tenants: the Laurer Family

The small attic bedroom under the eaves was vacant and Mary had planned to sleep there herself when the weather got warmer. However she received a letter from a Quaker, Piet Kappes, asking her to take in a 22-year-old woman, Ruth Laurer and her four-month-old baby, while she was being treated at the Buchinger Klinik. Mary met her and found her very pleasant. Ruth offered to keep the flat clean and to type any letters Mary had to write in German. A few days later, Mary discovered that Ruth's parents were also in Pyrmont and looking for accommodation. So she agreed that Frau Laurer could sleep in the attic room with Ruth and the baby and Herr Laurer, who would be away quite a lot, could have the couch in the sitting room adjoining Mary's bedroom. They could all use the kitchen and use Mary's coal until they were able to get their own supply.

But before Ruth's parents moved in, she began to show serious psychiatric problems. During a winter storm, she became hysterical and talked of hearing voices. She said she felt guilty and selfish, but was convinced that she could start a new life here. Ruth was very religious and talked about angels, of which she frequently made sketches. A few days later she settled down again and Mary felt they were getting on quite well. Mary enjoyed giving the baby a bottle and was happy to look after it occasionally. But two weeks later, when Ruth's parents moved in, more problems arose. The first night, Herr Laurer, whose bed was separated from Mary's part of the sitting room by a sliding glass door, cried like a baby in his sleep and then sang and prayed aloud. Such disturbances became a regular occurance. Frau Laurer needed to go to the toilet at night, and was constantly clattering up and down the wooden attic staircase to the bathroom.

The Knierim family, Mary's landlords, complained about the noise, and got their revenge by 'accidentally' removing the clothes' prop from the washing line, so that Mary's laundry fell in the mud. However, when old mother Knierim had her 95th birthday, Mary gave her a flowering geranium, after which the atmosphere improved.

Mary's diary, 1st February:

I felt impatient with all the Laurers, although I knew I had to make allowances for Ruth and her father, who had been through a lot and were obviously not in good health. They are so untidy and dirty and under my feet all day; they use my things, open my drawers and leave the cooker in a dreadful state. There are unwashed nappies all over the place. The baby is sick and cries a lot. I gave Ruth some carrots to cook for the baby, which she does not understand how to feed or look after. The baby has not been bathed for four days now.

Mary's diary, 4th February:

I went to Meeting, and got into trouble again. We were all to contribute items of clothing to send to our Friend Ernst Rummel, who had been bombed-out for the second time in Nuremberg. Hans Seutemann said I had given rags, which were not worth the postage. He then went on to say that I was always deciding which jobs needed doing in the Quakerhouse garden. I was very hurt, but said I would ask the nuns at Georg's Villa if they would cut the hedge. A few days later Hans did the job, which must have been his way of saying 'sorry'.

My own sympathies are with Hans over this episode, because in later years I often found myself in his position. He must have been a very kind person to go on helping Mary, in spite of so many irritations, though she was an experienced person who knew what needed doing. But her disabilities meant she simply had to rely on others. Hans, at the age of 46, was the most able-bodied man around, though often in pain from a wounded foot sustained in the First World War.

A few days later Mary's gardening problems were solved. The NSV (Social Welfare) occupants of the Quakerhouse had been allocated two Ukrainians and subsequently two Russians, on forced labour assignments. These men found Mary an easily satisfied taskmaster, who also gave them cups of tea and bread and jam. The mounting pressures of the final days of the war were undoubtedly resulting in everyone losing patience with each other.

Mary's diary, 11th February:

Now at last the baby is quiet and smiling, because the grandparents handle it with care and understanding. Such a normal display of contentment touches me so intensely, that I can scarcely keep from weeping. I have become such a poor weak thing, everything inside me feels hurt and raw. Will anyone ever be kind to me again? Lord make me stronger, to stop my heart from breaking.

Mary's diary, 17th February:

I called on the Seutemanns and found Hans in very great anxiety. Cilli had gone into hiding, having heard the rumour that Jews married to Aryans were to lose their 'special protection', and are now being rounded up. After she had left, a notice was delivered to their house commanding her to be at an appointed place at 4 pm. Because she did not show up, Hans was summoned to the police station and told that Cilli must report at the railway station next day with a small suitcase at 8 am to go to Hanover. Cilli of course remained in hiding and we were very anxious about her.

Mary's diary, 24th February:

Drinkuth and I went to the Quakerhouse to meet the NSV people who will be looking after the old folks. They seemed pleasant enough and agreed to my keeping a set of keys. I suggested at Meeting that some of us should volunteer to help for a couple of hours a week. But Friends thought it would be unwise to be so friendly.

Mary's diary, 25th February:

I visited Kurt Richter, who is still an invalid. He seemed cantankerous and expressed very nationalistic views. My visits don't give him any pleasure. Then I called on Gertrud and Albert Graf, neither family offered me anything to eat or drink and they both say they are always hungry. I send most of my bread ration to Leonhard, and manage without bread for breakfast and supper.

Mary's diary, 8th March:

There was a heavy raid on Chemnitz, by the advancing Soviet forces. I've written to Marie Pleissner to encourage her to come here with her sister. Martha Legatis has lost everything for the second time in an air raid. There was a very heavy air raid on Dortmund. We could hear it quite clearly though it is 120 kilometres away. Many Friends complain of hunger. I feel like a lodger among the 11 people with whom I share my home.

Mary's diary, 14th March:

I have received a Red Cross message from Grete Stendal, who saw Brenda in London and reported that she is full of energy and good spirits, but is anxious about Leonhard. I wonder if she, too, heard about the raid on Buchenwald? I feel convinced something has happened to him and have written to the Camp Commandant asking for information. I dread the possibility of facing the future alone.

The Laurer parents went to stay in Polle for six weeks, without saying anything to Ruth or to me. Ruth has been very withdrawn, she cries a lot and never speaks unless I talk to her. When her parents returned they did nothing but grumble at her. Her father left again for Bremen today, although Ruth begged him to stay for another three days, because she felt something dreadful was going to happen. At three o'clock this afternoon, Ruth said she had to go to confession, leaving me to look after the baby. I fed it at five and she eventually came home at seven with her mother and her sister, Sonia, who lives elsewhere in Pyrmont. Frau Laurer and I had a bite to eat in the kitchen, but Ruth who is still on Buchinger's fasting treatment, went into the bathroom for quite a time. We later discovered that she had stuck pins into her thighs and mutilated herself. We knew nothing about this when she emerged from the bathroom, but could see she was extremely distraught. Sonia, her sister, took her to see the priest again, while Frau Laurer went to speak to the psychiatrist, Dr Reinhart. He advised that Ruth should be taken to the police station, presumably because he recognised that she needed protection from herself, although he did not yet know about the pins. Ruth begged to be allowed to go, and said she wanted to sleep in a police cell. Finally her mother agreed to take her.

At the police station she declared herself insane and showed them what she had done to her body. They pulled out as many pins as they could and took her to the hospital. She was in a great deal of pain. It was after midnight when Frau Laurer came home, and we sat up in the kitchen talking until four in the morning.

Mary's diary, 21st March:

The big decisive battles have now started and it is frustrating to be without my radio, which has not worked for at least a month.

Arrival of the NSV Welfare Group at the Quakerhouse

Mary's diary, 22nd March:

Hans Seutemann was working with me in the Quakerhouse garden when two buses arrived bringing 90 people to stay. Many of them seemed to be deaf and blind. No preparations had been made to receive them. There was neither gas nor light and even the water was still turned off. Some bedsteads had been delivered months ago, but were not assembled. There was insufficient straw for bedding. Since there was no water from the taps, I carried pails of drinking water from our flat and helped people to settle in. The toilets could not be used, so I spent most of the night helping people out into the garden to relieve themselves. This is the second night this week I've not been to bed.

The water was turned on the next day, but the garden smells terrible and is a health hazard. All but 28 of the people were taken away to private homes, which makes things a bit easier. I lent the staff one of the galvanised tubs I use on wash day, so that those in need of it can be bathed in the kitchen.

Mary helped the young nurse in charge, by listening to the elderly patients and providing some packs of cards and table games.

Mary's diary, 29th March:

I was very relieved to receive another note from Leonhard, the first for six weeks. The post office has closed down and cannot accept mail. There has been very little food in the shops. I stood in line for two hours for ¼ litre of milk today and an hour for a loaf of bread. I only weigh 50 kilos.

There is a feeling of panic in the town. The Allies are reported to be 30 kms from Kassel and battles are raging at Paderborn, 50 kms from Pyrmont. I have seen Red Cross flags going up in the town. Willy Tangermann, a Quaker employed at the town hall asked me to visit him, and his office looked lovely with an open log fire burning. He asked me to prepare myself for a meeting with the American military authorities as soon as they get here. In order to avoid fighting over the town, Pyrmont intends to declare itself a hospital zone. I said of course I would be willing, if I was assured that the reasons were genuine.

All men are being called up for the *Volksturm* [an organisation similar to Britain's Home Guard]. They have even recruited our landlord, Knierim, who is 65 years old. His sisters and mother wept to see him go, but were relieved when he came home again in the evening, saying he had repulsed the enemy. My lodger Rohrman was also called on to go to Luegde, to make preparations for blowing up the bridge over the River Emmer. Hans Seutemann called in, to say he intended to disappear for a few days.

Mary's diary, 5th April:

'This is a red letter Day!' But I have no red ink. At ten this morning we heard the five-minute siren, the signal for everyone to go into their cellars, as street fighting was expected. I had not finished packing my emergency suitcase, although I had been up all night trying to decide what I should take with me, if we have to leave the house. I had intended to prepare cooked food and draw water. My lodgers, dressed in their best clothes, were sheltering in the cellar. I was at last ready to join them around 12.30 pm. Just as the potatoes were cooked, I heard a loudspeaker announcement from the street saying:

'People of Pyrmont. We stand outside your beautiful town. Will you surrender and let us pass through peacefully and save your homes and protect the wounded in hospital? If you surrender, not a shot will be fired. Signal your consent by hanging white cloths from your windows.'

I ran around our flat, taking the sheets off the beds to hang out of the windows. By the time I got to the balcony, I saw sheets appearing at the windows all over the nearby village of Holzhausen.

In the meantime, the people in the town hall could not decide what to do. Seebohm, the town clerk who favoured surrender, had retired on 1st April, but Ahrens, his deputy, and the SS Chief, thought they should fight to the last man and blow up the bridges as planned. However Dr Glaser, the town's chief medical officer, wanted the town to surrender to gain recognition as a hospital zone. A young Lance Corporal who was listening to all this while the minutes ticked by eventually took the decision himself. He got on his bike and hurried towards the American army in the Schulstrasse, waving a white cloth saying 'WE SURRENDER'. A few minutes later the Americans reached the Brunnen Platz and found Dr Glaser waiting to receive them.

Once this had happened the people were free to walk the streets. At three o'clock I decided to go into town and persuaded Frau Kuhl, who was very scared, to come with me. We saw no one looking miserable about the defeat. The Kuhls now openly declared themselves as refugees from Danzig and invited an American officer named Bedsall, to supper and to stay with them for the night. They invited me along too. We enjoyed some meat which the American soldiers had taken from an SS establishment in Detmold. The officer was terribly exhausted, he had not slept for six nights. We talked of England and America. He had obviously been very shocked by the experience of taking the SS establishment in Detmold. There had been 900 men and women there, but only 15 were left alive. He could not get over the fact that he had had to fire on a vehicle which was carrying 20 SS women, all of whom were killed.

CHAPTER XX

Leonhard Comes Home 1945

Americans Liberate Bad Pyrmont

Mary's diary, 8th April:
> Late on Sunday afternoon several American soldiers came to our house and called us all out to the doorstep. They said we had to vacate the house in one hour, to provide accommodation for 30 American soldiers. We could take anything we wanted with us, but must leave all doors and cupboards unlocked. I pleaded with him for us all, saying I was an English woman, whose husband was in Buchenwald. He was sorry, but he had his orders, and requested everyone to leave. However he agreed to check our situation with the Commander and would be back shortly. Fifteen minutes later he returned and we were very relieved to hear him say we could stay.

Mary's diary, 9th and 10th April:
> I was worried about the old people at the Quakerhouse, who were living in squalid discomfort and dirty conditions. There was still no gas or electricity and the food supply was meagre. I got on well with the young nursing staff there and realised that, now the Americans were in charge of the town, we could use our influence to improve conditions at the Quakerhouse. I consulted Otto Buchinger and spoke to Willi Tangermann, who was now Chairman of the Council [Landrat], since he had been a Social Democrat and was never a Nazi. They agreed I should ask to see the American Commandant responsible for the occupation of Pyrmont, to request no new patients be admitted to the Quakerhouse and that the building be restored to us. He was interested and friendly, saying it was American policy that places of religious worship should resume regular services.
>
> Mary heard how some local Nazis were faring. Ahrens, the Nazi district group leader, had voluntarily given himself up. Police officer Wenger and Seebohm, the former Town Clerk, had been taken to prison at Altenbeken. Several local Nazi leaders had hanged themselves and their families or had taken cyanide.

Mary's diary, 13th April:

There are many people walking about the streets who appear to have nothing to do. Some shops are open from 9-12 am, people form queues everywhere, but find nothing to buy. There is still no gas or electricity supply in the town; the railways are not running; the postal service remains suspended. But I have heard one may send letters to the USA and the UK through the military government.

Drinkuth has asked me to give him English lessons. This made me smile. He has no idea how many people are now asking for my help. The old people at the Quakerhouse still get no hot drink for breakfast or supper, so I have been taking over a big can of hot water twice a day.

In the afternoon I was visited by the Pyrmont police who asked me to find accommodation for a young woman and her child, who was working for them. I took the policeman over to the Quakerhouse to show him which corner the woman might occupy. While doing so I suddenly realised that since the Nazis were now ousted from power, the police could no longer enforce their demands on Quakers. We are free to decide how we wish to use our own building. So I simply said the Quakerhouse was temporarily designated for the care of the elderly, not for women and children.

Mary's diary, 14th April:

I had better luck with shopping today, and was able to use up all my coupons. They will be invalidated as from Monday, when the Americans take over responsibility for feeding the population.

I decided to talk with Herr Kropotke in the town welfare department about the appalling conditions at the Quakerhouse. He agreed to send someone at once to see about unblocking the toilets. I also asked them to transfer the elderly to a more suitable building and restore the property to Quakers as soon as possible. He agreed to try his best. While I was talking with him, a group of Ukrainian labourers came to complain of neglect and shortage of food.

Mary's diary, 15th April:

Friends held a Meeting for Worship in the office at the Quakerhouse for the first time since 24th May 1942. Fourteen of us were present. It was really nice, but we were too excited talking to each other to leave much time for worship.

In the afternoon I visited the Richters. As I walked along the Hamelin road, a stream of military vehicles rolled past me. Some 600 American and British soldiers are now stationed in Pyrmont.

I have heard that Buchenwald has been liberated by the Americans and that 5,000 people simply left the camp. I do hope Leonhard is safe, and that he will soon be here to share responsibilities.

The nuns at Georg's Villa have kindly invited me to lunch there regularly. I help at the Quakerhouse several times a day because the young nurses there are frightened of the American soldiers, who are often drunk and violate women. They come round to our houses asking for drink. They sell their handguns to the Poles for alcohol. The Poles use the guns to threaten, steal and revenge themselves on Germans.

Mary's diary, 16th April:

Herr Kropotke, the town Welfare Officer, came to discuss moving the old folks, which he thought would take at least a month to arrange. Kati Lotz came later and said she and Otto Buchinger felt we should ask the Military Command to give us back the Quakerhouse at once. But I feel we should not go over the head of Herr Kropotke, with whom we shall still be dealing long after the Military Command has left the town. Gertrud Graf and I have started checking our inventory. I invited the charge nurse and two of the old men to supper and made puddings for the others. I have had several of them in to meals with me over the last few days.

Mary's diary, 20th April:

Gerhard Richter came to fetch me to his home, because the negro soldiers billeted on him had stolen his wife's jewellery and items they had been looking after for Jewish families. I began to walk home with him, but before going very far, I decided first to discuss the problem with the Military Command. The Americans promised to deal with the situation that afternoon and said they would fetch me to go with them in a truck. They never came, but neither did Gerhard, so I assumed the matter had been resolved. However when I saw the Richters on Sunday, they blamed me for having done nothing and let them down.

Mary's diary, 22nd April:

Martha Seebohm came to see if I could plead for the release of her brother, the retired Town Clerk, from custody. After Quaker Meeting on Sunday, we discussed the many requests we were each receiving and decided to open an advice centre twice a week in the Quakerhouse. Hans Seutemann put a notice on the board by our gate and Kati Lotz and Cilli Seutemann agreed to be advisers. This was Cilli's first visit to our home since the Knierims had threatened her as a Jew five years ago.

Mary's diary, 24th April:

Frau Dr Wasch, a 32-year-old Czech lawyer from Prague University, came over from Steinheim to stay with me for four days. She had been arrested by the Gestapo in 1938 and was taken to Lublin in Poland, where she had endured terrible conditions in extermination camps. In one of them there had been 3,000 women and no piped water supply. They were dependant on daily water carts for drinking and cooking. For a whole year they had been unable to wash either themselves or their clothes. The women were provided with a dress, but no underwear. The SS men shaved off all their hair, including the pubic area. They had no shoes, though wooden clogs were later provided to improve their work output. When the Soviet armies entered Poland, the women were sent on a route march from Lippstadt towards Buchenwald. For part of the way they had to pull two railway carriages in which their SS guards were seated. Eventually, a few weeks ago, she managed to escape from this nightmare march with a few other Jewish women. She is staying with Frau Loewenstein, a distant relative of Hilde Sturmthal.

Mary's diary, 26th April:

Five American officers visited me for a social chat this evening. When they heard how frustrated I felt about being unable to hear the news, they promised to get me a good radio. They told me that some 800 children had been found living among the prisoners at Buchenwald, many of them had been sexually abused. They also mentioned the many infectious diseases there, typhoid, cholera, etc. The conditions were terrible, and many of the dead lay around unburied. The inmates had to be cleaned up and fed before they could be allowed home. The camp will need to be burned down once the prisoners have left. I am very anxious because I have still not heard a word from Leonhard.

Mary's diary, 28th April: **John Sutton**

I was very surprised and delighted to receive a visit from an English Quaker, John Sutton (1898-1988). He had been a prisoner for four and a half years. He was arrested by the Gestapo in 1940 while working in Paris for the US Embassy. But most of his imprisonment had been in the Hamelin gaol. He could only stay for half an hour this time, but will come again on Sunday. His hair and skin looked so grey.

Shortly after John Sutton's death in 1988, his second wife Madelaine wrote me a brief resume of his life. John was born in 1898 of an English father and French mother and grew up in France. As an adult he lived in England. He was a pacifist and a member of the Friends War Victims Relief committee in France 1914-15 and later joined the Society of Friends.

John remained in Paris after the First World War and helped to establish the Paris Quaker Centre with Justine Dalencourt. At the outbreak of war in 1939 he was working at the consulate section of the British embassy in Paris. When the city was occupied by the Germans in May 1940 and the embassy closed, he stayed behind to look after the remaining British citizens from an office in the American embassy.

In October 1941, three weeks after the death of his first wife, he was arrested by the Gestapo and charged with spying. He endured weeks of interrogation in the notorious prison at Fresnes and sentenced to life. He was then brought to Germany and kept in solitary confinement, first at Rheinbad near Bonn and later at Hamelin. When prisoners were ordered into the munitions factories, John refused to comply and was punished, being held for several weeks in complete darkness on a diet of bread and water.

When the Americans liberated Hamelin and took over the prison, they made John Sutton the Governor, until the area could be pacified and the prisoners sorted out for release. The Americans provided food for the prison and made a vehicle available for John, which enabled him to visit Pyrmont, where he remembered there was a Quaker group.

He came again on 8th May, laden with food to celebrate VE-Day with Mary. They listened to Churchill and King George VI on the radio. He brought 12 cans of peas, 10 lbs of corned beef, 10 lbs of cooking oil and a pound of tea. Mary was able to share this with 18 Quakers, giving each six teaspoons of tea, some biscuits and cooking oil to take home.

After the war in 1946 John resumed his work as British Consul in Paris and married Madelaine, his second wife. When he retired they purchased the historic Friends Meeting House at Congenies in the south of France near Nimes, converting it as their home.[1]

Mary's diary, 29th April:

> It was a great joy to go to our bank today, to cash a cheque for Leonhard's salary of 250 marks for the month of April.

For the next few days Mary and other Friends were busy clearing things left in the Quakerhouse attic by recent occupants. She planted seeds in the Quakerhouse vegetable garden, because food was likely to be in short supply for the foreseeable future.

Mary's diary, 9th-12th May:

> I made several trips to the town hall with my little cart to collect some of the books and stationery which the Gestapo had taken from Leonhard's office. There are still no trains running and no post. Thirty Quakerhouse chairs were returned to us today. The garden is looking lovely again, with the apple trees in blossom.

Mary's diary, 13th May:

We had a very good Meeting today with 45 people present. Afterwards we discussed starting an English language club, because many people now want to improve their English. This was John Sutton's last visit, as he is leaving for England tomorrow.

Mary's diary, 18th May:

I worry, because I still have no word from Leonhard. But I heard in town today that three Buchenwald men had passed through a neighbouring village. An American soldier called Ernst Becker-Burkes came to visit me. Before the war he had been a Jew living in Berlin.

Ernst wrote the following in Mary's guest book:

In the final year of this terrible war I thank Mary Friedrich with all my heart for her friendly welcome, after hearing all that has happened to my family and to hers, I give thanks for her understanding support.

Mary's diary, 14th May:

Today I have been able to buy some meat on my rations and have been cooking and bottling it, so as to have a good meal ready when Leonhard comes home. Some American soldiers came, hoping to see Ruth Laurer. She was out, but I invited them in and talked to them. The next day they brought me a wonderful radio and even sent an electrician to repair my electric wiring.

Mary's diary, 19th May:

People keep asking if I have any news from Leonhard. By their questions they suggest something may have happened to him. I went to the Military Commander to ask how I could find out. He said many men had been dispersed to smaller camps and it would be impossible to trace him at present.

Leonhard Comes Home

Mary's diary, Whit-Sunday 20th May:

We had our Meeting for Worship in the basement dining room. The old people have been moved out and the Quakerhouse really belongs to Friends again. I was the last person there and was walking up the internal stairs, when Leonhard came through the front door! What a wonderful surprise! I was so glad to have a good meal ready for him, though I had no idea that he was on his way. But of course our lodgers, including all the Laurers, were still in the flat. Later in the evening we went out to see the Richters.

Mary's diary, 21st May:

Leonhard is so happy and excited to be home again. He had a hot bath last night and he was so pleased to wear his own clothes again; the hair on his shaved head is growing and now he looks more like himself. He has lost his front teeth and says his eyesight is poor. We burned his flea-ridden red-striped Buchenwald clothing in the garden. We went together to visit Emma Raeydt and then to the Commandant this morning. He allocated three times the normal food rations for Leonhard. It is wonderful to feel so well off with plenty of milk and butter.

Mary's diary, 22nd May:

I went with Leonhard to see Herr Mokt, at the town planning department to talk about the Quakerhouse and the possibility of having our flat to ourselves again. We spent most of the day with Drinkuth, who fetched us in a car. Drinkuth is in trouble with the Americans and has had a house search. We met an American there who said he was a Quaker, so I asked him why he was wearing a military uniform? He said he was in non-combatant service with the military government and advised us not to be anxious about Drinkuth. They did in fact take him away and locked him up for 48 hours, actually in a cell with the man who had denounced him.

Mary's diary, 25th May:

This week has been full of exciting experiences for us both. Leonhard is impatient about getting our home and his office in order again. He says while he was away he learnt different ways of dealing with people and will not put up with getting the brush-off or waiting around in offices. We went to the bank together and to the paper mill, we will be able to retrieve many of our Quaker books, because the mill owner had deliberately left them aside.

Leonhard is very tired. His whole body seems puffed up and his face is very white. I do love having him home again and hope I can help him to recover.

Mary's diary, 29th May:

Today we were visited by two English Quakers, George Thorne and Alfred Bucknall, from the Friends Ambulance Unit (FAU). They are stationed at Vlotho near Osnabruck to work with the civilian population and brought us the first news of Brenda. They told us she had been married on 26th April at Friends House to Sydney Bailey, who had been in China with the FAU. I was able to write to Brenda through them.

On some occasions, such as Leonhard's return, six weeks after the liberation of Buchenwald, Mary's diary entries convey a rather low-key reaction to events, because they may sometimes have been written-up on a later day. Similarly I imagine that her delight at hearing first-hand that I was safe and well, was likely to have been tempered by feelings of sadness about the news that I had married young and would now have other loyalties.

It was with immense joy and relief that a few days later I received a letter in London dated 29th Mary, from FAU colleagues, George Thorne and Alfred Bucknall, telling me of their visit:

> Leonhard had arrived back from Buchenwald a few days before our visit. He has had a bad time, but has come through it all with the quietness and grace that is possible only to those who are grounded in true Faith. As we sat listening to his story, how he was arrested without warning and imprisoned for nothing more than being a Friend and helping the Jews, we felt humble to be with one who has suffered with such freedom from bitterness. Today they are extremely happy to be together and to hear news of you. We had a special celebration meal together on the balcony. Certainly no task we have done out here has been happier or more satisfying.

In the weeks that followed Leonhard and Mary had continuing problems with the lodgers. Ruth Laurer and her sister Sonia were discovered by Frau Kuhl, 'entertaining' American soldiers in the attic bedroom. Leonhard clearly needed a more peaceful home and was greatly relieved when all the Laurers left on 10th June, though Rohrman and Frl Weiss were not rehoused until July. During this time Leonhard and Mary enjoyed welcoming many visitors who just appeared on their doorstep.

Mary's diary, 4th June:

> Colonel Basil Reckitt drove a hundred miles to bring us news of Brenda at the request of his sister, Rachel, who is in charge of the Citizens Advice Bureau at Toynbee Hall, where Brenda is working. It is such a joy to have this contact and to learn about the support they are giving to people in the East End. In his book *Diary of Military Government in Germany 1945*, Colonel Reckitt described the family circumstances and then said: 'Leonhard Friedrich is recovering from his experiences, but was needing to rest in bed.'[2]

Mary's diary, 7th June:

> Bertha Maas, a member of the Meeting, has come to help Leonhard to create some order from the chaos in the office at the Quakerhouse. While in town shopping today, I met Oliver Ashford, a Quaker from Nailsworth. He is here to make meteorological enquiries for the RAF. He came home with me, and brought greetings from Gwen and Corder Catchpool.

Mary's diary, 10th June:

> I am so thankful that the awful years when I was mistrusted and despised for being an English woman, are now over. I feel such joy in my heart, with Leonhard beside me. We have lovely Meetings for Worship. The weekly English language club, attended by 25 people is very enjoyable.

Mary's diary, 15th June:

> Richard Vogt, a German Quaker, came to stay for a few days. He had walked most of the way from Czechoslovakia where he had been working in a flour mill. He is looking for his wife and three small children. While staying with us, he discovered that they were at Hildesheim. An FAU friend visiting us at the time was able to drive him there.

This was the first of many German Quakers who came to Pyrmont whilst tracing their lost relatives. On another day Sigried Gluckner came looking for her family, having cycled all the way from Hamburg.

Mary's diary, 1st July:

> Richard Wainwright and Donald Ractliffe from the FAU team in Vlotho came to Meeting and visited us. They brought the first letter from Brenda in reply to ours. Also a parcel of soap, hairpins, sewing cotton etc. and best of all, back issues of *The Friend*.

Richard, who later became a very well known Liberal MP, opened the head office in Vlotho for FAU teams who were to care for Displaced Persons, mainly people from the former occupied territories brought to work in German factories. (Illustration 33)

Mary's diary, 6th July:

> The postal services in the British zone are being resumed and we received the first delivery of mail since March. We heard that Marie Edert still has no news of her son, missing on the Eastern Front. Some Friends who tried to visit us, were not allowed through to Pyrmont, because we have a polio epidemic here.

Leonhard and Mary had surprise visits from Fritz and Martha Legatis who arrived from Nordhausen, about 100 miles south-east of Pyrmont.[3] It was first occupied by the Americans who had made premises available to hold Quaker Meetings and to organise welfare activities. The Legatis's had lost contact with both their sons. Gert had been a doctor with the army on the Eastern Front. His parents knew he had contracted tuberculosis and that Horst had been with the occupation forces in Holland.

Heinrich Otto and a number of Quakers had gathered in Pyrmont for the weekend of 14th July. Since August Fricke and Kati Lotz, members of the Yearly Meeting Clerk's Committee, were also there and only Hans Albrecht was missing, they had a quorum for holding the first Executive

33. *FAU friends visiting Leonhard and Mary.*
Unknown, Richard Wainwright, Johanne Schoenlank, Donald Ractliffe.

Committee meeting since 1943. The following Friends were accepted into Membership: Horst and Gert Legatis, Erna Peppler, and Henrietta Jordan.[4]

On 20th July Mary and Leonhard were visited by Waring Howson, a Canadian Red Cross worker who was pursuing an enquiry for 'missing persons' from Mary's brother in Sheffield. We still have the Red Cross Searcher Service form, on the back of which Mary wrote the following:

Dear Brother Bert and family,   20th July 1945

It is wonderful to have the chance to write to you while the Red Cross girl is sitting beside me, with her driver from Finsbury Park. Leonhard came home on Whit Sunday. He had a slightly easier time during his last year there when he worked as a sort of warehouseman. He could make a wood fire and eat the food I had sent, mostly just bread. It has not been too bad in Pyrmont. We were never bombed, nor was our town defended when the Americans came. Now we have a good vegetable garden and you know I am a good manager. Brenda has already sent us two very acceptable parcels of soap and things.

The war was a very hard experience for us both. I had constant trouble with the Gestapo and much anxiety. I never knew if I would sleep another night in my own bed, because I always feared they would fetch me away too. I have nearly always had other people crowded in with me, but now we have our flat to ourselves, and the Quakerhouse has also been returned to Friends' use. The Gestapo destroyed 172 cwt of Leonhard's books and took his two typewriters and everything else one needs to run a business.

In writing all this I realise how lucky we were not to be bombed out, or to live in the thick of the fighting. How has it been in Sheffield? So Margaret is married, and my Brenda also! I look forward to a newsy letter from Amy, which Brenda can send on to me. I weigh about seven stone and always feel tired. We both look forward to a rest and change. But there is no transport at present. Please don't worry about us: we have a better life now than most.

Lovingly, Mary.[5]

During August and September there were few diary entries, but from Mary's guest book it can be seen there were visits from 21 members of the Friends Ambulance Unit. Most Sundays a small group of people from the FAU headquarters in Vlotho would drive over in their ambulance to share in the Meeting for Worship with Pyrmont Friends. After Meeting they came to Mary and Leonhard's flat for lunch. They always brought tins of meat and vegetables and tea and instant coffee from the generous rations provided for those working under the Red Cross or Military Government umbrella. Some visitors also brought coal when they realised how difficult it was to obtain sufficient fuel to cook with.

Mary and Leonhard were so happy to be together again, and spent a lot of time filling in the gaps in their difficult years apart. Leonhard had to find his own way of dealing with the traumas he had gone through. It was difficult for him to understand how frequently Mary had been frightened and close to breakdown. But they both drew comfort from the many understanding young FAU visitors who passed through their home and Meeting.

CHAPTER XXI

Post-War Chaos 1945-6

Germany Torn Assunder

THE YALTA AGREEMENT DIVIDING Germany into four occupation zones left some uncertainty about the position of the German frontiers, but Stalin was determined to recover the Polish territories he had ceded to Hitler. Berlin, the former capital, well within the Soviet Zone, was similarly divided when Churchill and President Truman found difficulty in reaching agreement with Stalin. Only in exceptional circumstances would a German citizen be given a permit to cross from one zone to another. When the fighting ceased, the various armies were not in the positions agreed at Yalta, which necessitated many adjustments in the zones of military government.

The British Zone in north-west Germany stretched from Hamburg to Hanover, and from the Ruhr to Cologne. Frankfurt, in the south-west, was the centre of the American Zone. The French Zone was a smaller area carved out of the British and US Zones, at Churchill's insistence, who asserted that France would have an important role to play in post-war Europe. The Russians took control of the East. The Allied Control Commission organised 'de-Nazification' and war reparations, which Churchill said should be in materials, rather than in financial levies which had created so many problems after the First World War. This time whole factories were dismantled and taken away. The Allies were particularly interested in industrial techniques of the chemical, arms and space industries.

The bombing of the Ruhr had reduced much of Germany's major cities to rubble, where millions of people continued to live. Everyone realised they would face an extremely hard winter. Food was short, water pipes and sewers were broken and the electricity supply was intermittent. Many small family groups could be seen trekking along the roads, pulling a hand-cart with their possessions piled on top, searching for relatives who might be better placed. Others were out looking for food in the country, or for planks of wood and reusable old nails with which to repair their homes.

The Allies put the remaining German armed forces behind barbed wire, despatching them to POW camps in Europe but others scattered to distant areas from Egypt to the Arctic. Some 250,000 Germans were held in more than 600 camps throughout Britain. Prisoners taken in Germany were used as labourers for reconstruction. They piled up the rubble along the city streets to enable vehicles to move around the bomb craters. By 1947 most of the POWs had returned to their homes, but 2½ million were still missing; some were dead and others from the Soviet Union returned many years later.

The end of the war found many German families searching for one another. Many of the men between the ages of 16 to 60 had been posted all over Europe while serving with the German fighting and occupation forces. Their children had been evacuated to mountain areas with their schools. Homes were destroyed and the remaining occupants had moved away. There was great fear of epidemics of polio, typhoid and measles. Tuberculosis and malnutrition were common and spread as people from the Soviet Zone and others from concentration camps moved through the cities. There were up to 12 million foreign 'displaced persons' in Germany, who had been brought from the occupied territories to work in factories as slave labour or who had come as volunteers. After five years, many of these labourers had married and produced young families. The military governments were anxious for the speedy, humane repatriation of 'displaced persons', both for security reasons and because there was ill feeling between them and the Germans, also to reduce the number of people for whom shelter and rations had to be provided.

Between August 1945 and early 1947, another massive movement of up to 14 million people began. German citizens living in East Prussia, Poland, Czechoslovakia and Hungary were expelled from the Soviet Zone to the west, where they were housed in military barracks or redundant air raid shelters.

John Adamson, a member of the Berlin FAU team, wrote a graphic description of this movement in the FAU *Chronicle* of August 1945, which I have summarised.

There are 48 refugee camps in Berlin itself, which are said to be holding 30,000 people. The staff of the German Red Cross are working valiantly for them. Each expellee is allowed to rest in Berlin for only 24 hours, before moving on. But during this time they are provided with food, washing facilities, de-lousing, bedding and medical care, and inoculations against typhoid. The sick and infirm are cared for, but many children show signs of severe malnutrition. An orphanage has been opened for 200 children found travelling on their own. Around midday, queues of people form outside Berlin's main railway stations for night trains to the west. Train-loads of people eventually get dumped in some overcrowded disorganised west German city. Where they go from there and what they do is largely unknown.[1]

The policy of 'unconditional surrender' resulted in a power vacuum, leaving the military governments without laws or a constitution through which to govern. They were also hampered in their efforts to rebuild and normalise society by great piles of rubble everywhere and an inoperative system of communications.

Re-newed Activity at Quakerhouse

The Quakerhouse became a centre of information about Quakers and their families, and a haven for many Friends who did not know where to turn, especially as the Berlin Quaker office lay just inside the war-damaged Soviet Zone. Pyrmont had not been fought over, but the population of the town had risen threefold, to 22,000. It was overcrowded with hospital patients and Germans unable to return to their homes in the Soviet Zone. Visitors to Pyrmont were saddened to see so many young amputees. A 2,000-bed specialist hospital was later built for their treatment and rehabilitation.

The Quaker Meeting wanted to help the many distressed people to recover from war and develop plans for the future. Mary had the confidence of the Military Commander in charge of civilian affairs, who entrusted her with the task of setting up a voluntary welfare committee and generally supported Quaker activities. The Quaker Voluntary Committee first organised an advice and information centre. Then it held a series of open lectures and discussions, on topics relating to the future of society in Germany. One evening 300 people came to hear Dr Otto Buchinger snr. speak. The lectures also linked up with the English language group Mary had set-up a few weeks earlier.[2]

Sewing Room

Under the auspices of the Quaker Voluntary Committee, Mary, with the help of Cilli Seutemann, Bertha Maas and Gertrud Graf, established the Quaker Sewing Room in Brunnen strasse. It was opened on 12th October 1945 and was directed by Cilli until 1960. In the town it was generally seen as a place always offering a warm welcome for those in need. Many thousands of people on 'welfare benefits' were able to purchase clothing at nominal prices. It was largely manned by volunteers, though a tailor and several refugee seamstresses were later employed. In the early years it made use of bales of donated clothing sent by the British Friends Relief Service and the American Friends Service Committee.

Later on, Pyrmonters organised local clothing collections. The overhead costs were underwritten by the town council, though voluntary contributions were also needed.[3]

Youth Club

Mary and the Voluntary Committee set up a youth club in the town, with the enthusiastic support of the Military Commander. It provided a centre for 15-18 year-olds who lived in overcrowded homes. A beautiful carpeted room in the Kurpark arcade was made available and it opened in early October 1945 with a *sportfest* and a friendly football match with the British Army. Many of the parents helped to organise the festival, which was attended by 200 people. Hans Seutemann ran the club successfully for a time, but as the attendance grew he needed more help than was available. Eventually Mary and the Voluntary Committee decided the club had to be moved elsewhere.

Fragebogen – to establish who were Nazis

After the end of the war, everyone denied ever having been a Nazi. The Military Government was in need of German staff for its local services, and was determined to avoid employing former Nazis. It also needed to distinguish between those who had been nominal party members and those who should be prosecuted as war criminals. Every applicant for a job was required to complete a questionnaire. Leonhard kept a copy of his four-page form. The first 13 questions concerned Nazi affiliation. The next 36 questions related to participation in Nazi military organisations, including details of military service since 1930. The applicant also had to declare membership of Nazi professional associations, such as the leagues of Nazi doctors or solicitors and of organisations for women, young people and students. Applicants were required to detail their service in the civil administration in the territories annexed by the Reich. They were asked to list any articles they had published and to refer to any speeches made in public since 1923 and to give details of all employment and income since 1930. A further set of questions concerned overseas contacts and international political affiliations, anti-Nazi political activity and any persecution suffered due to race or passive resistance to the Nazi ideology.

My Own FAU Relief Work in Germany

Diana Close (later McClelland) and I had been selected as the first women to join the Friends Ambulance Unit team working for displaced persons in the district of Einbeck. We both had some experience of social work and my fluency in German was useful. Since there was no civilian transport, we travelled from London as military personnel and felt strange wearing our khaki uniforms with FAU shoulder flashes. We enjoyed our Channel crossing, and chanced to meet Roger Wilson on board, who was travelling for the Friends Relief Service. When the continental train eventually brought us to Vlotho on 23rd October, I was very excited to learn that Mike Rowntree had arranged for me to spend the first five days with my parents in Pyrmont and that Deryck Moore was going to drive me there that same afternoon.

It was a very emotional experience to return to my home, after six years of separation and to find both my parents surprised to see me, since they had not known which day to expect me. Their dear familiar faces, their way of talking, their gestures were so reassuring, though they both seemed older and smaller than I had remembered, when we had said goodbye in August 1939. Mary was really quite frail, but very talkative and lively.

We had supper at the kitchen table, eating off crockery Leonhard had brought home as samples from the porcelain factory where he had worked many years ago in Nuremberg. My first shock came when I tried to eat the supper that Mary had prepared. We had a large plate of bread soup, made from bread crusts cooked with potatoes and put through a sieve, with some sour apple sauce in the centre for flavour. This was accompanied by herb tea. I could scarcely swallow it, though I knew this was the sort of food they had become used to. I was dreadfully sick and in the bathroom I found a bar of mud-coloured soap which produced no lather.

I enjoyed sleeping in my old creaky bed, and the following days passed happily, meeting Quakers and neighbours, strolling around the somewhat shabby town and parks, listening to each other's experiences and simply being together again.

Leonhard was very pleased to have the pipe and tobacco that Sydney had sent him. They wanted to know all about my marriage to Sydney, who had been in China on the Burma Road with the FAU during the war. They were very pleased he had become a Quaker and had heard good things about him from other FAU people. But the situation could not have been easy for them to accept. I had left home as a 16-year-old schoolgirl and returned as an independent, 22-year-old married woman.

We made great efforts to understand each other, but it was not easy because we had lived in such different worlds. They had become more German and I had become more English. It was very painful to hear them describe their suffering, though I had been able to imagine much of it. I could only listen to so much at a time. I was pining for Sydney, whom I had left for the first time in the six months since our marriage. The experiences they told me about were so strange that I needed time and space to absorb them. It was then only four months since Leonhard had been released from Buchenwald and he had not fully recovered. He was thin, his clothes did not fit him and he had difficulty in remembering things that had happened before he was arrested. He had no patience with bureaucracy and he could not quite believe that he was now a respected citizen whose advice was sometimes sought by the Military Commander. I did not understand this and felt embarrassed by the inflated pleasure this gave him. He seemed most happy just listening to conversations when smoking his pipe or unravelling his untidy box of string. At other times he talked endlessly, without pausing to see if others wanted to speak.

FAU Work for Einbeck Displaced Persons

On 29th October, after five emotion-packed days with my parents, Grigor McClelland, whom I had known for four years, was now my FAU team leader, and came to drive me to Einbeck. The main displaced persons camp we served was in a former German military barrack which the Poles had named after their hero, General Sikorski. It housed some 500 displaced persons, in large dormitories partitioned into family units by hanging blankets. We also had responsibility for 14 smaller camps in the district, housing from 20 to 200 persons.

Our task was to compile a register listing names and numbers of displaced people in the district, to determine who wanted to be repatriated and to discover why others were reluctant to return. The Russians who had been in Einbeck had been repatriated before our arrival. There were many Poles and people from the Baltic countries, Romania and Yugoslavia. We needed to discover which families had special problems and to ensure that those who were sick received medical treatment. The people in our care had no employment or source of income. They understandably kept themselves separate from the German population. All were anxious about the future and could get no news from their home town. Many ugly stories were circulating about the Russian occupation of Eastern Europe. We tried to encourage some group activities and started several kindergartens, learning Polish nursery rhymes in the process. We organised a collection of wild rose hips from the hedgerows, to make a vitamin-rich syrup for the babies and discouraged the illicit distilling of schnapps.

One of the camps was a Polish stud farm under the control of a Polish cavalry officer. The Nazis had imported an entire stable of horses, along with the stable boys and their families to care for the horses. The Polish officer encouraged us to go riding with him on Sunday mornings. Most of us had never sat on a horse before, but were soon galloping over the hillsides of stubble fields with great abandon.

In its haste to repatriate displaced people from Germany, the Military Government directed us to prepare 400 people for return to Poland by freight train. Many were longing to return home, but we were sceptical about the living conditions they would face in Poland and anxious about the cold and discomfort they would experience on the five-day journey. We obtained straw for people to lie on and as they arrived on the railway platform we checked their documentation and survival equipment, giving them Red Cross food parcels, an army blanket and additional warm garments. Just before the train pulled out everyone was given a bowl of hot soup. The travellers were delighted with their send-off. (Illustration 34)

Quakers Meet Again in Pyrmont

During the weekend of 11-14th October the German Quakers held a second Executive Committee. The train services had just begun to operate though passengers had to travel in boarded-up carriages or goods wagons, because there was no glass available to repair the broken windows. Some Quakers from the American Zone managed to reach Pyrmont this time. German Friends were so pleased to have Fred Tritton from London and Errol Elliot from Indianapolis joining them, which they said felt like an opening of doors to the outside world. Friends talked about

34. *At Einbeck railway station, on 15th November 1945. Brenda handing warm clothing to families returning to Poland.*

the renewal of Quaker work, but also mourned those members who had died during the war. The Frankfurt Friends found it particularly difficult to restart their group without Alfons Paquet and Rudolf Schlosser. Joe and Albine Schindler were asked to reopen the Vienna Quaker Centre, which had been closed by the Nazis in 1942.

On 18th November many of us returned to Pyrmont for the wedding of Phyllis Stringer and Eric Turner, both British Quakers serving with the FAU. Leonhard, Mary and other Pyrmont Friends really enjoyed arranging and hosting a Quaker wedding.

Robin Whitworth, in charge of FAU overseas relief work, shared his reflections in *The Friend*, 30th November 1945:

> Germany is prostrate, and the Germans know they are beaten. Their minds are empty, but they are not cowed. 'We must work, work, and work', they say. In the midst the such fearful destruction caused by British bombs, it might be expected that they would be filled with hatred for us. But even in heavily-bombed Hamburg and the Ruhr there is a remarkable absence of resentment. The people feel they have been saved from something terrible, and are thankful that they live in the British Zone. They feel themselves to be in a spiritual vacuum . . . No matter how democratic Germans may now wish to be, they have forgotten the art . . . and have little understanding of the extent to which their name is hated throughout Europe.[4]

The Einbeck FAU Team Moves to Dortmund

As the winter got colder and the food shortages intensified, the Military Government became increasingly concerned for those in the Ruhr cities. Our Einbeck FAU team was asked to move to Dortmund. Two of us went ahead with Grigor McClelland to find out what would be needed. We were told our task was to support the German voluntary agencies who were valiantly trying to cope with the immense needs of the city.

Although I had lived in East London during the bombing, I was shocked to arrive in a huge industrial city which had been virtually destroyed. We first had to find somewhere to house our team. The Military Commander suggested we move into an empty villa in the British enclave, but this was too isolated from the community and far too grand. We were then offered two adjacent terraced houses, nearer the city centre at 214 Plettenburgstrasse, Gartenstadt. These seemed more appropriate, despite a substantial hole in the roof.

After this had been agreed, we were expected to assist the British army to make the residents leave, without offering alternative accommodation. I was horrified to realise that as relief workers we were making others homeless. But Grigor McClelland pointed out we could hardly survive the winter in tents. Had we chosen to move into the large empty villa in the British enclave, we might have felt easier, simply because we would not ourselves have taken part in an eviction, which had taken place months earlier.

When the removal day came, we encouraged the occupants to take all their personal possessions, including a sausage which a woman had accidentally left hanging from the curtain rail. But a basic amount of furniture had to be left for our use. It was with relief that we saw that the people we had evicted were taken in by neighbours in the road.

Our team was settled in and ready for work by mid-December. I was surprised to find myself the acting head of the Dortmund Red Cross Society, with a brief to restructure their organisation and to facilitate their essential welfare work. Germany's Red Cross leadership had been in the hands of the upper classes and was regarded as a Nazi stronghold.

We obtained and helped to distribute medical and other scarce supplies such as cod-liver oil, dried milk and soap to homes for children and homes for the elderly. We negotiated with the military government to get coal supplies for cooking and heating water. We started a Red Cross referral point at the main railway station, where German refugees from the East were directed to temporary accommodation.

On 10th January 1946, in a letter to my husband Sydney, I wrote:

I have been through hell this week with the Dortmund Red Cross, but I think things are now gradually going to function better. We have at last succeeded in appointing a director and have got the Nazis out. However, there is still a likelihood that the rest of the staff may leave in protest![5]

By now I had learned to drive the cumbersome field ambulances, though many of the streets were still cratered and impassable. Diana and I visited the voluntary welfare projects, which ranged from kindergartens, hostels for the homeless, homes for the elderly and the handicapped, finding out what they needed to function.

We created a co-ordinating council through which the voluntary bodies could report their needs to the Military Government. We helped them with materials and obtained permits to enable them to operate effectively. During our visits we sometimes discovered a complete breakdown of sanitary arrangements, where it was necessary to prompt the municipal authority to move cartloads of sewage. Some of the voluntary bodies provided accommodation for the homeless in six-storey bunkers. These were claustrophobic air raid shelters built above or below ground, constructed with five-foot-thick concrete walls.

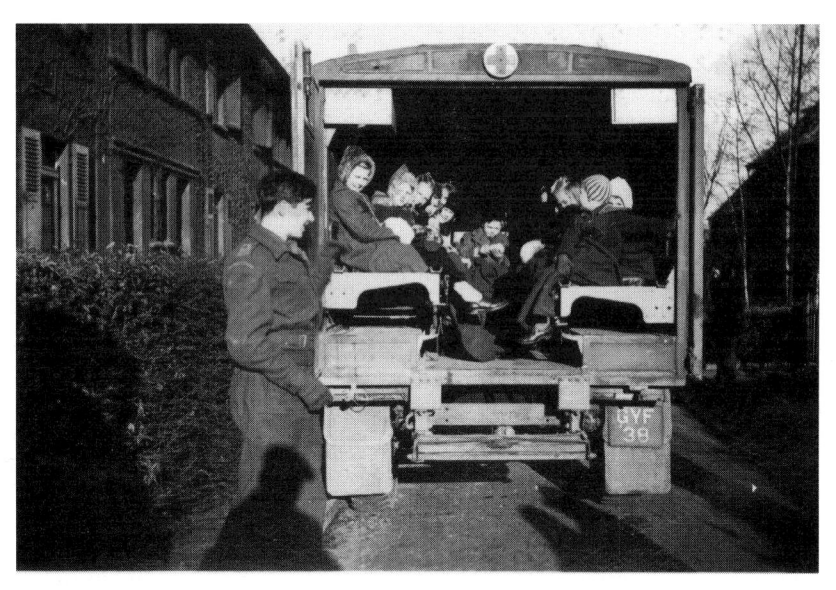

35. *Outside the FAU team house, Tony Trew taking children for convalescence.*

When the Military Government planned a school-feeding scheme, they asked us to discuss arrangements with head teachers, whilst we surveyed canteen arrangements. We obtained supplies for the welfare agencies through the Military Government, who occasionally uncovered a cache of Nazi stores. We could also draw on Red Cross clothing and blanket bales. After a few weeks we made collections of surplus food from army canteens. Many of the catering sergeants, during the Christmas season, willingly gave their surplus supplies for old folks and children's homes. Malnutrition among small children was a serious problem. We produced cans of banana powder for use in children's wards in hospitals. Eventually Dortmund Brewery made an infant malt/wheat carbohydrate formula for distribution, known as 'maltovena'. (Illustration 35)

The International Red Cross Searcher Service asked us to find missing persons. I looked for a number of Jewish people and after many abortive attempts of clambering around ruined buildings, I found three people. One Jewish woman had been married to a man who left her when he joined the SS, and became ashamed of his Jewish wife. Her two children had left for England on the Kindertransporte in 1938. She had gone into hiding, changing her appearance and moving from house to house in order to survive. I was able to take her a food parcel and register her for extra rations. Some weeks later, I delivered a letter from her children. She insisted on giving me a small silver brooch, which I was reluctant to accept, but is now a treasured souvenir.

Food supplies were extremely short in the British Zone. On 19th February 1946 the Military Government decreed that no more bread was to be sold after Thursday and that it would next week be a punishable offence to cook potatoes. All remaining potato stocks were to be kept as seed for spring planting. People started calling at our team house to ask for food. It was hard to refuse and we sometimes invited them for a meal in our kitchen. One blind man asked for kitchen scraps for his guide dog; he had no relatives to look after him and would have been helpless if his dog were to die of hunger.

CHAPTER XXII

Picking up the Broken Threads 1946-9

MY NEXT VISIT TO PYRMONT was 18-24 January 1946. Leonhard and Mary had been disappointed that work in Dortmund had kept me from spending Christmas with them, but we made up for it. My cousin Denys Holland, in the British army, had arranged for leave in Pyrmont to see Leonhard and Mary and was staying in a Hauptallee hotel for soldiers. Wolfgang Mueller, a young Friend who had left his parents in the Soviet Zone, was also there. Shortly afterwards he joined the FAU team in Essen as an interpreter and in 1949 came to live with Leonhard and Mary for three-and-a-half years. Leonhard regarded him as an apprentice and hoped he might become a partner to develop the Quaker publishing business. I was grateful to Wolfgang for this, because in some ways he filled the gap I had left in the family by marrying early. (Illustration 36)

Leonhard became very interested in the Nuremberg Trials, which had begun on 20th November 1945, when 22 leading Nazis were indicted. On 30th September the following year 19 were found guilty and were either sentenced to death or imprisonment.

When Leonhard recounted his Buchenwald experiences to fellow Germans, they often listened in disbelief. After people absorbed the shock of the appalling Nuremberg revelations, they seemed to submerge the facts from their conscious minds as though they had never happened. It is perhaps understandable that people who could hardly cope with the immediate problems of post-war life had little inclination to reflect on the shameful past. It was not until years later when the next generation of young adults began asking questions about the Nazi atrocities that many people examined their consciences.

Pyrmont Conference for Quaker Relief Workers, February 1946

Roger Wilson called a conference at the Quakerhouse to set out aims for the Friends Relief Service (FRS) work in Germany. Many of the FAU members had almost completed their wartime alternative service to conscription and were due for demobilisation over the next six months. The FAU had proved itself an adaptable relief organisation, filling the gaps between Military Government and German voluntary organisations. This enabled the FRS, who already had relief teams in Germany, to take over some of the longer-term work, along with younger members of the FAU who still had some years to serve.

Richard Ullmann, who participated in this conference, had come to Britain as a Jewish refugee in 1939, leaving his wife and child in Germany. In 1940 he had been interned in Britain and sent to an Australian prison camp with Germans suspected of being Nazis. On his return to Britain before the end of the war, he had been recognised as an original thinker in the Society of Friends and had trained relief workers for their service in Germany. Richard wrote about the relief workers conference:

When we arrived at the Quakerhouse, we found many familiar faces, among them was a German Friend who knew me by name, because he meets my wife Lena every Thursday in Bible study class, in

36. *Wolfgang Mueller, on the balcony standing behind Mary and Leonhard.*

Frankfurt-am-Main. It is strange to think he will see her again before I have done so.

Our German Friends contributed very creatively to the deliberations and were inspired by the depth of our concern and thoughtfulness. This was the best Quaker gathering I have ever attended . . . 20 young Friends speaking from much practical experience and inward concern. Nine sessions were crowded into 63 hours, during which we considered 19 types of work. Would that we could always live up to such inspiration.[1]

In December 1945 William Hughes, the Quaker prison visitor, returned to Germany to spend several months talking to the Nazis held in detention by the Military Government. He joined in the discussions during the prisoners' English classes and added reading materials to their bookshelves. He did this in much the same spirit as he had in earlier years visited Jews and political prisoners. During the war he was one of almost 100 British Friends who regularly visited German POWs on the Isle of Man, where he lived.[2] In a letter to *The Friend* on 7th December 1945 he wrote:

It was good to find Leonhard Friedrich apparently his own humorous self again. I was taken to a meeting of the Pyrmont Youth Committee, whose members faced many hardships, such as lack of shoes and heat. I was glad to see the direct way Mary Friedrich tackled the authorities on their behalf. At the weekend Brenda Bailey came home full of tales about what their FAU team had been doing with the Red Cross in Dortmund. We were about 50 people at Meeting for Worship on Sunday. Leonhard jokingly warned Friends to beware of becoming too popular![3]

Time For Me to Return to England

In March I heard from my husband, Sydney Bailey, that he had found a flat for us in north London, at 155 Brecknock Road, Tufnell Park. Since I was among the women who had now been released from conscription, I returned to England to look for a job to pay the rent. I visited Leonhard and Mary for the last time between 8-17 March. We eagerly planned that they should visit us in London at the end of May, to enable them to attend the London Yearly Meeting. Jim McNicol, the British Military Commander in Pyrmont, was impressed with what Mary had achieved through the Voluntary Committee and promised them seats on the military train service, since there was still no facility for civilian travel.

Rest Home Reopens

The Friends Service Council decided to re-open the Rest Home at St Joseph's House in Pyrmont, for people in need of further care following their discharge from concentration and labour camps. Bill Brown, who later became a well-known tenor singer, came to help Mary make suitable preparations. During this time he lived with Leonhard and Mary and was rather embarrassed one day to come back to find Mary mending his clothes. Elizabeth Fox Howard, then aged 70, was the first post-war hostess. Mary had eagerly looked forward to renewing their friendship. She had so much to talk about and wanted to understand what had happened to their mutual friends in Britain. Before the war they had gone together to visit Roehm at the Brown House in Nuremberg and the women's prison etc. Of all her friends, Mary felt Elsie would best understand what she had been through during these hard years. But there seemed to be a distance between them now. Elsie was preoccupied with the excitement of being in Germany again, wearing the Quaker grey battle dress like the young people and enjoying talking about how she had paid her taxi fare with a packet of cigarettes.

On 10th May 1946, the young Dr Ott Buchinger, who had been a POW in Canada, arrived back in Pyrmont. He had not been officially released, but Mary was able to have his discharge regularised with the help of Major Jim McNicol. From then on Ott was able to support his father, working as a doctor in the *Klinik* and gradually taking on more responsibility. In 1951, when he was 75 years old, Otto Buchinger senior left Pyrmont for Ueberlingen on Lake Constance, to help establish a second *Buchinger Klinik*, managed by his daughter Herta, and her husband Helmut Wilhelmi. This left young Ott and his wife Marlies, free to develop a new *Klinik* built on the hill-side overlooking Pyrmont, which opened in 1959.

First Post-war Visit to England 1946

At the end of May, Mary and Leonhard boarded the military train to London. On her return Mary wrote in her diary:

We were wonderfully looked after on the journey and so well fed, that I started feeling better straight away. However we found Sydney and Brenda's flat in Tufnell Park was rather basic. We slept in an attic bedroom with a sloping ceiling covered with posters to hide the war damage with only a small mat to cover the bare floorboards. Our brass bedstead was tied together with string. The bathroom and toilet were shared with two other families. Brenda and Sydney did their best for us, but they did not understand how to provide the comforts we longed for.

These comments of Mary's are almost mirror images of those I made in letters to Sydney during my first visit to Pyrmont. With her memories of a comfortable pre-war life in England, Mary was not prepared for the hardships which we had grown used to in Britain. They both enjoyed a visit to Woodbrooke, the Quaker college in Birmingham. There was much to catch up with among Quakers and with Mary's family.

On returning to Bad Pyrmont Leonhard struggled to re-establish the publishing business. He started by selling the books he had retrieved from the paper mill, at a time when there was nothing in the shops to buy. He applied for compensation for the unrecovered books and the office equipment which the Gestapo had taken, a process which took several years. But he was one of the first publishers in the British zone to be allocated paper and given a permit to reopen his business. He also got a permit to publish the monthly *Der Quaker* and the first issue appeared in July 1946.

Quakers throughout Germany were greatly helped by the CARE packages that began arriving from Quakers in Canada and the USA. These were standard cartons of 30 lbs of canned and dry foods. We received similar packages in Britain, which were particularly welcome when our first child was born in 1947. Mary was scrupulous about sharing her parcels with Friends and other needy people. Like many of her neighbours, she and Leonhard had virtually no income. The soldiers would give local girls packets of cigarettes for their favours, and these became the standard 'currency' for ordinary transactions, such as paying the plumber or getting one's shoes repaired. Fortunately CARE parcels always contained a few packs of cigarettes. Mary suggested the names of needy Quaker families to whom American Friends might direct CARE parcels, rather than distributing them all herself.

Leonhard was very sad to learn that his only brother, Bernhard, of whom he was very fond, had died at his home in Pennsylvania on 7th January 1947. His son Martin had served with the US forces in Germany and married a German girl from Chemnitz, but never visited his uncle.

Hard Times of 1947

This was the most difficult of Germany's post-war years. Initially the Germans showed remarkable goodwill towards the British occupation. Many recognised the evil of the Nazi dictatorship and began to take a lively interest in democratic institutions, frequently featured on the radio. The British Control Commission opened an educational division to prepare people for democratic life. Bertha Bracey, the Quaker who had led the work for German refugees in Britain, was now providing leadership training for women's groups in Germany through the Control Commission.

By 1947, when some normalisation of life in the cities was expected, large scale unemployment occurred while some of the German industries were being dismantled under reparation agreements. This led people to think that the promises of the Allies for a better life, were as hollow as Goebbels' propaganda. Confidence in democracy seemed to crumble. There were acute shortages of food, fuel and raw materials, and yet the UN Relief and Rehabilitation Administration (UNRRA) was being closed down.

Conditions in Britain during the winter of 1946-7 were also very hard. It was an exceptionally cold winter; food was rationed and the necessities of life were scarce. Europe seemed at a point of collapse. Winston Churchill, as Leader of the Opposition, put forward his vision for a United Europe in an article published by *The Times*, asking for responses to be sent to the home of Duncan Sandys, Churchill's son-in-law. Sacks of mail soon arrived from eminent supporters all over Europe. I was one of three young women temporarily employed to sort these out. We worked by candle-light in the basement of the Sandys' home, through endless power cuts, while Mary Sandys kept us going with cups of tea and hot water bottles. However, I enjoyed my few weeks working 'below stairs' in Sandys residence at Smith Square.

In the face of Germany's slow recovery from wartime privations, British Friends felt that it had become more important to take 'a message of hope' to their German counterparts than to continue the relief work. They opened several neighbourhood centres to encourage local initiative and offer support to people who were in a position to help others. One of these individuals observed: 'gaining the personal confidence to work democratically, was more valuable than a hundred books or CARE parcels'. At a political level Friends in the UK pressed for more humane and positive policies and supported Victor Gollancz, a radical publisher of Jewish background who pleaded for the return of POWs still being held in Britain, started a 'Save Europe Now' movement, enthusiastically supported by British Quakers. However some of the prisoners' families, who lived in the Soviet Zone, advised their men not to return, for fear of being deported to the Soviet Union as forced labour.

General Marshall launched the generous American aid plan for the recovery of Europe in 1947, from which 16 nations were to benefit. This excluded the Soviet Union enabling Moscow to tighten its control over Eastern Europe.

Yearly Meeting in Pyrmont 1947

The first post-war German Yearly Meeting was held in Pyrmont in July 1947. In spite of travel difficulties Quakers came from all parts of Germany. Willy Wohlrabe came from the Soviet Zone and once again a Nuremberg Friend, Hans Exmer walked all the way there and back, as he had done in 1932. The Friends present had survived great hardships and felt deep satisfaction in gathering together in freedom. They recognised that: 'Our own hearts were hardened and our characters were warped by living through years of violence, fear, dishonesty and selfishness. However, some of us found a new sense of fellowship in serving others'. Regret was expressed that British Quakers were unable to work in East Germany, where conditions were much tougher. Many people spoke of problems with the Russian soldiers in the Soviet Zone. Mary's guest book listed the names of 30 Yearly Meeting participants, among them was Ingrid Seutemann, from England, visiting her parents for the first time since the war, also Joan Mary Fry, Corder and Gwen Catchpool.

Currency Reform and the Berlin Airlift

Since the ending of the war the Mark had lost its value and a thriving black market economy emerged. On 20th June 1948 a currency reform took place in the British and American zones. This was necessary to restore confidence, but it was a disaster for Leonhard. His modest bank account was reduced overnight to one tenth of its value. The printers, who had been very slow in delivering the books he had ordered, completed their work overnight, demanding payment of 40,000 DM. This was the fourth time in his life that he had lost every penny: in the inflation which followed the First World War; when he would not join the Nazi Party and lost his job in 1933; when the Gestapo took all his assets in 1942; and again with currency reform in 1947. He felt helpless and did not know where to turn. Mary sold household items she could spare, took in paying guests and asked me to send small amounts of money from her savings in England.

Currency reform sparked off a chain of events which escalated the 'cold war' between the Western and former Soviet Allies. The Russians stopped all traffic from West to East Germany, blocking road, canal and rail traffic to Berlin. The Western Allies flew in supplies for their military personnel and the 2½ million German civilians in their part of the city, through the Templehof airport, which was still under their control. Food, fuel and other necessities were brought to Berlin by a round-the-clock airlift. This began in June 1948 and continued for a year, until the motorway access was negotiated. During this difficult period Ernst Reuter was the Mayor of Berlin while the citizens refused to be intimidated. On 11th October 1947, the Soviet Zone of Germany had been declared a separate state, known as the German Democratic Republic.

A Step Toward Retirement in 1948

In July Leonhard and Mary gave up their duties as wardens of the Meeting House. Reinhard and Erna Peppler, a Quaker couple who had arrived as homeless refugees from the Soviet Zone, took their place. They were ten years younger than Leonhard and Mary. Leonhard built a book storage room into the Quakerhouse loft and converted a bedroom in their own flat into an office.

Leonhard and Mary were relieved to be able to give up the hard work of looking after the Quakerhouse and grew fond of Erna and Reinhard. Leonhard was then 58 years old and Mary, at 65, felt ready to restrict her gardening to producing geraniums for the balcony. Leonhard was concerned about their financial position and had to take out a bank loan. But he established good relations with the Pyrmonter Volksbank, which invited him to become a member of their board. From then on he made more contacts in the town, which he had been wary of doing in the Nazi period.

In 1949 Leonhard applied for compensation for the books which he had lost at the printers during an air raid on Leipzig on 5th December 1943. He was told he should have made the application at the time, though when he said he was then in Buchenwald, he was given an emergency business loan of 2,500 DM.

Early in 1949 Mary again suffered from shingles and eczema, perhaps brought on by anxiety. Leonhard was not always easy to live with; there were times when he would not speak to Mary for weeks on end. After liberation there was much depression and many suicides among the concentration camp survivors. Some felt guilt at having survived at the expense of others weaker than themselves, perhaps having robbed them of bread. Some former prisoners engaged in frenzied rounds of pleasure.[5] Many Nazi victims found it impossible to share their feelings with their relatives and kept silent as Leonhard periodically did. Otto Buchinger took Mary into his sanatorium for a few weeks, during which time she wrote:

Away from my usual responsibilities and duties, I have found peace of mind here, such as I have not experienced since I was a child.

CHAPTER XXIII

The Later Years 1950-79

IN MAY 1949, WHEN MARY VISITED us again in London, we had moved to a larger flat at 156 Earls Court Road, SW5. She loved looking after our two babies, but quite rightly said that we had a lot to learn about bringing up children. Mary was once again a stalwart attender of London Yearly Meeting, not missing a single session of the five-day meetings and enjoying lunch breaks with old friends. After a few days with us, she travelled on to Dublin to take part in Ireland Yearly Meeting and spoke to several groups about German Friends. During her pre-war visits to Britain, Mary's talks had helped her to find overseas sponsors for refugees, now they helped to generate practical support for needy German Quakers and for their work in the community.

The German Yearly Meeting of 1950 was held in Berlin, to make it easier for the East German Quakers to attend. Some 250 Friends came and 39 new members were admitted. Leonhard announced his retirement as Treasurer, an office he had held for 23 years. He was now rebuilding his publishing business. (Illustration 37)

Douglas Steere, the American Friend who had visited Britain and Germany in 1941, came again in 1950 and wrote the following comments in his journal:

> In Germany I saw the stark and grim reality of ever present ruined city buildings, behind which I felt a bustling normality of life . . . But there were over a million expellees from the East, much unemployment and very low wages . . . A large proportion of women have lost their menfolk . . . In contrast to Britain, there is great apathy toward political activity.[1]

On 17th December 1950 Mary was visiting her close friend Helene Engel-Reimers and fell on an icy Pyrmont road as she was going home. She lay in the snow for an hour before being found. In hospital they discovered she had a seven-inch break in her shin bone, which was protruding through the wound. The fracture healed very slowly and she developed

37. *Leonhard Friedrich and Emil Fuchs joking with Friends at Yearly Meeting tea, 1951.*

osteomyelitis. She was kept in the St Georg's hospital, next door to the Quakerhouse, for four months and enjoyed being looked after by Sister Wendolini, a nun who had been kind to her during the war. Leonhard was very anxious about her.

Mary's Visit to the United States, Winter 1951-2

In November 1951 Mary visited us again in London, on her way to the United States for a five-month visit. She was still unwell; the leg wound had not entirely healed and she had sores on her face and ears. We were worried about her undertaking such a journey without Leonhard. After treatment with the new drug, penicillin, our doctor agreed to her travelling and she greatly enjoyed the two-week sea voyage. I wonder what was driving my frail 69-year-old mother to undertake such a long journey? It may have been her longing to see her four brothers and sisters who lived on that side of the Atlantic.

Arrangements for Mary's visit were made by the AFSC, in support of Quaker work in Germany. They planned her itinerary and arranged for her to give talks at Quaker Meetings and to other local groups. Once again, Mary interested people in the needs of German Friends and their work. As she travelled around she was amazed by the comfort and modern kitchens in many homes, but she found others who lived very simply. She met several of the former refugees she had helped to emigrate, and was delighted to be able to return some small family treasures. In New York she met Mrs Fleischmann and Mrs Wuga, two Jewish women who had been our neighbours in Nuremberg. She arrived at the home of her sister, Jennie Falconer, in St Louis for Christmas and spent a month in the Midwest. This visit was embarrassing at times, because Jennie and her daughter Joyce Mathews had become fundamentalist Christians, who prayed that Mary might be 'saved'. She also visited her widowed sister Kate Russell in Troy, Missouri.

Leaving St Louis, Mary visited the Barnesville Quaker School in Ohio, where she was very attracted to the simple life-style. A few of the Friends there still wore long dresses in Quaker grey, with bonnets and shawls and the men wore shirts with stiff collars, without lapels to their jackets.

On her way back to the East Coast, Mary visited Washington DC and Philadelphia, spending some time at Pendle Hill, the Quaker study centre. She stayed with Clarence and Lily Pickett, the Executive Secretary of the AFSC and visited Dora Friedrich, Leonhard's widowed sister-in-law. She then went to Canada to visit her brother Frank Tupholme and enjoyed being with her brother Will Tupholme, who had come from Vancouver to be with her in Toronto. Mary summed up her long tour saying she had travelled 20,000 miles, slept in 41 beds, had addressed 80 groups and written 322 letters. The fact that she had also consulted 13 doctors shows how unfit she still was. One doctor described her as still being 'extremely undernourished', which reflected the continued post-war food shortages in Europe. In thanking Philadelphia Quakers for their hospitality she said central heating was a wonderful invention. During the very cold winter months she had never, even once, had cold feet or hands.

We were relieved to see her back in London in May. She had enjoyed many experiences and adventures and had undoubtedly benefitted from them. Five months was a very long time to have left Leonhard. No doubt he would have liked to have been with her some of the time in America, but he needed to stay at home to re-build the publishing business, which was their livelihood.

While in the United States, Mary had met Rebecca Beard and was introduced to her writings. Rebecca was a Quaker doctor who practised faith healing and wrote about the influence of personal attitudes on health. Mary, steeped in the principles of the Buchinger fasting-klinik, found her writings wise and helpful. Over the next few years Leonhard published several of Rebecca Beard's books in German, notably *Was Jederman Sucht* (*Everyman's Search*), which sold well and also introduced some new readers to Quaker literature.

Return to Pyrmont 1952

It was now Leonhard's turn for a treat. American Friends, Ruth and Delbert Replogle had come over to Europe and hired a car to tour Scandinavia. They took Leonhard with them for an unforgettable four-week holiday in July and August.

In November 1954, Leonhard received his state retirement pension. He was also awarded an extra pension as a Nazi victim, with additional compensation for loss of health. From then on, after nine years of scraping to make ends meet, their financial situation improved. Eventually Leonhard also received compensation for the stock of books that had been destroyed by the Gestapo, though he was never compensated for the war-damaged stock held by his printers in Leipzig, because it was in East Germany.

During the next five years the life of Mary and Leonhard continued without the traumatic events of earlier times. With the help of one of Mary's Swiss friends, they managed to have a longed-for holiday in the mountains, taking Mary's Canadian brother Will Tupholme and her youngest sister Margaret Harbour along with them. Mary's widowed sister Kate Russell from America came to live with them in Pyrmont, but she was very deaf and spoke no German, so after nine months she returned to the United States. Sydney and I moved to New York with our children in 1954 in order to work as Quaker Representatives at the United Nations.

Max Born

In 1951 Max Born and his wife Hedwig retired to Bad Pyrmont and became friends with Leonhard and Mary. Before the war Max had been the distinguished head of the physics department of Goettingen University, where he had taught Klaus Fuchs. With the rise of Nazism, Born had left for Britain to accept a professorship at Edinburgh University, where he continued research in quantum mechanics. Born's attitude to his research work, which also influenced Klaus Fuchs, was summed by the Quaker crystallographer, Kathleen Lonsdale:

> The risk has always got to be taken that a person's work and achievement, good in itself, might later be abused. However, once it is known that the purpose of the work is criminal and evil, then the personal responsibility of the researcher cannot be evaded.[2]

Born's wife Hedwig, became an active member of the Quaker Meeting in Edinburgh. During their retirement in Pyrmont in 1954, he received the Nobel Prize for his work in physics and the town subsequently erected a bronze bust in the Brunnen Platz in recognition of their famous citizen.

Mary's Reflections – New Year 1957

At Christmas 1957 Mary packed over 20 parcels of food and clothing for Quakers in East Germany, who were still having a very hard time. During the New Year holiday, Mary reflected on her life:

I have been re-reading my diaries since 1901. My life seems to have been most productive during the years when I was between 20 and 40 years old. I am surprised to find how many talks I gave and how many papers I wrote about factory conditions. I managed this in spite of ill health. I also found time to make my own clothes. I dearly loved Brenda Voysey and was quite sentimental about Leonhard. He was the only man I ever took an interest in. I wonder if I would have given up the industrial welfare work I loved, if my health had been better? I got on well with the workers and was appreciated by my employers.

I have never felt as fulfilled since moving to Germany, but I do not regret having come. Through my overseas connections I have been able to help so many people. Looking back, I can see it has been too important to me to be liked, instead of finding satisfaction in being the channel of love to others.

Mary had now left behind the worst period of her life, when she had been almost totally isolated, suffering frequent Gestapo harassment and living in fear of arrest. Leonhard was home and she had close links with her family and friends. She did however, miss having an intimate woman friend, such as Edith Straus had been to her in Nuremberg. She ended her reflections with a quotation from *The Wisdom of John Woolman*, an American Friend who fought against slavery in the mid-18th century:

The Lord, who was the guide of my youth, hath in tender mercies helped me hitherto. He hath healed my wounds and helped me out of grievous entanglements; He remains to be the strength of my life, to whom I devote myself in time and eternity.[3]

Second Visit to the United States 1958

In April 1958 Leonhard and Mary came to visit us in New York for a month whilst we were working for the AFSC as Quaker Representatives at the United Nations. We lived in a brownstone house with garden at 247 East 48th Street in Manhattan, close to the UN buildings. We were in daily contact with UN Delegates and Secretariat members about issues of concern to Quakers, often inviting them for discussions over lunch or dinner. This was the exciting period of decolonization for Africa and sparked off my life-time interest in that continent. We came to the United States towards the end of the McCarthy period, when the Senator was promoting a witch-hunt against Communists. As Quakers we made efforts to establish good personal relations with the Soviet Ambassador at the UN Arkady Sobolev and members of his delegation. We were in touch with other East Europeans and also got to know many leading Africans and Asians.

Leonhard and Mary came to New York by boat from Hamburg. They went on to visit other relatives and Friends, but this time Mary left much of the travelling to Leonhard. Mary was delighted to find Margaret Jones on the New York Quaker staff. She had known Margaret in 1940 when she worked at the Vienna Quaker Centre. Margaret invited Mary to take part in a seminar on the economic problems of Africa, set up for Friends visiting from the Midwest. Mary took notes and gave several talks to German Friends when she returned home. She enjoyed being shown around Manhattan by her grandchildren, then eight and ten years old. They took her to Radio City Music Hall, to their school at the Friends Seminary, to children's concerts and the Delcroze School of Dancing and ice skating at the Rockefeller Center.

Friends World Committee Conference in Pyrmont 1958

Over a hundred Friends from 36 Yearly Meetings around the world came together at Pyrmont at the end of September 1958. Margarethe Lachmund, who had been the Clerk of the Yearly Meeting from 1948-54, spoke about the healing potential of Quaker faith in a divided world, which had particular poignancy for a Meeting held in divided Germany. She spoke of her experience of not showing fear towards an oppressor. With the power of love, she was able to overcome the evil she encountered. But if she was fearful, the appropriate words seemed to dry up inside her. Horst Bruekner from East Germany spoke persuasively about understanding the idealism of Communism. Kathleen Lonsdale, Professor of Chemistry and head of the Department of Crystallography at University College, London, spoke about the peaceful uses of atomic energy. Sydney Bailey, my husband, spoke about Quaker work at the UN, explaining how it grew out of our religious concern. He said that it involved working with people whose methods and outlook may be very different from ours, but stressed that diplomats have their own convictions and are just as concerned as Quakers to find peaceful solutions.

At the conclusion of this exhilarating conference, the Friends World Committee created a sense of spiritual unity among Quakers who had developed different traditions in many parts of the world, but had common roots in George Fox's teaching. Friends also supported the influential role their representatives in New York and Geneva could have as a non-governmental organisation working for peace at the United Nations. The

Quaker task at the UN was defined as being ready to help reconcile diverging viewpoints.[4, 5]

Looking after more than a hundred foreign Friends in Pyrmont in 1958 was no easy matter. Some discussion groups met swathed in blankets in the draughty Quakerhouse attic space, while others met in the Friedrichs' sitting room. Mary mentioned her pleasure in finding Sydney in the kitchen, washing up the coffee cups. (Illustration 38)

Leonhard's Tour of the Soviet Union 1960

For three weeks during July-August 1960 Leonhard joined a congenial group of mainly British Quakers on a tour to the Soviet Union. It was organised by Jack Catchpool, brother of Corder, who had started the Youth Hostels Association in the inter-war years. Jack hired a coach and arranged for 30 Friends to travel from London, driving through the Warsaw Pact countries. Leonhard joined them in Berlin, on their way to Moscow, Smolensk, Minsk and Prague. This was a real adventure in 1960, at the time of the Cold War. In Moscow's Red Square some of the party took mischievous pleasure in arguing with the police about taking a photo.

38. *1958 Friends World Committee in Pyrmont. Group session held in cold Quakerhouse loft.*

Coach travel gave opportunities for observing rural life and as they saw the huge wheat fields being harvested by hand because few tractors were available. The party was appalled by the squalor of the massive housing developments in the cities. Leonhard was glad to be home again, but had very much enjoyed the company and the understanding it gave him for those living under the Communist system.

Our family returned to London in the summer of 1960, partly because Sydney had a recurrence of bilharzia, contracted in China during the war, but also because we wanted our children, then aged 13 and 11, to feel their British identity. We had an enjoyable summer holiday in Pyrmont.

Sharing Experiences on Mary's Flower-filled Balcony

Mary gradually stayed at home more. She was now 78 years old and had mellowed in outlook, though several friends said: 'It is astonishing how fresh and young Mary remains in spirit'. She conscientiously made time for regular daily walks, in order to retain her diminishing mobility. She spent many hours on her balcony couch surrounded by the geraniums she grew from cuttings made each autumn and a magnificent tall oleander plant. The balcony was large enough for a table and chairs, and trapped the sun for eight months of the year. Many Friends remember sitting there, recalling the warmth and friendship with Leonhard and Mary, and the beautiful views it offered as the sun set against the hills.

Dr Otto Buchinger (1878-1966) was one of these many visiting Friends. Otto had helped Mary when she was ill and had supported her while Leonhard was away in Buchenwald. Now that he had retired, he enjoyed talking to her about his family and reflecting about Quakerism and the meaning of life. He told her about his intention of returning to Roman Catholicism after living for 40 years as a Quaker. One day, when he was about to leave for south Germany and was wondering if his age would prevent him from returning to Pyrmont again, he asked:

Mary, I have so much enjoyed my talks with you on this balcony. I shall miss them when I die. I would like to feel I could come back to you occasionally after I have gone. Would you mind?

Another Friend who meant a great deal to Mary and Leonhard was Dr Paul Oestreicher senior (1896-1981), who lived in Pyrmont from 1961-6, whilst working as a doctor and acupuncturist at the Buchinger Klinik. With his wife Maidi and their son Paul, he had left Germany in 1939 because he was Jewish. They emigrated to New Zealand, where they became Quakers. Their son Paul returned to Britain and became an Anglican clergyman, whilst later also becoming a member of the Society of Friends. His parents enjoyed the opportunity of returning to medical work in post-war Germany, for six years. After Leonhard's death Paul senior wrote: (Illustration 39)

> Leonhard and Mary were our closest friends for the years we lived in Pyrmont. Their memory is very precious to me. Mary was one of the most remarkable personalities I ever met in my life. She had such courage, integrity and strength of spirit. Her spiritual energy was an inspiration to many others. She seemed to be the heart and soul of the Bad Pyrmont Meeting. Her open mind and hospitality for all Friends, was unique.
>
> Leonhard had a much less developed ego, but was kindness itself and firmly stuck to his principles, for which he suffered bravely. I never forgot his jokes about being an ex-con. He was able to change and adapt himself to so many different situations in life, which is surely a sign of a well-integrated life.[6]

Yearly Meeting in Eisenach 1961

During the 1950s the effects of the Marshall Aid programme for West Germany gradually led to increasing prosperity, which was particularly noticeable in Berlin. In 1961 the Soviet Union built the Berlin Wall, to cut off all contact with the West, leaving the young East Germans looking enviously across the divide.

39. Dr Paul Oestreicher Snr.

These circumstances led to the Yearly Meeting of 1961 being held in East Germany. In August Leonhard and Mary crossed the Berlin Wall to reach Eisenach for the Yearly Meeting. Mary's diary, 28th July to 3rd August:

> The hotel in which we stayed had no more comfort than one would have expected a hundred years ago. But it was clean and the staff were kind. There were 200 Friends present for the Meetings, including Gwen Catchpool from London. I have been asked to become a Yearly Meeting Elder, which means having some advisory responsibility for the spiritual life of the Society, and being available for consultation about issues that are difficult to deal with at the local level. I was for instance, invited to hear 'Young Quakers' speak about their special problems. I am very pleased that the Yearly Meeting has decided to set up a *Quakerhilfe*, a German Quaker Service Committee.

Mary had been filling collecting tins for *'Brot für die Welt'* since she learned more about the problems of poverty in Africa during her visit to New York. The Yearly Meeting also organised a small group to visit Buchenwald, with Leonhard as their guide.

Etta Klingmueller's Reflections on Leonhard and Mary

Etta, who was Clerk of Bad Pyrmont Yearly Meeting, gave a talk at Woodbrooke College in 1966 in which she said:

> In pre-war years I used to think of the Berlin Quaker office as the 'head' of the Society, where letters were written and records kept, and of the Quakerhouse in Pyrmont as the 'heart', sending a pulse through the whole Society. Pyrmont has the lovely Quakerhouse, its atmosphere and beautiful scenery; the Quakerhouse also has the library and the cemetery and historic connections with an earlier era of German Quakerism. But the history of Quakerism does not lie in buildings, it exists in the lives of Friends, such as Leonhard and Mary Friedrich.
>
> I think of Mary, who has now reclaimed her British nationality, as always having been a 'Friend in Germany', whereas Leonhard is a 'German Friend'. It is never easy to change one's nationality, and I do not blame Mary for finding it difficult to identify herself as a German. Mary is outspoken and concerned about immediate problems, drawing our attention to opportunities for service. While Leonhard, as a Quaker publisher, represents Quakerism to the wider public, both through his documentary and historical work, and in his service as treasurer and trustee to the Society.

One day Mary had time to tell me about her work in Britain before she came to Germany. When I suggested she should write a book about it, she said:

'Oh no, Friends make so little use of our library, although it holds many interesting precious books. I don't want to add yet another.'

At the end of an Executive Committee Meeting in 1963, Mary asked to speak. The Clerk gave her the floor saying: 'Make it brief Mary, we are all rather tired'. After a few minutes Mary had the Meeting listening attentively, as she spoke of the vision she had for holding a Quaker Seminar. She had a tentative programme in mind, including the names of people to introduce topics. She had even made preliminary approaches for funding. This was recognised as the most exciting item on the agenda.[7]

Quaker Seminar – April 1965

Mary had introduced many people to Quakerism who were searching for more meaningful beliefs in the post-war world. She had for some time been considering how the German Society of Friends could be given a new impetus, and felt a series of annual Quaker seminars would satisfy this need.

She helped to organise the first seminar in 1965, very much in the style of a Woodbrooke course. Mary, who was 82 years old, was pleased by the number of young Friends who came. She felt that Konrad Braun from Woodbrooke had given a superb introduction. Mary admitted that Bertha Bracey's talk on the Advices and Queries was less well-received, because she read her paper. The informal part of the seminar had also gone very well, helped along by many cups of cocoa, thanks to supplies provided by Paul Cadbury.

Leonhard Disposes of the Quaker Publishing Business 1966

During the early 1960s Leonhard had been trying to find a way to keep the publishing business in Quaker hands, when he would have to give it up, but one solution after another failed to work out. He was now 76 years old and could not continue much longer, because Mary was needing more care. The Verlag had been started by British Friends in 1922 and 10 years later Leonhard took it over on behalf of German Friends. In 1939 it had to be transferred to the Leonhard Friedrich Verlag, because German churches were no longer permitted to publish. With his arrest in 1942 the business was closed and the books were carted to the papermill. Leonhard had invested half a life time to the venture. He had created a large and varied list of some 60 titles, as well as a similar number of Heritage leaflets. Small numbers of Quaker classics in German, such as George Fox's Journal, would always be needed, but nothing could turn them into best sellers. He said a Quaker Literature Committee could not be depended upon to make business-like financial decisions or look after the stock carefully. Friends could not afford to pay him for the capital he had tied up in the books. He therefore opened negotiations with several publishers. Eventually, in January 1966, a publisher *Turm Verlag*, agreed to purchase the business. After months of negotiation, Leonhard found himself having to accept a price less than half of what he had hoped for.

A few weeks later Leonhard watched sadly as five removal vans tooks away 60 boxes of books. However he gave DM 1,000 worth of books to the library and left more in the attic store-room, a few of which can still be found there to this day.

Leonhard and Mary Leave Bad Pyrmont

By October 1966 Mary had become quite frail and practically immobile with arthritis. They both decided it was time to move to Harbour House, a Quaker retirement home by the sea at Bridport in Dorset, to be nearer to us. They appreciated the care and comforts of living in a friendly small establishment. Despite visits from Margaret Harbour, Mary's sister, Gwen Catchpool and occasionally some German Friends, it was strange for them to be among people who had very little understanding of their past lives. No one finds it easy to give up the freedom of one's own home or to adjust to the few house rules that have to be respected.

Harbour House was a pleasant new building in which they occupied a self-contained flatlet, with meals provided. They enjoyed the peaceful life, the constantly changing light of the sea and getting to know other resident Friends. They had their own television set for the first time. Mary's mind was not always clear towards the end, and she used to tell me about 'that nice man Malcolm Muggeridge who came to visit us last night'. After Leonhard had been watching a Western she might tell me: 'there were some horrid people shooting around in our sitting room last evening, but they left without hurting us'. Leonhard enjoyed Bridport Meeting. It was a blessing that he remained healthy and strong enough to support Mary. I visited them for a weekend almost every month, driving them around the Dorset countryside and tracking down where the best pub lunches were to be had. Mary died peacefully on 11th November 1970, with both of us beside her. She was 88 years old. Leonhard had nursed her devotedly for three months.

Leonhard was at first devastated to be alone, and said he should have listened to Mary's counsel more often. After he recovered from the

40. *Leonhard, reading the newspaper (artist unknown)*.

extremely exhausting final months of Mary's life, he considered moving to London to be with us, or returning to Germany. But he eventually decided to remain at Harbour House, where he particularly enjoyed the company of Mildred Chattin, a Quaker in the next-door flatlet. They laughed a lot together and she was always there to help him when he needed it. He travelled with us on several family holidays abroad and introduced us to old friends in Nuremberg. He often came up to London, and enjoyed seeing the mini-skirted girls of the swinging sixties. Our two student-aged children got to know their grandfather well and heard about his life-experiences during the Christmas holidays, while sitting by the fireside, long after Sydney and I had gone to bed.

Leonhard returned to Pyrmont for several lengthy visits after Mary died, to stay with Dr Ott Buchinger jnr. at his new *Klinik* on the edge of the forest on the Bomberg hillside. He valued having medical check-ups, but refused to be put on a fasting diet. A visit to Pyrmont gave him the chance to renew friendships and to participate in Yearly Meeting activities as a backbench Elder. It also gave him the opportunity to meet Quakers from other parts of Germany and to see how the work that he and Mary had begun was developed by others.

In his last years Leonhard was troubled by deafness, attacks of dizziness and loss of appetite. If any of the well-meaning Harbour House staff tried to cajole him into eating, he was likely to lose his temper. He would say he had put up with enough of other people's demands in Buchenwald and now intended to decide for himself what to eat.

In some ways Leonhard was never able entirely to wipe from his memory the pain of interrogation and physical abuse of Buchenwald. He did well to talk and write so much about his experiences, but he never described the worst of his suffering, perhaps because we could not bear to hear it. Experiences we cannot talk about, cannot be put to rest. Leonhard suffered more frequently from these recollections in his later years, as did many other ex-concentration camp victims.

Like Mary, nine years earlier, Leonhard died peacefully in his room at Harbour House, on the 15th March 1979. Mildred Chattin and I had nursed him for the last 10 days of his life. The ashes of Mary and Leonhard were interred among their Friends in the 17th century Quaker cemetery in Bad Pyrmont, where their memorial plaques can be seen on the wall.

CHAPTER XXIV

Perspectives from the 1990's

WRITING ALMOST SIXTY YEARS AFTER Hitler came to power, it seems beyond belief that a nation of the highest culture could have organised such large scale barbarity.

In Germany, as in other Fascist countries, there were different reactions to Hitler's leadership: the spending on public services, roads and re-armament provided the unemployed with work and dignity; the opportunists made personal gains; the bullies and sadists were encouraged; the fearful person obediently faded into the background. Far too many people who understood what they saw, said nothing, kept quiet and tried to ignore what happened. Others risked their existence to save a life, or found personal, unrecorded ways to express sympathy with the persecuted. But the vast majority of Germans accepted the demands of the Nazi state and shaped their own lives around it. After the war I frequently heard people saying: 'What could I have done, I was only a little person'.

In 1973, Margarethe Lachmund was given an Honorary Doctorate of Law at Haverford, an American Quaker College. At a private meeting which followed she explained:

> During the Hitler years, Quakers in Germany, even in our own homes, frequently laid aside our cherished witness to truth. So often we were afraid, lacked courage and even shut our eyes to terrible occurrences ... We sometimes said nothing, when our hearts were full of bitterness and we could not find the right words to speak ... At other times we were consumed with hatred and self-righteousness and believed we had to tell lies to save ourselves and others who were in danger ... But afterwards we often felt that this hypocritical way of living had poisoned the whole of our lives.[1]

Now we live in a different world. Few of us have faced the dilemma of having to tell lies to save a life. But Margarethe's challenge to maintain the truth is as important as her conviction that 'perfect love casts out fear'. There are many instances of German Quakers taking risks for humanitarian reasons, but once the Gestapo had established the secret police, political action became impossible. Many Quakers had been members of the Social Democrats. Mary and Leonhard never joined the party, but voted for them as long as was possible.

My parents had no idea that I would one day write about their experiences, but as I said in the Introduction, they left me several boxes of documentation. Mary's diary, begun in 1901 when she was 19 years old, has given me both a feeling for her family and a personal flavour of the first half of the 20th century. I have also felt drawn towards Leonhard's relatives and their work in the vineyards and as fishermen in the twin villages of Marktbreit and Segnitz on the River Main. I have read the love letters of his mother, Christina, written to my grandfather, Martin Friedrich, while he was a conscripted soldier between 1884-6. At the turn of the century, Leonhard's parents left the countryside and moved to the city of Nuremberg with their two small boys, hoping to make a better living. They were part of the widespread population movement from rural to urban employment, which spread across Europe. My grandfather brought white grapes from the family vineyard and went by railway to Italy where he bought red grapes. He made and sold wine and opened a *Weinstube* in Nuremberg. After the First World War my father brought his British bride to live there, and this is where I, their only child, spent my early school years. The Nuremberg castle and the medieval city is part of my cultural heritage.

The Position of German Friends during the Nazi Period

In April 1933, after the Nazis had come to power, the Quaker Executive Committee decided it was necessary for their survival, to refrain from political statements and to affirm the corporate position of the Society of Friends as a religious body, whose essential task was to express their faith in direct relationship to God.

Bertha Bracey who was present, commented that these views were not easily accepted by the Meeting and some resignations from the Society followed.

At the beginning of the war there were just over 200 Quakers in Germany. Twenty-nine were teachers who lost their jobs because they had not taken the loyalty oath. A number had emigrated because they were non-Aryan, or had been politically involved in opposing Hitler. Many of those who remained were the unemployed, self-employed or housewives and pensioners, for whom it was a little easier to maintain non-conforming private attitudes to the Nazis. But there were also about 20 young men who faced the challenge of conscription.

Twenty-five Quakers are known to have suffered in varying degrees for their beliefs and opposition to the Nazi regime. Their experiences have been recorded in *Lebensbilder Deutscher Quaker*. There were also 24 Quakers on the confidential list of 'Trusted Friends' willing to help victims of Nazism. Records are incomplete and were not kept for security reasons. But there were many other Friends whose hearts went out to those who suffered and undertook courageous actions, sometimes without even telling their husbands or wives.

However, there were also a few timid Quakers who kept quiet and compromised themselves by following the outward forms of Nazi Germany. Some gave the Nazi salute and contributed to official charities, as Mary recorded in her diary. One Quaker school teacher said her protest was limited to having a fit of coughing when the Nazi anthem was sung. I have not heard of any Friend who joined the Nazi Party, though some had close family members who enrolled. I have noticed that Quakers around the world inevitably take on some of the prevailing mores of the society they live in.

There were so few members of the Society of Friends in Germany that one wonders why the Nazis even noticed them. The Gestapo could easily have ordered all the Quakers to be eliminated. However, during the pre-war period the Berlin Quaker office had sought interviews with the Nazi leaders to express concern about policies which threatened human rights and international peace, about Jewish emigration and made requests to visit concentration camps. The Nazis knew about and appreciated the prison-visiting which Quakers had undertaken for German POWs during the First World War, and hoped their prisoners in Britain would again be cared for. The Quaker school-feeding programme after the First World War was widely known, like an event of folk history.

Many people have asked me how German Friends survived the isolation and suffering of the Nazi period, because of the light it throws on our attitude to contemporary problems. I believe German Quakers have been too modest about their stand, because so little could be recorded. The Friends who felt most deeply about the destruction of civilised values never gave up taking risks to care for others. In their personal behaviour they showed a way of life which inspired others.

Pyrmont and the German Friends in 1994

In recent years I have returned to Bad Pyrmont for the Quaker Yearly Meeting, and renewed friendships which have helped in my writing. I often stay at the Buchinger *Klinik*. Young Ott Buchinger has retired and his son Andreas, is now the *'Herr Doktor'*. Andreas has built extensions to the fasting *Klinik* and has a son about to study medicine.

From the outside, the Quakerhouse appears almost unchanged, though the interior has been refurbished. The tall Canadian poplar tree has been felled, but the grounds have been newly landscaped and the perimeter fencing has been altered. Most of the wonderful avenue of trees from the castle up to the Bomberg tower remains. The St Georg's Villa, which had been a Catholic nun's convalescent home, is now a large hospital, with buildings coming right up to the Quaker fence. The Quakerhouse is partially protected by the fir trees Mary planted years ago. The Quakerhouse cemetery wall carries the small copper plaques bearing the names of many of the Friends to whom I have referred. The Jewish cemetery looks peaceful and respected. The lovely Knierim villa, where our family lived, has been demolished to make way for a hospital car park. The quiet, dusty Bismarckstrasse has become a by-pass road. But Pyrmont is still a delightful place, with renovated 17th century buildings and an exceptional variety of parks and woodland footpaths. Although the town planners permitted some very unsympathetic developments in the 1960s, recent renovations show appreciation for the charm of the old buildings. The Pyrmont Parks Department maintains a new circular flower bed outside the Quakerhouse gate, displaying the Quaker Star emblem in a changing pattern of bedding plants.

The moated castle has been beautifully restored and is used as the town museum and exhibition centre. The archivist, who has produced an historical picture book of Bad Pyrmont as it was at the turn of the century, is aware of the contribution of Jewish businessmen to the prosperity of the town, though not a single Jewish family survived the Nazi period in Pyrmont.[2] The archivist now hopes to gather material about former Jewish residents and to fix plaques on houses where they lived. It is encouraging that the post-war generation wants to acknowledge the contribution of Jewish citizens to present and future residents of Bad Pyrmont.

When I take part in the German Yearly Meeting I feel 'at home', as though among a group of cousins. I am able to talk with people of my own generation about their very different war-time experiences. I have renewed friendships with older Friends like Eva Hermann and others who remembered incidents of Mary and Leonhard's life. It is also lovely to build friendships with younger Friends who now carry responsibility and express Quaker beliefs in their daily lives. Mary would have been thrilled to see how active *Quakerhilfe* is in providing aid to the developing world. They also send young volunteers to serve in retirement homes for the holocaust generation in Israel, care for asylum seekers, and open-up contacts in Eastern Europe. There are now 500 German Quakers, who carry a continuity of Quaker faith among them.

A Clear and Honourable Stand

Leonhard's suffering was due to his organisational position as treasurer and publisher of the Society of Friends at the Quakerhouse, and to his personal uncompromising attitudes. He was helped to maintain this by his independent self-employed position, more easily than if he had been in other employment. The publication of two Heritage leaflets describing pacifist attitudes created problems for him. He also had the misfortune to become the focus of a personal vendetta from Gustav Willfuer, a prominent Nazi in Lueneburg, who resented the Society of Friends having inherited his sister's property.

Leonhard and Mary showed remarkable courage and persistence throughout the Nazi period, holding on to what they believed was right, though they sometimes faltered. In pleading with the Gestapo for Leonhard's release, Mary's letters did not always follow her own insights. At times she felt constrained by advice she was given by others. Left to herself, she might have taken a clearer stance and would perhaps have perished for it. She would never have signed off a letter with 'Heil Hitler' or have pleaded for Leonhard's release when his age group were called up for military service. At Leonhard's burial, Ott Buchinger likened him to a strong but knarled old oak tree, which had withstood the battering of a stormy life, expressing his beliefs in a compassionate warm-hearted way.

When young, I believed there was an indisputable difference between right and wrong, for which I would be prepared to die. However, with experience I gradually found that the complexities of human affairs often left me with the options of making choices in grey areas. I do still retain the principles which guided my youth, but have more understanding that nothing is more important than being honest and retaining a love for humanity.

Why Did Leonhard and Mary not Emigrate?

Looking back one might wonder why Leonhard and Mary did not leave Germany when they foresaw much that would happen. I do not remember asking them about this, because I was satisfied that they felt it was their God-given responsibility to stay, although they helped others to escape. I was surprised to read in Mary's diaries that she had enquired about emigration to the US in 1933, after Leonhard lost his job. His brother Bernhard in Pennsylvania, though not rich, could have provided an affidavit. Mary also had two sisters in America and two brothers in Canada who could have helped. But they decided to stay, to face the problems that would occur in the belief that Germany would never change if all those who believed in democratic values left the country.

As their daughter I have of course been deeply affected by their actions and beliefs. But I have never faced the challenges of my parents. We have lived different lives in different times and evolve our own morality to guide us. I have tried to be honest about my parents' shortcomings and strengths. They would have no wish for their lives to be seen as anything exceptional.

Some 20 years after the end of the war, when Leonhard and Mary retired to England, they received letters from all over the world expressing gratitude for what they had done in Germany. There are two tributes which seem to epitomise their lives:

MARY . . . The memory of her undaunting support for Leonhard, and her fearless protection of the Quakerhouse, her deep caring for people, stand out in our memory as a 'light' in times of gloom. She exerted a lively spiritual leadership among German Friends, and like a signpost, prepared the way for others. [Roger Wilson]

LEONHARD . . . What a courageous cheerful man he was, unwavering and steadfast, carrying his Faith through all the difficulties of life. [Hildbourg Braun]

In the concluding section of Leonhard's paper, *Guest of Adolf Hitler*, he explained why he had written this paper:

The main purpose of my writing is to help form realistic attitudes to these past events. I have met several former German POWs, who after talking with me at length about their experiences in captivity, said they could now understand why they had been treated with hostility, and occasionally experienced ill-treatment at the hands of Allied soldiers.

One can rightly say that people in charge of concentration camps were warped personalities for whom it was a matter of personal satisfaction to torture a victim. But this is no excuse for the German people who kept the National Socialists in power by repeatedly voting for them. Many people recognised the danger of Hitlerism far too late, but that does not excuse them from the responsibility of putting those 'benefactors' into office.

Our land is a heap of rubble. There is nothing to be gained by blaming anybody now, but we have to admit to having been inactive in the face of the evil that we perceived. We are all to blame for the situation in which we find ourselves.

If ordinary decent thinking people had come to grips with the anti-Semitism which developed in the 1920s, though no one could then have foreseen the future, something might have been done many years earlier to prevent the Jews' tragedy. Even today I hear people say 'But we knew nothing about it'. This would be a joke if it were not a fact that everyone first looked over their shoulder before expressing such an opinion. The *Deutscher Blick* demonstrates that everyone lived in fear of the Gestapo, and could not be sure that their thoughts were safe with anyone, not even with their parents or children.

We lived in extraordinary times. My article has no political motivation. It is told out of concern for humanity. I have shared my experiences as objectively as possible.

On my way home from Buchenwald I stopped at a small village and spoke with a simple woman, who asked if it had really been as bad in the camps as she had heard on the radio. When I told her it was all true, tears came to her eyes, and she said she was ashamed to be German. Whilst the German people may not have known everything that went on behind the wire fences of the concentration camps, most people suspected the truth, especially about what happened to the Jews. However, even universal fear of the Gestapo and their accomplices does not exonerate the people from guilt.

As I left the camp it became clear to me that I had two great duties, namely not to forget the 51,000 people who died and remain in Buchenwald, and secondly to show the world that German people are not what the Nazis and criminals made them appear to be. Anyone enduring the chains of our existence in the concentration camps will understand what it is like to be free again, without the constraints of having to look over one's shoulder. Having endured all this, we will find the courage to clear up the rubble and begin a new life.[3]

Perspectives of the Holocaust

We now believe that as many as 40 million people perished during the war. Many of them were from Eastern Europe and the Soviet Union and among them were six million European Jews. Since the recent break-up of the Soviet Union, we have learned that there are kilometres of archive shelving containing details of deaths caused by the Nazis, and by the Soviet authorities.

Anti-Semitism has ancient roots in the medieval Christian church and in society. It was endemic in Russia before the revolution and in many other societies. *Pogrom* is a Russian word. The anti-Semitism of the Nazis shook the world profoundly and led the United Nations to establish Human Rights conventions, banning racism. While this has not abolished discrimination and racism, it has set goals for achievement.

I am profoundly grateful that I no longer notice who is or who is not a Jew, though as a child growing up in Nuremberg I instinctively did so.

I am thankful that Jews and people of all races are free to practice their religion and are an integral part of British culture. But it is distressing that fascism and anti-Semitism are still latent in our society. They flourish in times of unemployment and hardship, when the normal controls of society and freedom of expression fail to function. We can best prevent such intolerance from ever occurring again, by offering friendship and personal support to the victims, by political action and maintaining a free press to expose the perpetrators. History does not repeat itself, but the challenge to create a better and humane society will never cease.

References

1. Items marked FHL can be consulted at the Library, Friends House, Euston Road, London NW1 2BJ.
2. Items marked QBP may be available at Quakerhaus, 9 Bismarckstrasse, 31812 Bad Pyrmont, Germany. Enquiries through Burobetreuung, because the library is not staffed.
3. For reference to publishers, please see Bibliography.

Introduction

[1] Leonhard FRIEDRICH, 'Guest of Adolf Hitler'. First given as a lecture at Quakerhouse on 6th October 1946, subsequently published in *Der Quaker*, July 1975, pp. 193-200 and *Quaker Monthly*, November 1979, pp. 201-9, FHL and QBP.
[2] Bruno BETTELHEIM, *The Informed Heart*, 1960, *Recollections and Reflections*, 1988, p. xiv.
[3] Mary Friedrich's diary and documents in author's possession.
[4] Nuremberg Quaker Minute book, QBP.
[5] Herta ISRAEL, *The Friend*, 9th August 1940, p. 471.

Chapter I – Life in Nuremberg 1931

[1] Ormerod GREENWOOD, *Quaker Encounters* Vol. 1, pp. 221-5, FHL.
[2] Richard CARY, *The Friend*, 9th January 1931, pp. 29-30.
[3] Naomi SHEPHERD, *Wilfred Israel – Germany's Secret Ambassador*, 1984.
[4] 136 Middle Lane, Palace View, Crouch Hill, London.
[5] Hans ALBRECHT, *Der Quaker*, December 1933, p. 303.
[6] Louisa JACOB, AFSC/FSC report, November 1931, in author's possession.

Chapter II – Nuremberg: Last days of Weimar Republic 1932

[1] William SHIRRER, *Rise and Fall of the Third Reich*, pp. 189-234, and Alan BULLOCK, *Hitler*, pp. 243-250.

2 Leonhard FRIEDRICH, Friedensthal, *Der Quaker*, March 1938, pp. 85-95 and October 1938, p. 289 and *Journal of Friends Historical Society* Vol. 48, Autumn 1958, pp. 260-267.
3 Fred TRITTON, Rebuilding Quakerhouse, *The Friend*, 17th June 1932, pp. 540-1.

Chapter III – Hitler Becomes Chancellor 1933

1 Corder CATCHPOOL, *The Friend*, 10th February 1933, p. 109 and *Quaker World Service*, 1st April 1933, pp. 1-2.
2 William HUGHES, *Indomitable Friend*, pp. 84-96.
3 Heinrich OTTO, *Quakertum*, pp. 297-9.
4 Bertha BRACEY, *Quaker World Service*, April 1933, p. 9.
5 Elizabeth F. HOWARD, *Across Barriers*, pp. 42-44.
6 Bertha BRACEY, *The Friend*, 25th May 1945, p. 346.
7 Corder CATCHPOOL, *The Friend*, 1st December 1933, pp. 1065-6.

Chapter IV – The Move to Bad Pyrmont 1934

1 Alan BULLOCK, *Hitler – A Study in Tyranny*, pp. 284-295.
2 William SHIRER, *Rise and Fall of Third Reich*, p. 278.
3 Therese HERZOG, 'Beauty of Quakerhouse', in author's possession.
4 Lawrence DARTON, 'Friends Committee on Refugee Affairs', pp. 7-8, FHL.

Chapter V – Consolidation of Nazi Regime 1935

1 Elizabeth F. HOWARD, *Across Barriers*, pp. 59-70.
2 Horace ALEXANDER, *The Friend*, 15th February 1935, p. 141.
3 Corder CATCHPOOL, *The Friend*, 26th April 1935, pp. 361-2.
4 Heinrich OTTO, *Quakertum*, pp. 315-8.
5 Elizabeth F. HOWARD, *Across Barriers*, pp. 89-91.
6 Ormerod GREENWOOD, *Quaker Encounters* Vol. 3, p. 309.
7 Alan BULLOCK, *Hitler*, p. 339.
8 William HUGHES, *Indomitable Friend*, p. 126.
9 Willis HALL, *Quaker International Work Europe 1918-38*, p. 150, FHL.

Chapter VI – Bad Pyrmont 1936

1 Alan BULLOCK, *Hitler*, p. 343.
2 Michael SEADLE, *Quakers in Nazi Germany*, p. 29.
3 Heinrich OTTO, *Quakertum*, p. 319.

Chapter VII – Mary's Commitment to the Jews 1937
1. Heinrich OTTO, *Quakertum*, p. 330.

Chapter VIII – Annexation of Austria and the Munich Crisis 1938
1. *Der Quaker*, February 1939, pp. 58-9.
2. Charles TUPHOLME, letter 1st May 1991, in author's possession.
3. Alan BULLOCK, *Hitler*, pp. 420-38.
4. Corder CATCHPOOL, *The Friend*, 6th May 1938, pp. 363-4.
5. Thomas KELLY, *Testament of Devotion*, FHL and QBP.
6. Roger CARTER, *Friends Historical Journal*, 1990, Vol. 56, no. 1, pp. 15-31, FHL.
7. Lawrence DARTON, *Friends Committee on Refugees and Aliens*, Appendix IV and pp. 58-9, FHL and William HUGHES, *Indomitable Friend*, pp. 133-139.
8. Ratcliff Meeting declaration, *The Friend*, 7th October 1938, pp. 856-8.
9. Corder CATCHPOOL, *The Friend*, 7th October 1938, pp. 858-9.
10. Roger CARTER, Prague report, 27th September 1938, at FHL; Box Berlin FSC/GE/9.
11. Tessa ROWNTREE/CADBURY, letter 2nd January 1991, in author's possession, and FHL.

Chapter IX – Kristallnacht 1938
1. Bernt ENGELMANN, *In Hitler's Germany*, p. 113.
2. William SHIRER, *Rise and Fall*, pp. 525-9.
3. Elga STURMTHAL, letter 4th December 1990, in author's possession.
4. Heinrich OTTO, *Quakertum*, pp. 319-332. Union Verlag '85.
5. Bertha BRACEY, letter 10th March 1986, in author's possession.

Chapter X – War becomes Inevitable 1939
1. *Der Quaker*, March 1939, p. 89.
2. Naomi SHEPHERD, *Wilfrid Israel*, p. 150.
3. *The Friend*, 28th April 1939, p. 345 and *Der Quaker*, May 1939, pp. 143-4.
4. Enid HUWS-JONES, letter 4th January 1988, in author's possession.
5. Emil FUCHS, *Mein Leben* Vol. 2.
6. Norman MOSS, *Klaus Fuchs*.
7. Robert C. WILLIAMS, *Klaus Fuchs – Atom Spy*.
8. Leonard KENWORTHY, *An American Quaker Inside Nazi Germany*, p. 31.

9 Homer MORRIS, *The Friend*, 24th November 1939, pp. 931-2.
10 Bernt ENGELMANN, *In Hitler's Germany*, p. 209.

Chapter XI – Hitler's Domination of Europe 1940
1 Leonard KENWORTHY, *Living in the Light* Vol. II, pp. 209-211.
2 Douglas STEERE, report 'Quakerhilfe Germany 1940', AFSC Archives, and FHL.
3 *Lebensbilder Deutscher Quaker 1933-45*, pp. 32-37, QBP and FHL.
4 Annetta FRICKE, letter 14th May 1990, in author's possession.
5 Leonard KENWORTHY, *Living in the Light* Vol. II, pp. 113-4.
6 Leonard KENWORTHY, *An American Quaker in Nazi Germany*, p. 60.
7 *Lebensbilder Deutscher Quaker 1933-45*, pp. 79-82.
8 'SEUTEMANN file', FHL, QPB.
9 Bernt ENGELMANN, *In Hitler's Germany*, p. 208.
10 GURS, *The American Friend*, 25th July 1940, pp. 28-9.
11 Relief supplies for Gurs, *The Friend*, 17th January 1941, pp. 33-4.
12 Alice SYNNESTVED, letter 31st March 1990, in author's possession.
13 Anon, *The Friend*, 20th December 1940, p. 696.

Chapter XII – The Suffering Intensifies 1941
1 Leonard KENWORTHY, *American Quaker in Nazi Germany*, p. 68.
2 Oswald DICK, *The Friend*, 5th November 1943, pp. 741-2.
3 SEUTEMANN File, FHL and QBP.
4 William SHIRER, *Rise and Fall of Third Reich*, pp. 993-998.
5 Alan BULLOCK, *Hitler*, p. 643.
6 Alan BULLOCK, *Hiter*, p. 656.

Chapter XIII – Expulsion of the Jews 1942
1 FSC European News Sheet 14, 26th February 1942, FHL.
2 Anna S. HALLE, *Quakerhaltung und Handeln im NS Deutschland*, pp. 23-6, QBP.
3 FINK'S record of Pyrmont Jews, available from Pyrmont public library archives, and in author's possession.
4 Bernt ENGELMANN, *In Hitler's Germany*, pp. 229-238.

Chapter XIV – Leonhard's Arrest 29th May 1942
1 Leonhard FRIEDRICH, 'Guest of Adolf Hitler', published in *Der Quaker*, July 1975, pp. 193-200 and in *Quaker News*, November 1979, pp. 201-203, QBP, FHL.
2 Eugen KOGON, *Theory and Practice of Hell*, p. 66.

3 Heinrich OTTO, *Quakertum*, p. 316.
4 Hans ALBRECHT, letters 9th and 21st July 1942, in author's possession.
5 Christobel BIELENBERG, *The Past is Myself*, pp. 230-2.
6 Hans ALBRECHT, letter to Hagenbruch 7th August 1942, in author's possession.

Chapter XV – Initiation to Buchenwald 1942-3

1 Christopher BURNEY, *The Dungeon Democracy*, p. 144.
2 Pierre d'HARCOURT, *The Real Enemy*, pp. 104-111.
3 Leonhard FRIEDRICH, 'Guest of Adolf Hitler', QBP, FHL.
4 Stan SATTLER, *Buchenwald and Auschwitz*, pp. 31-2.
5 Eugen KOGON, *Theory and Practice of Hell*, pp. 272-5.

Chapter XVI – Mary on her Own 1943

1 Bernt ENGELMANN, *In Hitler's Germany*, p. 260.
2 BAFFOR and FRISBY, *Helmut von Moltke*, p. 218.
3 William SHIRER, *Third Reich*, pp. 1159-1164.
4 Alan BULLOCK, *Hitler*, pp. 707-711.
5 William SHIRER, *Third Reich*, pp. 1207-8.
6 Georg SCHNETZER, *Friends Quarterly*, July 1987, p. 313, FHL.
7 Eva HERMANN, *In Prison Yet Free*, FHL, QBP, and letter 23rd March 1992, in author's possession.
8 Eugen KOGON, *Theory and Practice of Hell*, p. 76.

Chapter XVII – The Allied Invasion of Europe 1944

1 Bertha BRACEY, 'Europe's Displaced Persons and Related Problems', article *International Affairs*, Chatham House, April 1944 (pamphlet at FHL).
2 Copies of 11 letters written by Mary FRIEDRICH to Margarethe LACHMUND between February and October 1944, in author's possession.
3 *Lebensbilder der Deutscher Quaker 1933-45*, pp. 29-30.
4 Margarethe LACHMUND, *Der Quaker*, January 1965, pp. 5-11 and *Lebensbilder Deutscher Quaker*, pp. 83-6.
5 Ott BUCHINGER, *The Friend*, 29th September 1944, pp. 635-6.

Chapter XVIII – Final Year in Buchenwald 1944-5

1 *Observer* newspaper, 13th October 1991, p. 20.
2 Eugen KOGON, *Theory and Practice of Hell*, pp. 109-124.

3 Letters between Leonhard and Mary, 4th and 12th February, in author's possession.
4 Leonhard FRIEDRICH, 'Guest of Adolf Hitler', QBP, FHL.
5 Eugen KOGON, *Theory and Practice of Hell*, pp. 251-7.
6 Pierre d'HARCOURT, *Buchenwald: the Real Enemy*, pp. 170-80.
7 Christopher BURNEY, *Dungeon Democracy*, p. 232.
8 HM Stationery Office, Command paper 6626, 1945.

Chapter XIX – Ending of the War 1945
1 Alan BULLOCK, *Hitler*, pp. 755-801.

Chapter XX – Leonhard Comes Home 1945
1 Ormerod GREENWOOD, *Quaker Encounters* Vol. II, pp. 64-79, and letter from Madelaine Sutton 20th July 1988, in author's possession.
2 Basil RECKITT, *Diary of Military Government 1945*, p. 62.
3 *Observer* newspaper, 13th October 1991, p. 20.
4 Heinrich OTTO, *Quakertum*, p. 359.
5 Red Cross letter from Mary FRIEDRICH to her TUPHOLME family, 20th July 1945, in author's possession.

Chapter XXI – Post-war Chaos 1945-6
1 John ADAMSON, *FAU Chronicle* 76, 6th October 1945, pp. 4-7, FHL and in author's possession.
2 Heinrich OTTO, *Quakertum*, p. 359.
3 *Pyrmonter Zeitung*, 10th October 1960.
4 Robin WHITWORTH, *The Friend*, 30th November 1945, pp. 808-810.
5 Letter from Brenda to Sydney Bailey, 10th January 1946, in author's possession.

Chapter XXII – Picking up the Broken Threads 1946-9
1 Roger WILSON, *Quaker Relief*, pp. 273-5.
2 Heinrich OTTO, *Quakertum*, pp. 367-8.
3 William HUGHES, *The Friend*, 7th December 1945, pp. 835-6.
4 Primo LEVI, *Auschwitz and Buchenwald*, pp. 54-6.

Chapter XXIII – The Later Years 1950-70
1 Douglas STEERE, duplicated Journal 1950, FHL.
2 Bernt ENGELMANN, *Germany Without Jews*, p. 211.
3 Reginald REYNOLDS, *The Wisdom of John Woolman*, p. 106.
4 Lore HORN, *Der Quaker*, February 1959, pp. 23-7.

[5] Howard DIAMOND, *Friends World News*, January 1959.
[6] Letter from Dr Paul OESTREICHER senior, December 1970, in author's possession.
[7] Etta KLINGMUELLER's Woodbrooke speech, autumn 1966, in author's possession.

Chapter XXIV – Perspectives from the 1990's

[1] Heinrich CARSTENS, *Margarethe Lachmund Festschrift, Zum 80 Geburtstag*, pp. 37-41.
[2] Dieter AFTER, *Brunnenstrasse: Fotografiert von 1880-1930*, in author's possession.
[3] Leonhard FRIEDRICH, 'Guest of Adolf Hitler', *Der Quaker*, July 1975, pp. 193-200, and *Quaker Monthly* Vol. 58, November 1979, pp. 201-3.

Bibliography

Publications marked FHL, can be consulted at the Library, Friends House, Euston Road, London NW1 2BJ, UK, telephone 071 387 3601.

For publications marked QBP, enquiries can be made at Quakerhaus, 9 Bismarckstrasse, 31812 Bad Pyrmont, Germany, telephone 0581/4413. However, enquirers should approach the Burobetreuung, because the library is not staffed.

Dieter AFTER, *Brunnenstrasse: Fotografien von 1880 bis 1930* (Schriftenreihe 15, Museum im Schloss Bad Pyrmont, 1990).

M. BAFFORT and J. FRISBY, *Helmut von MOLTKE* (Macmillan 1972).

S Payne BEST, *The Venlo Incident* (Hutchinson 1950).

Bruno BETTELHEIM, *The Informed Heart* (Peregrine 1968); *Recollections and Reflections* (Thames & Hudson 1990).

Christabel BIELENBERG, *The Past is Myself* (Chatto & Windus 1968); *The Road Ahead* (Bantam Press 1992).

Lilian BIRT, *The Children's Home Finder* (James Nisbet & Co., London 1913).

Mary BOSANQUEST, *Life and Death of Dietrich Bonhoeffer* (Hodder and Stoughton 1968).

Bertha BRACEY, *Europe's Displaced Persons: Problems of Relocation* (Reprint International Affairs, Chatham House, April 1944), FHL.

Alan BULLOCK, *Hitler: A study in Tyranny* (Penguin 1962); *Hitler and Stalin: Parallel Lives* (Harper & Collins 1991).

Christopher BURNEY, *Dungeon Democracy: Solitary Confinement* (Papermac 1960).

William CARR, *A History of Germany 1815-1985* (Hodder & Stoughton 1985).

Heinrich CARSTENS, *Margarethe Lachmund, Zum 80 Geburtstag* (Sensen, Vienna 1976), QBP.

Lawrence DARTON, *Friends Committee for Refugees and Aliens 1933-50* (duplicated volume 1954), FHL.

Tegla DAVIES, *Friends Ambulance Unit 1939-45* (Allen & Unwin 1947).

Der Quaker, Monthly Journal, QBP and FHL.

Pierre d'HARCOURT, *Buchenwald: the Real Enemy* (Longmans 1967).

Bernt ENGELMANN, *In Hitler's Germany* (Methuen 1988); *Germany without Jews* (Bantam 1984).

FAU Chronicle 1940-6 (duplicated volume), FHL.

Hans J. FLIEDNER, *Judenvervolgung in Mannheim 1933-45* (Verlag Kohlhammer).

Victor FRANKLE, *Man's Search for Meaning* (Hodder 1987).

Leonhard FRIEDRICH, *Als Gast bei Adolf Hitler in Buchenwald*. First given as a lecture at Quakerhouse, 6th October 1946. Published in *Der Quaker*, July 1975, pp. 193-200, the 50th Jubilee issue of the German Yearly Meeting. Published in *Quaker Monthly* vol. 58, November 1979, pp. 201-203, with the title *Buchenwald and After*.

The FRIEND, Weekly Journal, can be seen at FHL.

A. Ruth FRY, *Ein Quaker Wagnis:* 9 Years of Relief and Reconstruction 1914-23 (Quakerverlag Nuremberg 1933), FHL and QBP.

Emil FUCHS, *Mein Leben Vol. 2* (Koehler & Amelang 1959).

Alfred GARRETT, *One Mystic,* an autobiography (privately published, USA 1945), FHL.

Ormerod GREENWOOD, *Quaker Encounters,* 3 volumes (William Sessions, York 1977), FHL.

Willis HALL, *Quaker International Work in Europe 1918-38* (Thesis Inst. Hautes Etudes, Geneva), FHL.

Anna S. HALLE, *Thoughts are Free* (Pendle Hill Pamphlet 265, 1985), FHL; *Quakerhaltung und handeln im National-socialisten Deutschland* (Deutsche Jahresversammlung 1993), obtainable from QBP.

Eva HERMANN, *In Prison Yet Free* (12 pp, 1948); *Profit & Loss Account* (8 pp, 1947), both at FHL and QBP.

Elizabeth F. HOWARD, *Across Barriers* (Chigwell Press 1941); *Midstream* (Friends Book Centre 1945); *Barriers Down* (Friends Home Service Committee 1950), FHL.

William HUGHES, *Indomitable Friend – Corder Catchpool* (Allen & Unwin 1956); *Those Human Russians* (Victor Gollancz 1950), both at FHL.

Thomas KELLY, *Testament of Devotion* (Hodder & Stoughton 1943), obtainable FH Book Centre, FHL.

Magda KELBER, *Quakerhilfswerk 1945-8* (Leonhard Friedrich Verlag 1950), FHL and QBP.

Leonard KENWORTHY, *An American Quaker in Nazi Germany* and *Living in the Light*, vol. 1 and 2, FHL (Quaker Publications, Box 726 USA, 1982), FHL and QBP.

Thomas KENEALLY, *Schindler's Ark* (Hodder & Stoughton 1982).

Eugen KOGON, *The Theory and Practice of Hell* (Secker & Warburg 1950).

Margarethe LACHMUND, *Begegnung mit dem Judentum* (Leonhard Friedrich Verlag 1962), FHL and QBP.

H. D. LEUNER, *When Compassion was a Crime* (Oswald & Wolff 1966).

Primo LEVI, *Auschwitz & Buchenwald* (Michael Joseph 1988).

Karl LOTZE, *Sprudelnde Quellen erzaehlen...* (Leonhard Friedrich Verlag 1948), QBP.

Bruce MARSHALL, *The White Rabbit – Yoe Thomas* (Greenwood Press 1987).

Norman MOSS, *Klaus Fuchs* (Grafton 1987).

Johannes OBST, *Gurs – Deportation und Schicksal 1940-5* (Gesellschaft Christlich – Juedish zusammen arbeit, Mannheim 1986).

Heinrich OTTO, *Quakertum – Seine Entwicklung in Deutschland* (Sensen Verlag Vienna 1972), FHL and QBP.

Clarence PICKETT, *For More than Bread* (Boston Littlebrown 1953).

QUAKER MONTHLY, Journal, FHL.

Myrtle RADLEY, *Norwegian Diary 1940-5* (Friends International Relations Committee), FHL.

Basil N. RECKITT, *Diary of Military Government in Germany 1945* (Stockwell Ltd 1989).

Stan SATTLER, *Buchenwald and Auschwitz – Prisoner 68 Months* (Kelley Books, Melbourne, Australia).

Michael SEADLE, *Quakers in Nazi Germany*, pamphlet, published USA, 1980, FHL.

Seutemann File 1940-1, correspondence with Margarethe Lachmund about sending welfare parcels to concentration camps. To be seen c/o A. S. Halle, Berlin, QBP, FHL.

Naomi SHEPHERD, *Wilfrid Israel – Germany's Secret Ambassador* (Weidenfeld 1984).

William SHIRER, *Rise and Fall of the Third Reich* (Pan Books, Secker & Warburg 1964).

W. von STADEN, *Nacht ulber dem Tal* (Eugen Diederich, Dusseldorf, 1979).

Jack SUTTERS, *Archives of the Holocaust, AFSC 1932-45* (Garland Publishing inc. London, New York, 1990), FHL and AFSC Archives, 1501 Cherry Street, Philadelphia 19102/1479, USA, published 1980.

Kate TACKE, *Lebensbilder Deutscher Quaker waehrend 1933-45* (Published by Deutsche Jahresversammlung 1993), FHL, obtainable QBP.

Herbert WILLIAMS, *Klaus Fuchs – Atom Spy* (Harvard University Press 1987).

Roger WILSON, *Quaker Relief 1940-48* (Allen & Unwin 1952), FHL.

Index

AACHEN 68, 169
Abraham, Solly 91
Abrahams, Edith 90, 98
  Hans 90, 98
Adamson, John 230
Ahrens, - (SS) 217, 218
Air Force *see* Britain; USA
Albrecht, Hans 94; clerk, BPYM 8, 30-31, 40-41, 63, 70, 103, 135, 141, 226 and QH 144, 174, 175, 180, 186 and LF arrest 145, 146, 148, 149, 151, 175
Alexander, Edith 131-132, 147, 179, 190
  Horace 61
America *see* USA
American Friends Service cttee 50; relief in Ger. 7, 9, 14-15, 16; post war 231, 249; peace movement 21; under Nazism 66, 89, 107, 109-110, 112; France 124ff; Austria 112, 144; and UN 252
Ames, William 30
Amsterdam (Holl) 60, 178
Angell, Norman 18
Ansermoz, Felix 122
Antwerp (Holl) 189
Arnhem 189
Aschburger, - 102
Ashford, Oliver 225
Attendorn 65
Attlee, Clement, MP 38, 114
Aus Frommer Morgen Stille 74
Auschwitz camp 137, 163, 193
Australia 98, 241
Austria 18, 53, 77 AFSC work 112, 144; annexation 79-80, 82; Fds 80, 81; annexed 79-80, 82; Jews 128-130; *see also* Vienna
Axis 77, 114

BAD PYRMONT
  Fds in 4, 29-31, 53, 68, 72, 97, 104, 109, 122, 124, 128-129, 135, 137-139, 143ff, 152, 156ff, 172, 173-175, 177-182, 181, 191, 193, 213, 214, 219ff. 225ff, 321-233, 235, 253, 256, 257; archives in 93, 137; Meeting House & burial gd. 5, 30-31, 50, 54, 55, 57, 74, 185, illus. 9; *see also* QH; AMF & LF arrive 54, depart 259; baths 186; bombed 186, 192; bombing victims 184ff; epidemic 226; hospital 158; Jews in 58, 74, 90-94, 97-100, 111, 128, 133-134, 137-139, 141, 172, 220, 265; liberation 216-217, 227; municipality 172, 173, 175, 179, 181, 219, 224, 265; occupied 219, 231-232; police 146, 174, 190, 211, 214, 219; womens' prison 64, 84
Bad Pyrmont YM
  24-25, 74, 112, 122, (1932) 29-31, (1933) 48-49 (1934) 54, 55-56, 94 (1935) 64-66, (1936) 70-71 (1937) 74-75 (1938) 81 (1939) 102, 103-105 (1940) 120 (1947) 245-246 (1950) 248 (1951) illus. 37 (1961) 256-257 (later) 264 (1988) 91; archives 4; childrens group 65, 74; conscription and 63; Executive cttee 22, 40 41, 48, 97, 110, 120,

281

128, 129, 133, 135, 152-153,155, 157, 176, 226-227, 235, 258, 263; Finance cttee 141; Lecture 50; and Nazism 40ff, 70-71, 81, 118-120, 128-130, 145, 150-151, 153-155, 157ff, 171, 173-175, 178, 189, 191, 192, 263-264; property dispute 144, 150, 159, 174-175, 192, 266; publishing *see* Quaker Verlag, LF; QM 97, 111, 135, 139; Relief cttee 48; Service cttee (*QuakerHilfe*) 257, 265; sewing group 130, 135, 231; voluntary & youth work 231, 242

Badoglio, marshal 173
Baeder, fr. 211
Bailey, Brenda birth 47; childhood 1, 9-14, 16-18, 28-29, 33, 34, 36-38, 54-55, 57, 60-61, 67, 73, 78, 81, 159, 171, 268; schooling 47-49, 73, 100, 107, 108, 113; and Nazism 36-37, 42-43, 47, 51-52, 57-58, 84, 100, 268; leaves Ger. 107; wartime 116-118, 183-188 *passim*, 197, 214; university 184, 188; and FAU 133, 146, 188, 232ff, 236ff, 240, 242; LF's arrest 146; marriage 206, 224, 233; re-encounters parents 233, 240; postwar life 242, 245, 248, 255, 261, 264, 268; UN work 251, 252, 255 *see also* Saffron Walden, Sidcot; illuss. 5,6,18, 34
Bailey, Sydney 242, 248, 254, 261; in FAU 206, 224, 233, 237; UN work 251, 252, 253, 255
Baptist Church 5
Barclay, Robert 30
Barkas, Rosalind 81
Barmen 177
Bauman, Adolf 19
 Magda 136
 Theodor 136
BBC 12, 114, 159, 178, 179; banned 89
Beard, dr. Rebecca 250

Beck, gen. 176
Becker-Buerkes, E. 223
Becker, Heinrich 41
 Otto 207
Belgium 113-114 *see also* Brussels
Bell, bishop 82, 176
Belsen camp 47
Benes, Edward 85, 86
Berlin 65, 77, 85, 132, 133, 179; Fds' work in 4, 23, 38, 46, 48, 50, 51, 66, 69, 81-82, 86, 94, 95, 97, 99, 107, 109, 111, 112, 113, 128, 135, 136, 145, 146, 148, 149, 152-153, 157, 176, 193, 257, 264; Friends in 19, 33, 70, 81, 99, 119, 122, 148, 152-153, 157, 194, 248; Jews of 10, 223; bombed 105, 115, 135, 139, 176, 180, 195; Gestapo in 94, 135, 143, 148, 149ff, 168, 170, 184; anti Hitler plot 188-189; SS in 192; fall 209-210; occupied 229, 230; Airlift 246; Wall 257
Bernadotte, ct. Folke 210
Bernhardt, Edwin 94
Bettelheim, Bruno 2
Bielenberg, Christabel 149
Bigland, Edith 98
Bird, Anne 17
Birmingham (Eng) 18, 102, 184, 187
Birt, Lilian 51
Bizerta 173
Blumhart, Christof 149-150
Bock, Peter 146
Bonhoeffer, Dietrich 52, 176
Bonn 102
Born, Hedwig 251
 Max 106, 251
Bowles Chester 16, 21
 Minnie 16
Bracey, Bertha 40, 42, 48, 55, 69, 82-83, 95, 96, 101, 123, 244, 258; illuss. 12
Brandstetter, Anna 22
Braun, Eva 209, 210
 Hildeborg 267
 Konrad 258

Braunschweig 185
Bremen 131, 140, 147, 156, 180
Breslau 109
Brest-Litovsk 108
Bristol (Eng) 69, 73, 105-106
Britain, British
  193, 209-210, 222; Air Force 108, 115, 131, 132, 135, 140, 153, 175, 179, 188, 193, 225; Army Pioneer corps 100; Axis 77; conscription 89, 107; crisis (1940) 114; Cz. and 101; economics 19; Ger. re-arms 62-63; intelligence 172, 176; internment 241; and Jews *see* Jews (emigration); Norway campaign 110; nuclear weapons 106; occupies Ger. 3, 219, 226, 229, 230, 236, 238, 242, 244; Poland, treaty 106; POWs in 15, 230; prisoners in Ger. 199, 200, 202, 204, 206; USA and 132-133; war with Ger. 107, 115-118, 132-133, 172, 175, 176, 179, 188 *see* also Bailey, BBC, Germany Emergency, Jews (emigration), London
British Wives Club *see* Nuremberg
Broadstairs (Eng) 18
Brown, William 243
Brueckner, Horst 253
Bruening, Heinrich (chancellor) 19, 21, 25, 27, 36
Bruchsaal 142
Brussels (Bel) 189
Buchenwald camp
  2,3, 5, 90, 140, 141, 142, 171, 176, 180, 191, 221; LF arrives 155; imprisonment 157-159; conditions 158, 160ff, 186, 195-201; bombed 191, 214; Christians in 198; closure 207; Jews in 162-163, 168, 170, 195, 199, 210; liberation 201-208, 210, 220; museum 165, 207; organization 170, 195ff, 199; post-war 207; prisoner nationalities 210, 204, 208; resistance 199, 201-202; revisited 165, 207, 257; illuss. rear cover, 29-32
Buchinger, Andreas 264
  Beate 97
  Elsbet 73
  Hans 97, 193
  Ingrid 97, 171
  Marlies 90, 93, 180, 243
  Ott, dr.,jnr. 90, 115, 147, 155, 156, 193, 243, 261, 264, 266; illus 28
  Otto, dr., sen. 29, 68, 83, 84-85, 112, 115, 146, 159, 174, 180, 182, 186, 193, 231, 243, 247; illus. 27; his klinik 68, 84-85, 156, 212, 243, 247, 250
Bucknall, Alfred 224, 225
Bueckeberg 36, 89, 102, 136, 189
Burney, capt. 200, 202, 204
Burnitz, Leonora 136, 211

CADBURY, Emma 144
  Paul 258
Cadbury co. 18
Canada MF in 5; 87, 106, 125, 243, 244
CARE 244
Carter, Roger 82, 86, 94, 97, 99
Cary, Ellen 50, 55
  John 50, 55
  Mary 16, 51, 55
  Richard 8, 33, 50, 81, 57, 104
Catchpool, Corder 36, 43, 46-47, 50, 62, 63, 64-66, 69-70, 80, 86, 225, 246; illus. 11
Catchpool, Gwen 38, 43, 69-70, 225, 246, 257, 259; illus. 11
  Jack 254
  Jean 81; illus. 11
  Pleasaunce 81; illus.11
Catholic Jewish committee 112
Catholics, Ger. 23, 83
censorship *see* BBC, Manchester..., Radio...
Central Jewish organization 94
Centre Party (Catholic) 25, 36
Chamberlain, Neville MP 85-86, 108, 113

Chattin, Mildred 261
Chemnitz 121, 214, 244
Chichester, bishop of 52, 82
Childrens Sheltering Homes 51
China 5, 224, 233
Christian Peace Conference 106
Christiansen, Friedrich 94
Churchill, Winston, MP 114, 115, 179, 187, 222, 229, 245
Citizens Advice Bureau (Eng) 188
Clark family 28
Clark, son & Morland co. 118
Clark, C & J co. 6, 28
Close, Diana 232
Cohen, Anne-Marie 72, 94, 120
   Rudolf 94
Cold War 106, 246, 253, 254
Cologne 101, 11, 229; bombed 140, 153
Communism, communists Ger. 35, 36, 64, 105, 164, 170, 200; (Eng) 62; (USA) 252; (USSR) 140, 255; *see* also USSR, &c.
Concentration camps 2, 46-47, 88, 90, 94, 96, 110, 114, 121, 122-126, 134, 137-139, 140, 141, 142, 153, 154, 160ff, 189, 192, 195ff, 243, 247; and conscription 181; *see* also Buchenwald, Dachau, Gurs, Germany, Poland &c.
Conscription *see* Britain, Germany
Confessional Church (Ger) 82
Council for Ger Jewry *see* London: Council
Country Schools 85
Curtis, Anna 10
   Lionel 172
Czechoslovakia 69, 77, 80, 85-88, 101, 105, 226, 230

DACHAU camp 2, 46, 153, 191, 192, 194
Daily News 87
Dalencourt, Justine 222
Danzig 108, 217
Darlington (Eng) 37
Davis, John 94

DAW factory 164
de Gaulle, Charles 189
de Haas, Charlotte 99
   Marianne 98
   Margarethe 98
   Max 99
   Tilly 98
Denmark 113; Fds 109, 126, 148, 200; prisoners 199
Der Quaker 2, 4, 60, 97, 101, 135, 141, 144, 148, 178; closure 137; reopened 244
Der Stuermer 25, 84
Derby (Eng) 126
Detmold 134, 217
Deutsche Edelstahl co. 78
Dewsbury (Eng) 19
D'harcourt, P. 204
Ding-Schuler, dr. (SS) 196, 201
Disarmament conference 21, 27, 50
Dixon, Helen 28, 31, 60, 83, 101
Doenitz, Admiral 210
Doerr family 177
Dolfuss, dr., president 53
Doncaster, L. Hugh 73
Dortmund 175, 214, 236, 240, 242
Dresden 27, 106
Drinkuth, Aenne 193
   Daniel 187, 193
   Heinrich, legal advisor to QH & MF 144, 152, 155, 172, 180, 181, 184, 193, 212, 214, 219, 224
   Marlies 147
Dunkirk (Fr) 114
Durrbeck, Magda 21
   Paul 94

EARLHAM college (USA) 73, 97, 193
Edert, Marie 48, 180-181, 182, 226
Egypt 132, 230
Einbeck 232, 234-235
Eindhoven (Hol) 189
Eisenach 256
Eisenhower, gen. D. 209
Elberfeld 177
Elkington, Anna 75
   Howard 75, 109, 113, 120

'Ella' 10, 34; illus. 6
Elliott, Errol T. 235
Emanuel, Jenny 138
Emigration, Jewish *see* Germany;
  LF; MF
Engel-Reimers, Helene 156, 194,
  248
Engelmann, Bernt 124
England *see* Bailey; Britain; LF; MF;
  London, &c.
Erbgut leaflets 136, 149, 259, 266
Essen 140
Estonia 110, 132
Exmer, Hans 29, 33, 245

FALCONER, Jennie 28, 250
Falkenstein-Taunus 59
Fellowship of Reconciliation 89, 136
Finch, Ruth 125
Fink, Walter 91-93, 137
Finland 110, 111, 128
Fischer, Hilde 102
Fleischman, fr. 10, 250
Flossenburg camp 202
Fox, George 30, 34, 128, 253, 259
  Marion 13
France: post world war I 8, 222;
  diplomacy and 22, 61, 62, 68,
  77, 85-86, 101, 139; Fds 16, 29,
  33, 36, 66, 122ff, 189, 221, 222;
  invaded 113-114, 187, 188; Gurs
  camp 122-126, 146; liberation
  189; occupies Ger. 229; *see* also
  Paris
Frankenberg, Anne 109
Frankenberg, dr. 109
Frankfurt Fds 2, 43, 82, 120, 122,
  151, 236; relief post WWI 6, 8;
  bombed 140, 185
Frankfurt-Main 142, 185, 242
Frankfurter Zeitung 185
Fresnes (Fr) 222
Freundschafts Heim 89
Fricke, Annetta 119, 156
  August 94, 135, 137, 148, 156,
  226
Friedensfreunde 149

Friedenstahl 29-30, 58, 91, 108,
  113, 156, 185
Friedrich, Bernhard 35, 75, 113,
  155, 181, 244; illus 20
  Brenda *see* Bailey
  Christina 6, 263
  Dora 75, 250
  Hildegard 75
  Martin sr. 6
  Martin jr. 75, 244, 263; illus. 20
Friedrich, Leonhard
  in Berlin 48, 128, 135; and
  BPYM 18, 24, 31-33, 70, 110,
  112, 115, 133, 248; Brenda,
  reunion with 233; Buchenwald
  liberated 205ff, 233; Buchenwald
  revisited 257; Buchenwald in
  157, 158, 171, 178 180, 182,
  186, 196ff, 240, 242, 255;
  Buchenwald conditions 158,
  160ff 186, 187, 196-200;
  Buchenwald camp war work 164,
  168, 178, 195ff; Buchenwald
  release request 154, 181, 184;
  childhood and origins 5, 13, 35,
  67, 77, 83, 263; deNazification
  232; early employment 7, 18, 24,
  37; England visits (1933) 49-50,
  51 (1946) 244; retirement in 9,
  259ff; family origins 13, 263;
  health 72, 131, 143, 145, 146,
  152ff, 166, 167, 224, 240;
  imprisonment 67 *see* also
  Buchenwald; indictment 150,
  153, 154; Jews assisted 94, 98,
  122, 150, 225; meets Fds 6, 18;
  Nazism and 1, 4, 34, 42-43,
  47-49, 67, 83-84, 89, 101, 111,
  246; at Nuremberg 9-16, 19-23,
  24-28, 31, 48, 53, 59, 233;
  nurses MF 259; and QH 31,
  53-54, 59, 60-61, 70-71, 73-74,
  112, 126, 133, 136, 141, 246;
  publisher 34, 55, 60, 83, 112,
  133, 136, 137, 149, 152, 228;
  readjustment 224ff, 234, 242,
  247, 256, 261; Rest Home and
  59, 60; retirement 247, 251;

returns home 223, 225, 227, 268; threatened 94; USA visits 75, 78, 252; USSR visit 254; death 261; assessed 256, 257, 261, 266-267; illuss. title, 3, 5, 15, 19, 33, 36, 37, 40

Friedrich, Mary
childhood 5; joins Fds 6; nationality 190, 257; employment 2, 6, 17, 28-29, 182, 252; Brenda and 9-10, 16-18, 28-29, 34, 36-37, 38, 56, 60-61, 73, 78, 81, 159, 182, 184, 190, 197, 214, 224, 225, 228, 233, 242; Berlin visited 48, 128, 195 see also BPYM Exec. cttee; and British Wives Club 14, 15, 22, 23, 49, 67; bombing, assists after 177-180, 184ff; evacuees hosted 184, 186, 212, 214, 225; Fds, relations with 156-157, 174-175, 182, 213-214; *Gestapo* and 143ff, 150ff, 157,186, 182, 184, 192, 211, 218, 228, 252; health 13-14, 23, 28, 29, 31, 58, 72-73, 101, 112, 137, 139, 143, 145, 146, 156, 181-182, 185, 186, 247, 248-249, 250, 252, 255, 256, 258-259; home economy 12-14, 68, 81, 111, 112, 113, 148, 152, 156, 159, 177, 179, 182, 190, 194, 216ff, 246; assists Jews 94, 97-103, 106, 109-110, 111, 122, 126, 128, 129, 134, 135, 137-140, 150, 158; Voluntary cttee 231-232, 242; LF imprisoned 141ff, 157-159, 164, 168, 171, 172, 180ff, 184ff, 187, 191, 193, 197, 210, 211, 214, 221; Nazism and 36ff, 44-49, 51, 64, 69-74, 80-83, 84, 89-95, 139, 143-145, 191; *see* also Gestapo; LF; and QH 31-33, 49, 53-57, 60, 67, 70-71, 73-74, 80-81, 90, 120, 131, 133, 143-145, 153, 154, 156, 171, 173-175, 179-181, 186, 190, 192, 207, 213, 215, 218-228, 231, 240, 242; retires 247; Rest Home and 59, 60; England, visits (1931) 16-18, (1932) 28-29, (1934) 51, (1935) 60-61, (1936) 68-69, (1939) 101-102, (1946) 244-245, (1949) 248, (1950) 250, retirement in 259ff; Ireland visited 248; USA visited 10, 249-250, 252; death 259; assessed 256-257, 266-267; illuss. title, 4, 5, 17, 33, 36

The Friend 4,8, 62, 86, 100, 101, 109, 125, 127, 128, 176, 185, 189, 226, 236, 242

Fds Ambulance Unit, (Ger.) 4, 110, 118, 128, 133, 188, 189, 225, 226, 228, 230-231, 232, 234-235, 236ff, 240, 242; illus. 34; (China) 224, 233

Fds Of Peace 35, 62

Friends Quarterly 177-178

Fds Relief Service 4, 47, 231, 233, 240-241

Fds Service Council 31, 34, 40, 46, 66, 82, 94, 112; and Cz. 69, 86; and German relief 7, 9, 14-15; and Ommen school 27, 55; Rest Home 59, 242; *European News Sheet* 135

Fds War Victims Relief cttee (1914) 6, 221

Fds World cttee 253; illus. 38

Fds World conference (1937) 75; illus. 19

Fritchley (Eng.) 126

Fry, A. Ruth 13

Fry, Joan Mary 31, 55, 65, 75, 246; illus. 24

Fuchs, Emil 8, 41, 48, 54, 65, 68, 104-106, 120, 128, 133, 136, 156, 181; illus. 37

fr. 104

Elizabeth *see* Kittowski

Gerhardt 105, 156, 157

'Gusti' 153, 177

Klaus 104-106, 133, 181, 251

Kristel (Heinemann) 105

Fuerstenau 134

Fuerth 19, 49, 136

GANDHI, M. 136
Garrett, Alfred dr. 16, 21, 33, 55; illus. 15
Gehringer fr. 15, 49
hr. 49
Geneva (Sw) 21, 27, 62, 126, 135, 253; Convention 195
George VI, king 73, 222
German Armament Works *see* DAW
German Democratic Republic 106, 246, 256-257
Germany: Abwehr 172; North African war 132, 173; Air Force 52, 114, 116, 188; Allies occupy 207, 219ff, 229-231, 232ff, 235, 237ff, 241, 242, 246; Allies invade 189, 191, 200, 209-210; Austria annexed 79-80; and Italy 77; Bel. and 113; bombed 175, 185, 193 *see also* city names; censorship *see* BBC; Manchester...; Radio; churches in 19, 52, 54, 79, 82, 104, 176, 258; conscription 63, 118-119, 150, 153, 181, 190, 263; Cz. annexed 69, 85-88, 101; deNazification 229, 232, 242, 244; Denmark and 113; displaced persons 226, 230, 234-239; Fds origins 20; food shortage 113, 125, 139, 210ff, 229, 245; France and 113-114, 126, 187, 188, 222; Hol. and 113-114, 192; invasions of 1940 113-114, 192, 222; Japan and 133; Jews in 1, 3, 19, 36ff, 46ff, 66, 69, 73, 77, 81-85, 94, 97-100, 102-104, 109, 110, 112, 113, 118-120, 123, 128, 130, 134, 137-140, 146, 148, 150, 178, 180, 220, 238, 267; *see also* Jews; MF; Kristallnacht 89-94, 103, 109; League of Nations *see* League of; medical corps 115; naval war 175; Nazism 51, 53, 55, 59, 60-66, 84, 108-135, 136-140, 185, 187, 191, 192, 195, 199, 210, 240, 262, 266ff;

Nazism, rise 8, 15, 25-26, 29, 35ff; Norway and 113; Poland and 101, 107-108, 110, 113, 118, 230; post WWI 7, 8, 42, 52, 101, 151, 168, 264; postwar currency 246; racial Laws 66, 81ff; rearms 62-63, 67, 81; Rhineland 69; Saarland 61-62; Sudetenland 69; surrender 210, 216; Sw. and 114; USSR and 132-133, 135, 140, 172-173 189, 207, 209-210, 214; Weimar republic 24-26; *see also* BPYM, Berlin, LF, MF, Gestapo, Hitler, Jews, &c.
Germany Emergency cttee 4, 65, 65, 82, 87, 101, 123
Germany YM *see* BPYM
Gestapo (State Security) 3, 38, 40, 62, 70, 72, 79, 84, 90, 94, 103, 113, 121, 128, 135, 137, 139, 152, 221, 222, 262, 264; and QH 143-145, 150, 154, 155, 156, 157, 158, 159, 171, 172, 173, 180, 182, 186, 252; LF's arrest 141-155, 157, 184, 246, 251, 252; at Buchenwald 164, 168, 170, 196, 199, 200, 201; at BP 211
Gillett, Henry dr. 98
Lucy 100
Gingerich, Josef 94
Glaser, dr. 217
Glauner, Helene 136, 145
Gleichschaltung 37, 43
Gluckner, Sigrid 226
Goddard, Alvana 33
Goebbels, Paul Josef 89, 179, 209
Goering, Herman 25, 35, 188
Goettingen 105, 251
Goetze, Anna 131
Gollancz, Victor 245
Goodhue, Elizabeth 16, 21
Graf, Albert 171, 191, 214
Gertrud 191, 214, 220, 231; illus. 19
Grafenberg 23
Greene, Ben 95
Grenstein, - 102

Groel, August 207
Grosse, Otto 207
Gruber, Heinrich 82
Grynszpan, Hershel 89
Guildford college (USA) 113
Gurs (Fr) 122-126, 178
Gustloff II factory 164, 197, 199; illus. 29
Guttmann, Helmut 207
Gypsies 135, 162, 165

HAARLEM (Hol) 27, 60, 114, 192
Hagen 102, 148, 190
Hagenbruch, - (SS) 148-158 *passim*, 184
Hahms, - 103
Halle 155
Halle, Anna Sabine 122, 129
  Gerhard 33, 48, 119
  Olga 48, 66, 157, 176
Hamburg 40, 75, 98, 226, 229, 253; bombed 175, 236
Hamelin 74, 131, 132, 147, 179, 190, 211, 219, 221, 222
Hamilton, duke of 132
Hanfstaengl, dr. 61
Hanover 5, 29, 56, 72, 78, 90, 94, 102, 110, 111, 112, 137, 138, 142, 171, 180, 184, 207, 214, 229; Gestapo 143, 153, 156, 157, 171, 186; and LF 142-143, 145-148, 152, 154, 155, 187; Jewish Home 146
Harbour, Margaret 17
  Wilfred 17
Harbour House (Eng) 261
Harris, Barbara D. 87
Heath, Carl 104
Hecht family 102
Heilbron, rabbi 43
Henkel, dr. 103
  Dorothy 190
Henlein, Konrad 69
Henderson, Arthur, MP 27
Henniker family 177
Herbeck, Ilse 98
Herrmann, Carl 94, 123, 178, 193
  Eva 94, 122, 123, 178, 193, 265

Herzog, Elise 48, 54
  Therese 54, 57, 182
Hess, Rudolf 132
Heydrich, Heinrich 135, 139, 192
Heyman, Anna 98, 138
  Israel 98, 138
  Rudi 98
Hildesheim 226
Himmler, Heinrich 80, 135, 188, 200, 201, 209, 210
Hirsch, Otto 94
Hitler, Adolf 25-26, 35-38, 46, 52-53, 55, 61, 63, 68, 69, 79-80, 81, 85-87, 89, 101, 107, 115,132, 135, 140, 151, 194; to power 35-36; pact with USSR 106; Britain, war with 107, 114, 115 &c.; invasions 113-114; of USSR 132-133, 140, 172-173; and Japan 133; and Italy 173; decline 175-176; opposition 172, 176, 188-189, 199, 263; attempts on life 172, 176, 188-189, 193; death 209-210
Hitler Youth 3, 51-52, 53, 173-174, 176, 190
Hocheimer, fr. 126
Hocheimer, Otto 99
Hodgkin, David 36-37
  Edward 37
Hoffman, Franz 122, 148, 152, 155
  Lotte 48, 122, 148, 152, 155
Holbeach (Eng) 73
Holbeck, Helga 126
Holland 24, 27, 48, 54, 60, 73, 84, 94; Fds 109, 114-115, 181, 191; invaded 113-114; liberation 189; Jews 192; *see also* Haarlem, Ommen, Arnhem, &c.
Holland, Denys 240
  Jessie 17
Holm-Seppensen 84
Holzhausen 216
Homer, Otto 103
Homosexuals 165
Hoover, Herbert 7, 19, 21
Horsnaill, Elizabeth 24
  Headley 24

INDEX 289

Howard, Elizabeth F. 8, 43-46, 61, 646, 65, 84, 103, 135, 243; illus. 4
Howson, Waring 227
Hoxter 102, 110, 126
Huber Jordan Koerne co. 7, 18
Hughes, William R. 40, 46-47, 65, 242
Hungary 199, 201, 230
Hutchinson, George 100

INDIA 16
Institute of Personnel Mgt 6
Inter Church Council for Refugees 82
Inter Govt cttee for Refugees 185
Ireland YM 248
Israel 125, 265
Israel, Herta 5, 82
  Wilfrid 13, 95, 100
Israelsohn, fr. 109
  Henny 98, 99, 109
  Max 99
Italy 73, 77, 189, 210, 263 *see* also Mussolini

JACOB, August 41
  Gertrud 21, 33
  Louisa 21, 22, 27, 33, 58, 60
Japan 16, 133
Jehovah's Witnesses 64, 119, 165, 198
Jerusalem 65
Jewish Board of Guardians 83
Jewish Refugee Aid cttee 83, 95, 101
Jews
  in Austria 80, 128-130; Buchenwald 162-163, 168, 170, 195, 199, 201, 210; converts 130; emigration 66, 69, 77, 81-83, 95ff, 109, 111-112, 125, 127, 150, 238, 241, 255, 264; in France 124, 125; in Germany 1-3, 19, 29, 35ff, 43-47, 51, 52, 58, 74-84, 85, 90-94, 97ff, 103, 111, 119, 121, 122-123, 126, 128, 129, 133-134, 136, 137-140, 141, 146, 148, 172, 178, 213,
223, 238, 242, 250, 267, 268; in Holland 192; in Hungary 199; Nuremberg laws *see* Germany; Ommen school 27, 55, 114, 192; orthodox 130; Palestine 65; in Poland 110, 119, 125, 127, 128-130, 173, 188, 199, 221; USSR 140; *see* also Non Aryans
Jews & Non Aryans assisted by LF & MF *see* separate list
Jodl, gen. 210
Johannsen, John 109
  Meta 109
Jones, Enid H. 103
  Margaret 112, 252
  Rufus M. 75
Jordan, Hannah 136, 177
  Henrietta 227
  Mitzi 136
Jordans (Eng) 18, 98

KANDERS family 134
Kappes, Elise 68
  Heinz 65
  Piet 212
Kara co. 7
Karle, fr. 102, 106
Kassell 54, 142, 181, 207, 216; Fds 156
Katowice (Pol) 101
Kaufman, hr. 72
Kelly, Thomas 81
Kenworthy, Leonard 109, 120, 128
Kershner, Howard 126
Kharkov (USSR) 172
Kiel 104, 175
Kiev (USSR) 172
Kindertransporte 95ff, 100, 125, 238
Kittowski, Elizabeth 104-105
Klingmueller, Etta 257-258
Knierim family 111, 177, 184, 216, 220, 264
Kogon, Eugen 142, 169, 196, 201ff
Korte, Reinhold 131
Kose, Jaroslav 69
Kovno (Lith) 66
Kramer, Hans 98
Kraus, Herta 41, 59

Krefeld 78
Kropotke, hr. 219, 220
Kuhl, fr. 177, 186, 194, 225

LACHMUND, Hans 120, 187
  Margarethe 48, 95, 119-120, 130, 153, 171, 176, 187, 190, 194, 253, 262
Lack, Max 102
Lausanne *see* Disarmament
Landesmann, Kurt 100
Latvia 110, 132
Laurer family 212ff, 223
  Ruth 212-213, 214-215, 225
  Sonia 225
Layton, Margaret 87
League of German Girls 51, 54, 107, 176, 180
League of Nations 21, 50, 61, 62, 81, 114, 122
Legatis, Fritz 157, 226, 227
  Martha 95, 157, 214, 226, 227
Leipzig 8, 106; bombed 185, 251
Lenhardt, Helmut 207
Lesage, Gilbert 36
Lichtenstein, Berta 137
  Fritz 137
  Hedwig 137
  Laura 129, 137, 138
Liebel, - 43
Lieftink, Miep 60
Lippstadt 221
Lithuania 66, 101, 110, 132, 151
Liverpool (Eng) 5, 51
Livingstone, Florence 22, 102
  Laura 82
Locarno pact 68
Loewenbaum, - 103
Loewenstein fr. 221
London
  BB in 16, 73, 107 116-118, 146, 168, 188, 206, 225, 232, 244-245; bombed 115-116, 187; Fascism in 69; FAU in 188, 225, 232; Fds House 2, 16, 82, 99, 206; Fds in 66, 82, 86, 120; post war 244; refugee work 95, 98,

100 *see* also Germany Emergency &c.; YM 60, 63, 68, 102, 248
Lonsdale, Kathleen 251, 253
Lotz, Kati 70-71, 111, 145, 174, 176, 178, 182, 185, 220, 226; illus. 19
Louvain (Bel) 189
Lowensen 113, 152, 186
Lowenstein, Dinah 99
  Ilse 99
  Marion 99
Lubeck 209
Lublin (Pol) 128, 129, 221
Ludwig, Henny 95
Luedecke, Frieda 174
Luegde 99, 134, 186, 216
Lueneburg 111, 115, 144, 150, 159, 175, 192, 266; *see* also BPYM: disputed property
Lutheran Church 52, 83, 104, 176

MAAS, Berta 111, 128, 138, 225, 231
McAfie, Effie 16, 21
McClelland, Grigor 234, 236
MacNichol, James 242
Mai family 155
Malin, Patrick 185
Mallon, J.J. 188
Man, Isle of, internees 6, 242
Manchester Guardian banned 51, 79, 89
Mannheim 12, 123, 178
Marktbreit 13, 83, 84, 171, 263
Marseilles (Fr) 125-126
Marshall Aid 245, 256
Marx, Alice 145
  Trudy 178, 179
Marxism 150
Mathews, Joyce 250
Matsuoka, - 133
Mayr, Max 207
Mehlmueller, fr. 126
Meld, Hermia 102
Memel, Memelland 66, 103, 151
Mensching, Wilhelm, pastor 33 89, 136, 189
Mergel, Trudy 103, 128, 145, 147

Meyer, fr. 102, 106, 111, 134
  Giesela 100, 111
  Heinrich 109, 111
  Meyer, Kurt 100, 111
  Margot 100, 111
Miklas, Wilhelm 80
Military Command, Government *see* Germany: occupied
Minden 5, 98
Ministry for Ecclesiastical Affairs 52
Missouri (USA) 28
Moebus, Konrad 207
Mokt, hr. 224
Montauban 124
Montgomery, gen. 172, 209, 210
Moore, Deryck 233
Moorestown (USA) 21
Morris, Edna 109-110
  Homer 109-110
Moscow 133, 254-255
Mossberg, - 102
Mueller, I (Gestapo) 147, 148, 153, 154, 156
  Ludwig, bishop 52
  Wolfgang 240; illus. 36
Muenster 192
Mundhenk, fr. 146, 154, 159
Munich 176; Crisis 85-88, 89; Fds 120
Mussolini, Benito 77, 114, 132, 173, 189, 210

NANSEN, Fridjtof 111, 136
Narpits, Tony 21
National Socialist Party 8, 25-26, 35-36, 44, 53, 77, 85, 111, 115, 159, 187
Nationalist Party 36, 37
Nazism *see* Germany, Hitler, LF, MF, Nazi Party &c.
Neal, Muriel 18
Needlers & co. 6
Neter, Eugen dr. 123, 124-125
Netherlands *see* Holland
Neubrand, Lydia
Neumann, Rosel 99
Neumann, Sigmund 99
New York 10, 16, 251, 252, 253

New Zealand 255
Niemann, Almuth 131, 147
Niemoeller, Martin 52
Nijmegen (Hol) 189
Non-Aryans 81, 82, 109, 111, 120, 128, 129, 178, 192, 195, 213; *see* also Jews
Nonne, - (Gestapo) 143, 145, 147, 154
Nordhausen 195, 226
Norlind, Emilia F. 109
Norway 110, 113, 206, 210
Nuclear espionage 106-107
Nuremberg 58, 95, 102, 132, 243, 263; Fds 4, 5, 7, 9, 14, 19-22, 26-28, 46, 54, 60, 72, 126, 183, 261; illuss 7, 8; after WWI 6; bombed 176, 213; British Wives Club 14, 15, 22, 23, 49, 67; *Der Sturmer* 25; Jews of 10, 13, 37ff, 43, 66, 99, 102, 111, 250, 268; LF & MF at 6, 7, 9ff, 18-33, 34, 36-37, 53-54, 72, 183, 245; municipality 15, 24, 49; Nazi rally 85; *Quaker Verlag* 34; Reichstag session (1935) 66; War Crimes court 207, 240; Youth House 36
Nuthmann, Charlotte 105, 119
  Kurt 105, 119

OESTREICHER, Maidi 255
Paul jr., rev. 255
Paul sr., dr., 255-256; illus. 39
Ommen (Hol) Fds school 19, 48, 55, 60, 114, 181
Osbourne co. 17
Otto, Dietgard 78; illus. 18
  Heinrich 48, 65, 74, 78, 93, 226; illus. 18
Oxford 98, 99, 100

PADEBORN 99, 216
Palestine 58, 65, 100
Paquet, Alfons 16, 55, 74, 78, 184, 236; illus. 15, 19
Paraguay 98, 138

Paris 73, 89 114, 189, 221 ; Fds work 16, 66, 69, 82, 105, 124, 146, 222
Passau 202
Patton, gen. 189
Pau (Fr) 123
Paulus, gen. 172
Peace cttee, Fds (Eng) 69
Peace Society (Ger) 94
Pearce, Freda 100
Pemberton, John 57
Pendle Hill college (USA) 105, 250
Penemuende 175
Penn, William 30
Peppler, Erna 227, 246-247
  Rheinhold 246-247
Perpignan (Fr) 48, 122, 124
Petain, Henri, marshal 114, 124, 126
Peterborough 16, 18, 28, 34, 47, 51
Pfalz 123
Philadelphia (USA) 55, 125, 250
Phillipson, - 102
Pickard, Bertram 62, 108
Pickett, Clarence 9, 21, 89, 250
  Lily 89, 250
Pino, Karl 102
Pister, col. (SS) 157, 164, 167, 202
Pleissner, Marie 95, 121, 214, illus. 24
Poland 164; concentration camps 2, 110, 122, 124, 134, 137ff, 173, 199, 221; deportations to 128-130, 134, 137-139, 173, 221; diplomacy and 52, 100, 106; Jews of 110, 118, 122, 188, 199; occupied 118; prisoners 208, 220, 234, 235; refugees from Nazism 87; war v. Germany 107, 108, 110, 111, 113, 121; post war 229, 230
Pollack, hr. 101, 102
Pollatz, Karl Heinz 192
  Lili 27, 60, 94, 114-115, 192
  Manfred 27, 60, 94, 114-115, 191-192; illus. 15

Prague 85-88, 101, 106, 107, 206, 221, 254; Fds 88
Prisoners of war 164, 173, 193, 195, 198; assisted 122, 128, 136, 148; German 230, 242, 243, 245, 264, 267
Propaganda, Ministry 61
Protestant Mission Relief 112
Pumphrey, Ruth 21
Pyrmont *see* Bad Pyrmont
Pye, Edith 189

QUADE, Sigrid 157
QuakerHouse 1-3, 48, 49, 54, 56-58,59, 64-65, 68, 70, 73-74, 84, 111, 112, 115, 126-127 133, 135-136, 137, 141, 153-156 *passim*, 186, 210ff, 219-228 *passim*, 240-241, 246, 253-254, 257, 264, 268; rebuilt 30-31; advice centre 220, 231; closure 143-145, 150, 154, 158, 159, 171, 172, 180; damage 190; hospital 192; hostel for bomb victims 176, 180; for old people 211, 215; requisitioned 173-175, 179, 180, 186, 211; repossessed 219ff; illus. cover, 2, 9, 10
QuakerHilfe see BPYM
Quaker Monthly 141
Quaker Verlag 34, 55, 60, 83, 258
Quakers, German *see* BPYM, Nuremberg, QuakerHouse, LF, MF, &c.
Quisling, Vikdun 113

RACTLIFFE, Donald 226; illus. 33
Raeydt, Emma 30, 54, 55, 57, 185, 224
Radio Luxemburg, banned 89
Ramallah school 58
Ranoch, frl. 33
Ravensbruck camp 121
Reckitt co. 6
Reckitt, Basil, col. 225
  Rachel 225

INDEX

Red Cross 120, 128, 134, 146, 156, 184, 197, 207, 210, 214, 216, 228, 235, 242; German 230, 237; Search service 227, 238
Reformed Church 32
Refugees 98, 185; *see also* Germany: displaced persons; Inter Church; Inter Govt
Reichspresse Kammer 137
Replogle, Ruth 251
  Delbert 251
Rest Home, Quaker 59, 60, 61, 64, 178, 242
Reuter, Ernst 61, 246
Rheinbad 222
Rhineland 68
Richborough (Eng) 100; (USA) 102
Richter, Agnes 177, 179
  Eugen 177, 179
  Kurt 95, 156, 182, 214, 219, 223
Rieber, Johanna 95, 152
Rodwell, Henry 126
Roehm, Ernst 25, 44-46, 52-53, 54, 94, 243
  Martha 66, 157
Rohrman, hr. 184, 186, 211, 216, 225
Romania 211, 234
Rome 73 *see also* Axis
Rommel, Erwin, gen. 132, 172, 193
Roosevelt, Franklin 125
Rosenberg, fr. 126
Rosier, Erna 95
Rossiger, Peter 149
Roth, - (Gestapo) 151
Rowntree, Tessa 87
  Michael 233
  Seebohm 58
Royal Air Force *see* Britain: Air Force
Rummel, Ernst 176, 213
Ruhpolding 126, 145, 152
Rupp, Babette 84
Rupp, Lily 13
Russell, Kate 28, 250, 251
Russia *see* USSR

SA *see* Sturm Abteilung

Saarbruecken 68
Saarland 61-62, 123
Sachsenhausen camp 199
Saffron Walden school 43, 49, 51-52
St. Louis (USA) 28, 250
Salamon, Adolf 91
Salomon, Anna 138
  Ellen dr. 98
Salomyxin, Johann 206, 207; illus. 32
Samuel, lord 95
  Minnie 116
Sandys, Duncan MP 245
Sattler, Stan 167-168
Save Europe Now 245
Schadow, Walter 41
Schaffer, Alice 112
Scharrer, fr. 103
Schelleman, Kaetchen 13, 54
Schindler, Albine 236
  Joe 236
Schlosser, Rudolf 41, 95, 211, 236
Schnetzer, Georg 177
Schoendorf family 29, 177
  Hans 31, 99, 101
Schoenlank, Johanne illus. 33
Schroeder, Elinore 158
Schubert, Sophie 22
Schulemann, 'Ru' 22, 23, 73
Schulze, Leo 189
Schuettemeier, fr. 54
Schutzstaffl see SS
Schweitzer, Albert 136
Seebohm, - Bgmstr. 173, 181, 186, 217, 218
  Ludwig 58
  Martha 58-59, 146, 152, 173
Segnitz 7, 263
Seitel, Giesela dr. 165
Seutemann, Cilli 98, 111, 114, 122, 128, 129, 130, 133, 148, 155, 181, 213, 220, 231; illus. 25
  Hans 98, 122, 148, 152, 213, 215, 220, 232; illus. 26
  Ingrid 98, 246
Sheffield (Eng) 6, 68, 99, MF family 17, 28, 51, 68, 73, 78, 227-228
Shipley, Elizabeth 109

Sidcot school 47, 57, 68, 73, 98, 100, 102
Siebert, Ludwig 95
Simon, John, sir 62
Slater, Eleanor 124
Smythe, Audrey 102
Social Democrat Party (Ger) 36, 61, 94, 104, 218, 263; (Aus) 80
South America receives emigrés 69, 99, 109
Soviet Union *see* USSR
Spain 123, 144
Spargenthal family 100
Specht, Jangeborg 95
   Minna 95
   Alma 138
   Berta 138
   Selma 138, 139
SS 8, 53, 93, 114, 160, 162, 173, 192, 217, 221, 239; at Buchenwald 160-170, 191, 196, 210-202
Stalin, Jozef *see* USSR
Stalingrad 135, 140 172-173
Steere, Douglas 118-119, 120, 122, 248
Stein family 134
   Gertrud 99, 134
   Kurt 99, 134
   Richard 99
Steinheim 99, 126, 138, 139, 192, 221
Stendal, Grete 214
Straus, Edgar 23, 116; illus. 23
   Edith 12, 14, 18, 22, 27, 36, 37, 49, 57, 60, 61, 67, 101, 107, 116, 252
   Willi, dr. 14, 22, 27, 37-38, 43; illus. 13
Street (Eng) 6, 24, 47, 118
Stringer, Phyllis 236
Sturm Abteilung (SA) 8, 15, 25, 35, 37, 43-46, 49, 52-53, 75, 93
Sturmthal, Elga 74-75. 90, 94, 98, 102; illus. 21
   Gerda 98; illus. 21
   Gustav dr. 58, 75, 82-83, 91, 93, 98, 99, 104, 172; illus. 21

Hilde 91, 98, 99, 104, 126, 221
Lina 91, 104
Nicholaus 90, 99, 104, 108, 113
Stuttgart 2, 141, 143, 145, 150
Sudetenland 69, 85, 89, 151
Suez 132
Sumpf, Grete 120, 122, 128-130, 153, 156
Sutton, John 221-222, 223
   Madelaine 222
Sweden 98, 109, 110, 138, 172, 176, 190, 209, 210; *see* also Protestant Mission
Switzerland 21, 27, 105, 109, 126, 190, 193

TACKE, Eberhard *see* cover
   Kate 153
Tangermann, Minnie 190
   Willy 173, 216, 218
Theresienstadt camp 10
Thomas, Yeo 199
Thorne, George 224, 225
Timmendorf 84
Tirlewangler, - (SS) 201
Toynbee Hall (Eng) 188, 225
Treblinka camp 173
Trew, Anthony illus. 35
Trier 68
Tritton, Frederick 235; illus. 19
Tucher, dr. 84
   Heinz 16
   Karen 16
Tunis 173
Tupholme, Amy 17, 28, 73, 228
   Beeston 5, 17, 73
   Bert 17, 28, 68, 73, 227-228
   Charles 78-79
   Constance 12
   Frank 250
   Margaret 12, 16-17, 35, 79, 228, 251, 259
   Norman 61
   Sarah 16-17, 28, 34-35
   Will 250, 251
Turm Verlag 259
Turner, Eric 236
Tysz, William 101

UEBERLINGEN 243
Ukraine 195, 213, 219
Ullman, Lena 241
   Richard 241
Ullrich, fr. 102
Ullrich, Elizabeth 102
United Nations 268; relief 185, 245; Quaker work 251, 252, 253-254
Ursell, Erich 99
   Julius 65
   Lisa 98, 138
   Margarethe 98, 138
   Martha 138
United States
   10, 18, 30, 55, 64, 99, 102-103, 105, 106, 109, 114, 118, 126, 128, 133, 155, 221, 222; Air Force 175, 185, 190, 209; Cold War 106, 246; emigrés in 116; Fds 55, 75, 124-125, 224, 235, 244, 249, 250, 251; Fds school 250; visited 75, 250, 252; world war II and 132-133, 141, 175, 185, 189, 190, 209-210, 216; liberates Buchenwald 201ff, 220, illus. 31; occupies Ger. 220ff, 229, 230, 235; *see also* American Friends Service
USSR
   62, 104, 106, 108, 110, 115, 125, 140, 164, 187, 206, 207, 211, 268; aid to 175; war v. Ger. 132, 135, 175, 189, 207, 209-210, 214; post war 229, 230, 234, 245, 246, 252, 257; visited 254

VAN ETTEN, Henry 29
Van Oordt, Toot 16, 124, 146
Versailles treaty 50, 52, 54, 61, 62, 63, 101, 145, 151
Vienna 79, 209; Fds work 2, 24, 80, 81, 84, 107, 109, 111, 112, 120, 122, 128-130, 153, 236, 252
Vlotho 225, 226, 228, 233
Voelker, Friedrich 30
Volkischer Beobachter 198
Vogt, Richard 226
Volksturm 216

von Bentheim, Konstantin 201
von Hase, Paul, gen. 155
von Hindenburg, marshal Paul 9, 25, 36, 37, 53, 55
von Moltke, Helmut, gen. 172-173, 189
von Papen, Franz 25, 26, 35, 53, 79
von Schleicher, Kurt, gen. 26
von Schussnigg, Kurt 53, 79-80
von Stauffenberg, Klaus Lt-col ct. 188-189

W -, Lydia 136
Wainright, Richard 226; illus. 33
Waldeck, prince 29-30
Walker, Barbara 81, 108
   John 108
Wallenberg, - 176
War Crimes court 207, 240
Warriner, Doreen 87
Warsaw (Pol) 98, 110, 134, 137, 138, 150, 211; ghetto 173
Washington DC (USA) 250
Wasch, fr. dr. 221
Wasserberg 146
Watson, Henry 17
   Kathleen 17
Weimar 160, 166, 195, 201, 206
Weiss, frl. 184, 186, 225
Weisselberg, Martina 102
Wempen, Franz 94
Wendolini, sr. 186, 249
Wenger, - (Gestapo) 144, 171, 173-175, 186, 192, 211, 218
Werner, fr. 67
   Michael 29
Whitworth, Julia 61, 64
   Robin 236
Wiedel, Friedel 90
Wieding, Martha 94, 145, 146, 153, 180
   Rudolf 70, 72, 94, 145, 146, 153, 180
Wiesner, Paul 207
Wilhelmi, Helmut 180, 243
   Herta 243
Willfuer, Gustav 144, 192, 266
   Marie 115, 144, 175, 192

Wilson, Roger C. 86, 189, 233, 240, 267
Winter Aid Fund *see WinterHilfe*
WinterHilfe 52, 156
Witzenhausen 68
Wohlrabe, Willi 245
Womens International League 27, 87
Wood, Carolina 21
Henry G. 50
Woodbrooke college (Eng) 18, 48, 49, 50, 51, 188, 244, 257, 258
Woolman, John 252
Woore, Alfred 126, 143, 145, 146, 148, 152, 190
Wuertenberg 190

Wuga, fr. 10, 250
Heinz 10; illus. 6
Wuppertal 177, 179

YALTA 207, 229
Yarnell, Howard 49
YMCA 122
York Retreat 98
Youth Hostels Assoc. 254
Yugoslavia 234

ZAYD, dr. 21
Zantner, Irmgard illus. 6
Zankel, Peter 88
Zhukov, Georgi, gen. 133

JEWS & NON ARYANS ASSISTED BY MARY FRIEDRICH: FAMILY NAMES

Aschburger
Emanuel
Fischer
Fleischman
Frankenberg
Grenstein
Hahms
Hecht
Heilbron
Henkel
Heyman
Hocheimer
Homer
Israelsohn
Johannsen

Kanders
Karle
Lack
Lichtenstein
Lowenbaum
Lowenstein
Mehlmueller
Meld
Mergel
Meyer
Mossberg
Phillipson
Pino
Pollack
Rosenberg

Salomon
Scharrer
Schoendorf
Speyer
Stein
Sturmthal
Tucher
Ullrich
Ursell
Weisselberg
Wuga
see also lists pp. 97-100, 102-103 and references to Bad Pyrmont archives on p. 137